AUTHOR	CLASS
HENSHALL, P.	623.45119HEN

TITLE	
The nuclear axis	

THE
NUCLEAR
AXIS

GERMANY, JAPAN AND THE
ATOM BOMB RACE,
1939–1945

PHILIP HENSHALL

SUTTON PUBLISHING LIMITED

First published in the United Kingdom in 2000 by
Sutton Publishing Limited · Phoenix Mill
Thrupp · Stroud · Gloucestershire · GL5 2BU

British Library Cataloguing in Publication Data
A catalogue record for this book is available from the British Library.

ISBN 0-7509-2293-1

08077780

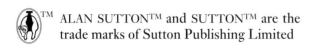

TM ALAN SUTTON™ and SUTTON™ are the
trade marks of Sutton Publishing Limited

Typeset in 11/12pt Ehrhardt.
Typesetting and origination by
Sutton Publishing Limited.
Printed in Great Britain by
Butler & Tanner, Frome, Somerset.

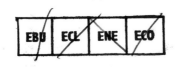

Contents

'You are correct when you say that the full story of the German rocket and atomic programs has not been told. With the passing of time, it probably never will be told.'

Arnold Kramish, Manhattan Project physicist and scientific historian, in a letter to the author dated 7 August 1994.

'The references you made to nuclear energy, "Uranmaschine", nuclear payloads, the "Korsett" (and also, what did you mean by V4?), are absurd, this presents a false picture of WW2 historical events.'

Dr Ernst Stuhlinger, Peenemünde rocket propulsion expert, who also worked with von Braun after the war in the USA. Part of letter to Dutch journalist dated 9 April 1996 after interview in USA. In 1945 Dr Stuhlinger was detained by ALSOS at the Stadtilm nuclear site.

'Was he God or Mephistopheles, Mailer asked at one point, as he watched the charismatic German scientist holding forth to a huge room full of applauding scientists, industrialists and politicians. Von Braun never ceased to tantalise Mailer, always looking as if he had some secret to hide . . .'

From 'A Giant Leap for God or the Devil' by Christopher Booker, *Daily Mail*, 17 July 1999. Based on Norman Mailer's 1970 book on the moon shot, *A Fire on the Moon*.

'We have a German doctor friend whose father is a professor of chemistry. . . . and despite having open dialogue on most wartime issues, including the SS, when we asked about the history and function of the Watten V2 bunker, the discussion ended.'

Private correspondence to the author, 14 April 1986.

Acknowledgements

I would like to thank the engineers and scientists in the aeronautical, defence and nuclear industries with whom I have worked over the years and who have provided much help and assistance; the ex-members of the RAF and photographic interpretation unit (ACIU) for information on the offensive against the V-weapons; the French naval authorities at Cherbourg for assistance in examining sites such as Brécourt and Castel Vendon, as well as the many French citizens of the 1940s generation in the countryside from Calais to Cherbourg for their help and hospitality, remembering events of over fifty years ago as if they were yesterday; the veteran British author Tom Agoston, the first to put the spotlight on SS General Dr Hans Kammler in his book, *Blunder*, who is still continuing in his quest to unravel the Kammler mystery, for his friendly help and assistance; the Dutch and German media contacts who are also investigating the subject of German nuclear weapons in the Second World War; Bob Wilcox, author of *Japan's Secret War*, for his assistance on the question of Japanese nuclear weapons in the Second World War; US scientific investigator Charles Stone, who has the uncanny knack of getting on the scent of a story and finding the right information; and the many other people who have been of assistance.

I also owe a great debt of gratitude to the friendly and helpful staff of the Imperial War Museum, London; the Public Record Office, Kew; the Smithsonian National Air and Space Museum, Washington DC; the US National Archives, Washington DC; the Bundesarchiv, Freiburg; and the National Institute for Defense Studies, Tokyo.

Lastly, I thank my wife Jean for her support over this long project, especially with the computer aspects, and Victoria and Richard who spent many family holidays in northern France and 'cut their teeth' on rocket sites.

List of Figures

Introduction

This book tells two stories. Firstly it includes the 'official' history of German and Japanese nuclear weapons in the Second World War; of brilliant nuclear physicists including Nobel Prize winners before the war, apparently struck by some strange malady which turned them into incompetent bunglers during the Second World War; of the Peenemünde team who produced the world's first large rockets within a short space of time, but only because they were interested in space flight. But, from 1943 to 1945, this same Peenemünde team, now considerably larger, appears to have been suffering from a similar 'sickness' that affected the nuclear workers, because nothing new emerged from Peenemünde in one-and-a-half years, only paper rockets.

The second story tells of nuclear programmes using materials that even America did not have and facilities at least as large as anything on the Manhattan Project. It also tells of rocket scientists and engineers building rockets and launch sites at any cost in human lives, launch sites that were capable of handling rockets much larger than the V2. It also tells of the transfer of ideas and materials between the two main Axis partners, which became ever more desperate as the war progressed.

It is easy to say that the Cold War dictated how the official history of the Second World War was going to be presented to the public. But the Cold War is now history and the truth about the Second World War is long overdue, otherwise Henry Ford was right, 'History is bunk.'

CHAPTER 1

German Long-Range Weapons

INTRODUCTION

By the end of the war in Europe, Germany had designed, built and used four long-range weapons. They ushered in the era of the guided missile in all its forms, from the ICBM and the cruise missile to the super-gun of Iraq. These four weapons all had either a conventional or nuclear/chemical/biological capability.

In the 1930s, as the German armaments industry finally threw off the restrictions of the Diktat, the Versailles Treaty of the First World War, its innovative military thinkers were once more directing their thoughts towards the next conflict. In the First World War the chemical industry had provided artificial nitrates for explosives and fertilizers, and 25 years later Emil Fischer was to provide the fuel for modern warfare, petrol and oil from coal, which, together with artificial rubber, 'Buna', added the *Blitz* to the *Blitzkrieg*.

The major industrial companies with interests in munitions, Krupp, Rheinmetall-Borsig, Henschel, Deutsche Edelstahlwerke and the Krupp of the Saar, Hermann Rochling, were once more thinking of the modern versions of Big Bertha and the Paris Kanone which in their time had been at the forefront of military technology. But technology had moved on, aircraft could now fly at speeds unthought of in the First World War and manned bombers could deliver their bomb load over distances which had transformed the meaning of war. But there was still one major problem with this new aerial weapon: it needed men to fly them, and hence there was always the crew to train, to protect, and they were fallible. But what if the weapon could be un-manned? This was the prize, this was something that focused the minds of the new military men emerging under cover of Hitler's new Reich.

If technology was moving on, national boundaries of the major countries had changed very little since the First World War and to Hitler the old adversaries were still there in Europe. They could all be reached by land apart from one, England, and Hitler the land-soldier never really thought in terms of conquests from the sea. Hence for any new land-based, long-distance weapon, the main requirement was that they had to be able to reach the UK from bases in France and the Low Countries. This meant a minimum range of 150 miles (240 km) at least, and ideally 350 to 400 miles (560 to 640 km).

Hitler became the new German Chancellor at 5 p.m. on 30 January 1933, and from then onwards events throughout the Third Reich began to move, slowly at first but with an ever-increasing momentum.

The basis for what was to become the V1 flying bomb and V2 rocket now began to take shape. The initial interest by the Reichluftministerium (RLM) was for target drones which were given the title Flakzielgerat (flak target equipment), or FZG, an abbreviation that was eventually applied to the V1, or FZG-76, code name Kirschern, or cherry stone.

The V2, or A4, also started from humble beginnings with the 1930s interest in rocketry and space travel in Germany. This original amateur interest eventually caught the attention of the Heereswaffenamt (Army Weapons Office), or HWA, and their Ballistics and Munitions Office under General Becker and another, younger, officer, Walter Dornberger. Although both the V1 and V2 originated before 1939, the remaining two weapons both started development after the war had started. The engineering and armaments firm Rheinmetall-Borsig was given a development contract by the Army in 1941 for a multi-stage, solid-fuel, unguided rocket using R-B's experience in the supply of the Army's and Luftwaffe's solid-fuel rockets for various purposes, including the assisted take-off of aircraft. The final weapon has also lived on to the present day, but in more bizarre circumstances. With conventional artillery there is a practical limit to the maximum range of a shell. Lengthening the gun barrel and increasing the explosive propellant charge eventually results in engineering limitations on the overall weight and size of the weapon that limit the range to about a hundred miles. But what if the barrel was very long, around 150–450 ft (50–150 m), and after the initial explosive impulse the shell was boosted by additional explosive charges at regular intervals along the barrel, each one accelerating it until it emerged from the nozzle at a velocity that was unobtainable with a conventional weapon?

The potentional speeds were too high for rifled barrels, which imparted a stabilizing spin to the shell; instead, small stabilizing fins would have to deploy as soon as the projectile emerged from the nozzle. This was the complicated solution, but the simpler answer was just to add the boosting charge to the shell as it emerged from the barrel, doing away with the stepped charges along the barrel.

The idea had been around for some time, and during the First World War the French had considered such a project in retaliation for Krupp's Paris Gun, but nothing came of it.

Hermann Rochling, of the Rochling Eisen und Stahlwerke in the Saar, was one of Alfred Krupp's 'buddies', and these two, together with Walter 'Panzer' Rohland of the Deutsche Edelstahlwerke, ran the Reichsvereingung Eisen (Reich Iron Association). The RVE supplied Hitler with the raw materials for his armaments and they were among the most powerful men in Germany. Although Rochling was not particularly a weapons producer, he probably thought it was a good idea to get in on the act, and since he had access to Hitler and Armaments Minister Albert Speer, getting their attention for his new project was not a problem. One of his senior engineers, August Coenders, dug out the plans for the original French project, and within a few weeks model testing was under way with a 20 mm (0.79 in) diameter shell. The idea of being able to fire five or six hundred shells an hour towards London from the French coast for very little outlay appealed to Hitler, and by August 1943 Rochling had a contract that bypassed the usual Heereswaffenamt (HWA) channels of approval, enabling him to carry out full-size testing at the Army's ranges. As usual the project had a codename, Hockdruckepumpe (HDP), or High-Pressure Pump, but it later became known in the Army as Fleishiges Lieschen, Busy Lizzie.

The timing of the award of the contract, as we shall see, was highly significant.

THE V2 TO THE BEGINNING OF 1943

When the amateur rocket society, the Verein fur Raumschiffart (VfR), operating from a firing range on the outskirts of Berlin, was closed down by the security services in 1933, this signalled the beginning of a serious interest in rocketry by the Army. By 1933 Captain Walter Dornberger of the Ordnance Office had been slowly assembling a small team of specialists at the Army's testing ground fifteen miles south of Berlin, at Kummersdorf. Among the team were two names that were to become well known years later as major architects of America's Apollo project, Wernher von Braun and Arthur Rudolph. Dornberger's first task had been to convince his Army chiefs that the solid fuel devices of the VfR and other 'amateurs' in Germany were not the way ahead; controllable liquid fuel motors offered the best chances of providing the weapons of the future. By the end of 1933 the small team had built the first rocket, the A1, or Aggregate 1 (Assembly 1), fitted with a 650 lb thrust motor powered by liquid oxygen and alcohol. Static tests showed that the 5 ft long × 15 in diameter A1 was basically unstable, and a test flight was abandoned to avoid an embarrassing failure, but the motor worked. The next few months were spent refining the design, and with assistance from instrument firms who were experienced in the gyroscopic fire control of large naval guns, a simple control system was produced and installed in the A2, dimensionally similar to the A1. It was obvious by now that a rocket-firing range only a few miles from Berlin was not the ideal location, especially for a top-secret project, and the almost deserted island of Borkum in the North Sea was chosen for the first test flights of the A2 in December 1934. This time there were no major problems, and both the A2 test vehicles were launched successfully, reaching heights of around 1.5 miles. These test flights of the Army's first gyro-controlled, liquid-fuelled rocket were not the first of such experiments, as in Russia and America similar tests were being carried out. The difference was that in Germany the work was being carried out for the Army, an Army that was rapidly looking for new weapons to add to its armoury. By 1936 Dornberger, with his team of 150 scientists and engineers, was able to give a demonstration at Kummersdorf to Army chiefs of the three rocket motors with thrusts of 650 lb, 2,200 lb and 3,500 lb. Being able to control such powerful devices at the flick of a switch was impressive, and before the party left, the C-in-C, General Werner von Fritsch, had agreed to provide more money and, most importantly, gave orders that in future all rocket work was to be moved to a new secret location, to be chosen by Dornberger.

Wernher von Braun already had a site in mind: his father had gone duck shooting on the island of Usedom, jutting out into the Baltic Sea, and the tip of the island faced down the Pomeranian coast, providing an ideal combination of isolation and unobstructed range for the new, larger rockets being planned. The site was called Peenemünde.

With agreement from the Army the Luftwaffe was to share the construction costs, and they would have a research and test establishment complete with airfield at Peenemünde. They would also benefit from some of the Army facilities, such as wind-tunnels, in their work on high-speed flight. Despite the involvement of the Luftwaffe, overall control at Peenemünde was to be in the hands of the Army, with Dornberger as director. Hence, by 1937, with most of the construction work at Peenemünde complete, Dornberger was virtually in control of Germany's rocket work. By now Dornberger's team had been formed into several specialist departments, with von Braun as Technical Director. Other department heads were Steden, Administration; Rees, Workshops; Steinhoff, Electrical (instrumentation, guidance, telemetry); Schilling, Testing; Huter, Ground Installations; Steuding, Trajectories; Herman, Aerodynamics and Wind-tunnel; Thiel, Motors and Fuel; Rudolph and Schubert, Production; and Riedel, Design Office. The next rocket to be built was the 25 ft A3, a huge advance on the 5 ft A2, and most likely Dornberger and his team were carried along by the general military freedom that was sweeping through Germany by 1937. All branches of the armed forces were racing ahead with new projects after Hitler publicly rejected the Diktat, aided and abetted by the armaments industry.

Four A3s were available for launch in the winter of 1937/8, and as Peenemünde still had many construction workers on site, a temporary launch pad was built on the adjacent island of Greifswald Oie. However, all four launches were failures, the rockets only reaching a few hundred feet before losing stability and plunging to the ground. It was clear from the post-test meetings that the A3 had been too large a step forward without sufficient system testing and verification that the new design worked. The A3 was immediately redesigned as the A5, the A4 already being on the drawing board as the definitive weapon. The A5 was subjected to an extensive test programme in the wind-tunnel and using unpowered models dropped from He111s at heights of up to 25,000 ft. Industry was also involved to a greater extent than before, including the elecrical firm Siemens and various universities. The result was that from 1939 to 1941 at least 25 A5s were launched, initially from Greifswald Oie, and later Peenemünde, without a single failure. In configuration the A5 was similar to a scaled-down A4 (V2), but with one major exception, the liquid fuel in the A5 was forced into the combustion chamber by compressed nitrogen stored in cylinders on the rocket. In the much larger A4 this was impracticable due to the vast amount of fuel used, over 7.5 tons per minute. Eventually the Kiel firm of Hellmuth Walter provided the solution with their expertise in the use of hydrogen peroxide (HTP), which with a suitable catalyst produces high-pressure steam. Walter designed a miniature steam turbine which drove the separate liquid oxygen (LOX) and alcohol fuel pumps, experience which was later used on other projects, including the V1 catapult, the Me163 and U-boats. By 1941 the construction work at Peenemünde was largely complete and all the facilities were operational. This included the very advanced supersonic wind-tunnel, the first in which aerodynamic forces could be measured on models at supersonic speeds. The 14 in square working section could operate at between Mach 1.2 and 4.5, and this was achieved by evacuating the air from a 41 ft diameter sphere at one end of the tunnel and allowing dried and turbulent free air to rapidly replace the vacuum. At its busiest time during the finalization of the A4 (V2) design, the tunnel was operating for 500 hours a month, although this also included work carried out for the Luftwaffe at Peenemünde-West.

Peenemünde had all the facilities required for a town of 20,000 inhabitants, including its own power station and docks.

Despite the success of the A5 and the progress being made with the A4 (V2), Dornberger was having a constant battle from 1939 to 1942 with the projects priority rating, and there was even the possibility that Peenemünde might be closed down. Despite support from the Army C-in-C, Field Marshal von Brauschitsch, and General Fromm, Head of the Army Weapons Office, the success of the conventional forces, especially in the defeat of France in June 1940, meant that establishments like Peenemünde working on new and untried weapons systems were always going to have to struggle for survival. However, the failure of the Luftwaffe to defeat the Royal Air Force later in 1940, through to 1941, meant that a reappraisal was carried out on the future of long-range rockets, and once more the priority ratings were raised and the future of Peenemünde looked assured. Rocket development at Peenemünde received the highest priority rating, SS (Sonderstufe), while the production facilities were downgraded to S. Work was proceeding on the first A4 (V2) test vehicle, 001, the programme being to launch 001 in June 1942, followed at intervals of two months by 002 and 003, by any standards a fairly leisurely timescale, especially in wartime, but the actual deployment of the A4 (V2) was still not guaranteed. On 13 June 1942, before an invited audience of military and industrial chiefs, including Albert Speer, 001 was rolled out to the launch pad, an impressive sight, 46 ft tall and 11.5 ft across the fins, with a launch weight of 28,500 lb and a maximum thrust at lift-off of 25 tons. Unfortunately 001 barely cleared the launch table before falling back on the pad and exploding in a massive fire-ball as nearly nine tons of highly volatile fuel ignited. The problem was judged to be fuel pump failure.

On 16 August 1942, 002 appeared to make a successful launch, only to break up after 45 seconds while travelling at over Mach 3. From telemetry records the structural failure was considered to be due to the sudden deceleration after motor stoppage. Despite these failures, 003 was launched as planned on 3 October 1942, without any watching dignitaries, and this time both launch and flight down range were carried out without a hitch, the rocket coming down in the Baltic, 120 miles along the coast. The rocket's trajectory was tracked initially by a Würzburg-Riese (Giant Würzburg) radar located five miles behind the launch pad. Originally developed by Telefunken as a fighter ground-control and height-finding radar, the original aerial dish had been increased from 10 ft to 25 ft diameter to improve the range, changing it from being mobile to a fixed emplacement. A string of Würzburgs followed the rocket down the range, and at the required height and velocity the fuel pumps were stopped by radio signal, allowing the rocket to continue on a purely ballistic trajectory. During the flight, information was transmitted from the rocket, such as temperatures and pressures, via a coded telemetry link to a ground receiver. This first successful flight also achieved several 'firsts' in flight. It was the first time a guided missile had exceeded Mach 1, it had reached a height of 60 miles before plunging earthwards and it had used technology in the guidance and control system which had never before been used in such an environment.

On 8 February 1942, Dr Fritz Todt, the Armaments Minister, had been killed when his He111 had mysteriously exploded when landing at Hitler's HQ in Rastenburg, East Prussia. Todt had been a critic of the vast sums of money and resources being expended at Peenemünde, but his replacement, Albert Speer, was more amenable to Dornberger's requests for assistance and recognition. Dornberger and von Braun had issued a report in November 1942 outlining progress so far and giving details of a programme in which 4,000 V2s would be produced in a year, obviously as part of a sustained attack on Great Britain, since no other similar target existed within the range of the V2. Despite these production claims in the report, no mass-production facilities existed nor had the V2 been specifically designed for mass production. It was assembled by hand by a very skilled workforce and many of its components did not lend themselves to mass-production techniques due to the close tolerances required.

The report had been circulated to military and industrial leaders, and apart from some adverse comment from the military establishment (Dornberger was only a colonel at the time) it was generally agreed that planning for mass production should go ahead. This was endorsed by Speer, who appointed his own candidate for the task of organizing production, Gerhard Degenkolb. Degenkolb had transformed locomotive production at Krupp and Henschel by using standardized designs in place of traditional craft techniques, and production rose from 1,900 locomotives in 1941 to 5,500 in 1943. Final endorsement of the change to mass production came from Hitler as the mass-bombing raids against German cities began to take effect from early 1942 onwards. Production of the V2 was to be moved to the Zeppelin GmbH works at Friedrichschafen and the Henschel-Rax works at Wiener-Neustadt. Production figures were optimistically put at 300 per month, rising to 900 per month by December 1943.

This was the situation at the beginning of 1943, but all these plans were soon to be overtaken by events which had come to a head by July of that year.

THE V1 TO THE BEGINNING OF 1943

The Air Ministry's (RLM) interest in target drones and pilotless battlefield surveillance aircraft crystallized such that by 1939 a specification had been prepared for a small pilotless aircraft carrying a one-ton bomb load to a maximum range of 300 miles. Based on earlier work the project was given the codenames Flakzielgerat 76 (flak target equipment) and Kirschern (cherry stone), later to be called the V1. The power plant was to be a single ram (pulse) jet mounted above the fuselage and using low-octane petrol. The Argus company, producer of engines for light aircraft, was given the contract for manufacturing, testing and developing the powerplant under the supervision of Dr Fritz Gosslau.

Production of the airframe and guidance/control equipment was contracted to the Arado and Lorenz companies respectively. By April 1941 flight-testing of the ram jet was being carried out with it slung underneath the fuselage of a Gotha 145 biplane, and this confirmed the low-speed performance and reliability of the powerplant. The design of the definitive production V1 now passed to the Fiesler company, famous for its Storch slow-flying communications aircraft, under the supervision of designer Robert Lusser, Arado having more urgent work associated with their jet aircraft projects. The finalized design for the V1, known to Fiesler as the Fi 103, was presented to the RLM in June 1942. It comprised a mid-wing monoplane with the following approximate dimensions: wingspan, 17.3 ft; tailplane span, 6.8 ft; overall length, 27 ft; maximum fuselage diameter, 2.8 ft; motor length, 11.3 ft; loaded weight, 4,800 lb.

Fuel capacity was 150 gallons, which gave a range of 150 miles at a nominal operating height of 8,000 ft, and the warhead comprised 1,800 lb of high explosive. The airframe and motor used non-strategic materials, mild-steel and wood wherever possible, and the motor had very few moving parts. At the front of the 1.9 ft diameter tube, a spring-loaded grid-valve opened and closed at around 50 cycles per second, giving the weapon its characteristic 'buzz', and immediately behind the grid-valve fuel was injected and ignited initially by a single sparkplug. The pressure of the igniting fuel closed the spring-loaded grid and the exhaust gases exited at the rear of the tube, providing the thrust of around 800 lbs, enough for a cruising speed of 350 mph. The main disadvantage of the ram jet is that the motor must have some forward speed to compress the fuel-air mixture in the combustion chamber. Hence the V1 had to be accelerated along its firing ramp by some form of catapult, or alternatively it could be launched from an aircraft.

The failure of the Luftwaffe in the Battle of Britain also boosted the acceptance of the V1, and on 19 June 1942 at a top-level Air Ministry meeting chaired by Field Marshal Erhard Milch it was decided that the V1 should by given top priority, with all development work being transferred to Peenemünde-West, where motor testing at operational speeds started, using Me109 and Me110 aircraft, with full-size air-launches from Fw200s at various heights and speeds to confirm the aerodynamic performance of the weapon. The contract for the guidance and control system was given to the Askania company, which had experience of aircraft auto-pilots, the brief being simplicity and hence reliability and low cost.

With this in mind only two moving control surfaces were provided: elevators in the tailplane for height control by varying the pitch attitude of the nose, and a rudder for horizontal directional control. A vertical two-degrees-of-freedom gyro linked to a sensitive aneroid barometer controlled the elevators, the signals being transmitted by servo valves working at 20 lb/in^2 from the vehicle's 1,000 lb/in^2 air storage system. The horizontal control was achieved by a directional gyro which indicated the direction of flight from a heading reference based on a compass pre-set on the bearing of the target. This simple method of directional control had two main disadvantages:

1. The V1 had to be launched on a direct straight-line bearing with the target. If a side wind was encountered during flight, the rudder provided the necessary side force to keep the target bearing on the correct alignment, the vehicle adopting a crab-like flight path. The amount of side force generated by the rudder was limited and hence strong or turbulent side winds produced a poor target accuracy.

2. A directional gyro requires stops on the inner gimbal axis to prevent it becoming locked to the outer gimbal axis. These stops, at ± 85° from the horizontal axis, perform satisfactorily unless the horizontal axis of the vehicle is rotated to an angle more than ± 85°. This results in the inner gimbal stops striking the outer gimbal axis, which then rotates through 180°, causing the 'tumbling' which destroys the vehicle's orientation and hence its stability. This effect was discovered accidentally by Allied fighter pilots who flew alongside the V1 and noticed that gently raising the V1's wing-tip with their own resulted in the V1 losing stability and crashing. But the simplicity of the control system did have its advantages. Because the V1 had no wing-mounted ailerons and therefore in theory could not roll, one of the main sources of error in pitch attitude was removed. This error is due to the fact that a vertical-pitch gyro cannot distinguish between gravity and centrifugal force caused by a roll movement. This causes the basic vertical gyro reference to be in error, which results in height errors. The absence of this source of error at least ensured that the V1 flew at the correct height. Although the V1 did not have ailerons and hence in theory could not change direction, this being achieved in a normal aircraft by first rolling using the ailerons and then turning using the rudder, it was possible by using a small amount of positive dihedral (when viewed from the front the wings have a slight upward V configuration) to change direction. Later in the V1 offensive, some V1s utilized this ability and were fitted with a timing device to provide a pre-set change in heading of a few degrees. This enabled the launch ramp to be aligned off the target bearing, a feature of the original launch sites which had alerted Allied intelligence to the site's purpose. The target range of the V1 was set via a propeller-driven counter which fed impulses to a timer detonator in the arming system. After a pre-set number of impulses had been recorded, the warhead was armed, the fuel supply stopped and spoilers below the tail plane activated, putting the V1 into a pitch-down attitude from which it dived onto the target.

By the end of 1942, free-flight launches from aircraft and similar in-flight testing of the ram jet had confirmed that the flight characteristics of the V1 were satisfactory. Ground launches were the next crucial part of the programme, and two ramps were built by Rheinmetall-Borsig (R-B) at Peenemünde, facing out over the Baltic. Initially the idea was to use solid-fuel booster rockets to accelerate the V1 along the ramp, but after a few trials this method was abandoned in favour of a Walter steam-driven catapult using HTP and a catalyst, the Walter system giving more accurate control over launch velocity.

The first ground launch using the Walter catapult took place on 24 December 1942, and this first flight was a complete success, the V1 droning on along the coastline for 130 miles.

The main part of the ramp was a 12 in diameter tube into which a 3 ft long, 300 lb steel piston fitted, which engaged with a lug on the underside of the fuselage. Steam entered at one end from a portable HTP-catalyst generator, forcing the piston and V1 along the inclined ramp (the angle varying slightly depending on ramp length, though it was usually about 6 to 10°) until at the end of the ramp the V1 was launched at 200 mph, the piston being ejected from the tube to be recovered and used again. Unfortunately the piston left tell-tale scars on the ground where it had landed which were another sign that a launch site was in use.

During early 1943 ramp launches continued with relatively trouble-free progress, the main problems being poor target accuracy due to the simple control system, and reduced speed and range due to higher than expected drag and weight. Speed was down to 350–400 mph instead of 450–500 mph and maximum range was 200 miles, but these were similar problems to those encountered with a new aircraft and the Luftwaffe was confident that gradual improvements could be achieved. On 26 May 1943 a demonstration was arranged before a VIP audience of Ministers, Party officials and military chiefs. The two V1s launched both plunged into the sea after a few seconds' flight, whereas the two V2s launched behaved perfectly; nevertheless, this did not affect the programme.

Mass production was planned at the Volkswagen plant at Fallersleben starting in September 1943, the target being 1,400 V1s by January 1944, rising to 8,000 per month by September 1944. From these figures it is clear that the V1 was intended to take over a large part of the manned bomber offensive against the UK, the initial range of the V1 enabling targets to be reached from Bristol across to the Wash on the east coast when launched from northern France. In addition the successful air-launch stability during the test programme had not gone unnoticed: after release the V1 developed no pitching oscillations and only a slight lateral movement that quickly damped itself out. Although operational air launches would extend the range, this tended to nullify the whole concept of using the V1 as an unmanned bomber; nevertheless, work started in the late spring of 1943 to use the Heinkel He111H as a launch vehicle. Although being phased out as a front-line bomber, the docile flying qualities and solid structure of the He111 provided a suitable platform for carrying a V1 under the port wing.

The Luftwaffe now started the formation of both ground and air personnel to service and launch the operational V1. For the ground launches a new regiment was formed from heavy anti-aircraft personnel and given the name Flakregiment 155 (W) under the command of Colonel Max Wachtel. Total staff was 3,500 men, comprising four Abteilung, each with two service, maintenance and supply sections and four firing teams. Each firing team was capable of manning four launch sites, and hence, in theory, 64 V1s could be launched simultaneously. To train the operational staff, two new launching ramps were built, complete with accommodation and service buildings, adjacent to Peenemünde at Zinnowitz. For the air-launches a new battle-group was formed, Gruppe III of Kampf-geschwader 3, with a complement of forty He111H-22s, its personnel being specially selected from those engaged on secret assignments since 1940.

This was the situation regarding the V2 and V1 as the summer of 1943 approached, and now two more weapons were about to join the arsenal.

THE RHEINBÖTE, RHINE MESSENGER

The heavy engineering and armaments firm of Rheinmetall-Borsig had considerable experience in solid-fuel rockets, short-range weapons for the army and assisted-take-off equipment for the Luftwaffe. Work started, as with all the new weapons, from 1934 onwards, and the project went through the usual problems associated with its acceptance by the Army Weapons Office, the Heereswaffenamt (HWA). By May 1941, with the V2 still awaiting its first successful launch, the go-ahead was given by General Leeb of the HWA for a multi-stage, solid-fuel, unguided rocket with a range of at least 100 miles and a warhead of 2,700 lb. This figure was soon revised since it was realized that to deliver such a payload would have required a massive launch stage, but it was clear from the outset that the thinking was along similar lines to the V2. A team at Rheinmetall was soon set up under a Dr Heinrich Klein, and the project was given the designation Rh Z-61 and Raketesprenggranate 4831 (high-explosive grenade rocket) by the HWA. First trials were carried out later in 1941 from the Leba firing range, 160 miles further down the coast from Peenemünde, the rockets being launched towards the island of Bornholm. The development progressed from single-stage rockets to two-, three- and four-stage versions with an overall length of 36.6 ft and a weight of 3,700 lb. Body diameters varied from 1.8 ft for the first stage to 0.6 ft for the warhead, and each stage was equipped with six swept-back fins, the rocket being spin-stabilized. As no guidance and control system was fitted, the rocket was aligned accurately on the target before launch, and the high velocity of the rocket, with its maximum speed slightly higher than the Mach 5 of the V2, ensured that there was little deviation from the planned trajectory. The angle of launch effectively determined its range, an angle of 65° producing the maximum.

The Rheinböte, like the V2 initially, suffered from a lack of resources, materials and manpower, due to its low priority rating, and only twenty of the long-range, four-stage versions had been launched by the middle of 1943, the first long-range version being demonstrated to members of the HWA in April 1943. The overall length of the four-stage rocket had increased to 42.3 ft, and by the summer of 1943 the maximum ranges achieved were over 140 miles, with a maximum lateral deviation at the target of 12 miles, and the definitive design and arrangement of the fins and structure had been finalized.

THE HOCHDRUCKEPUMPE (HDP), HIGH PRESSURE PUMP

After acceptance of Herman Rochling's plans by Hitler for a long-range gun capable of firing up to 600 shells an hour at London from northern France, and confirmation by Engineer Coenders from model tests that the project was feasible, work started on building two full-size test rigs at the Hillersleben firing range twelve miles north-west of Magdeburg and at Misdroy on the island of Wolin near Peenemünde. The initial trials used a barrel and breech with a total length of 405 ft, and 28 sequential explosive charges were detonated from side-branches as the shell passed along the length of the barrel. Various shell configurations were tried, with typically an overall length of 9 ft, maximum diameter over the stabilizing fins of 5.9 in and minimum diameter of 3.9 in. The project was also given the unofficial names Tausendfussler (millipede), since from above the numerous short side-branches resembled the legs of a millipede, and Fleishiges Lieschen (Busy Lizzie).

The project had one overwhelming advantage over the other long-range weapons in that Herman Rochling had the personal attention of Hitler, and this meant that the project could bypass the usual HWA appraisal and assessment procedures. One of the obvious advantages of the HDP was that it cost very little in terms of resources, including strategic materials and manpower, which appealed to Hitler, and if it could be made to work, the effect of several thousand shells in a few hours, although they were relatively small, on a city like London would be devastating.

Testing at Hillersleben and Misdroy started with short barrel lengths, and the sections gradually increased until the full-size barrel lengths were achieved. Two main technical problems soon revealed themselves. Because the barrel was not rifled as in conventional artillery, the shell was not spin-stabilized but would have to rely on small fins deploying as the shell left the muzzle to provide a rotary motion. And in order to achieve a range of at least 100 miles the muzzle velocity would have to be a minimum of 5,000 ft/sec. The maximum muzzle velocities of conventional artillery were around 3,500 ft/sec and no one knew if the HDP shells could be stabilized at these velocities. Also, the timing of the sequential explosive charges along the barrel was critical, and this was proving difficult to arrange with the split-second accuracy required.

This was the basic situation with the fourth and last of Hitler's long-range weapons, and the thinking behind the overall programme was predictable. No one puts all his eggs in one basket, especially when it involved so many new technical features. If the development potential varied for each of the weapons, they all had at least one basic similarity – they could be used to bombard England – and hence out of the four it was not unreasonable to think that at least one would be finally available for this purpose.

CHAPTER 2

The German Military Situation and the Four Weapons, 1943 to 1945

At the end of 1942 the signs for the Third Reich were ominous. The mass-bomber raids had started in March and April with Lübeck and Rostock. On 16 May 1942 it was Kiel's turn, followed by Dortmund on 25 May. The first 1,000-bomber raid was on Cologne on 30 May, and these raids continued through into 1943, with Hamburg and Berlin among the regular targets. Goebbels wrote in his diary, 'We are facing problems [in Hamburg] of which we had no conception even a few weeks ago.'

At sea, the 'happy hunting days' for the U-boats were over as the Allies started using long-range air cover, better surface protection and radar in their fight against the U-boats attacking the Atlantic convoys, the life-blood of the Allies. Between April and May 1943, 109 U-boats were sunk for the loss of 550,000 tons of Allied shipping, an approximate rate of one U-boat per ship, an unacceptable ratio, and Admiral Doenitz was forced to review the whole U-boat strategy. Despite the introduction of measures such as the Snorkel, which allowed U-boats to run their diesels while submerged and recharge their batteries, this was really only a defensive improvement and did nothing to remedy the real problem, the lack of underwater speed. On land, 1943 had started badly and was getting worse. On 30 January 1943 the newly promoted Field Marshal Friedrich Paulus had surrendered at Stalingrad with what was left of the 300,000 men of his Sixth Army. Never before had a German Field Marshal surrendered on the battlefield, and on 1 February Hitler vented his anger on senior Army commanders at a military conference. On 12 May the last of Rommel's famous Afrika Korps surrendered to the Allies in Tunisia, with the loss of over 240,000 German and Italian troops and most of their equipment.

But worse was to come, and this time there was no obvious scapegoat for Hitler, it was his own plan. Russian forces had recaptured the city of Kursk and the Kursk salient between Orel and Belgorod in the winter of 1942/3. In the early summer of 1943 they had concentrated huge armoured forces in the area ready for a campaign to recapture the Briansk/Orel region in the north and to head south into the Ukraine to push the Germans out of the capital, Kharkov. The bulge in the Russian forces was an obvious weakness, and to Hitler it seemed like a golden opportunity to repeat one of the classic pincer movements of 1941/2 and destroy the very same Russian armies that had been victorious at Stanlingrad, before pushing on towards Moscow in the north and back to Stalingrad in the south. But the Russians had prepared massive defences in depth for just such an eventuality. Under the personal command of Marshals Zhukov and Vassilevsky, the defences included unprecedented numbers of tank and anti-personnel mines, trenches, pillboxes and barbed wire, in some sectors extending to a depth of sixty miles, and thousands of guns of all calibres. The importance of the battle to Hitler and to the German armed forces cannot be over-exaggerated. The build-up of German forces had carried on throughout the spring, with a slight hiccup due to the situation in Italy when Hitler thought Mussolini was about to capitulate, but by the end of June the men and equipment were ready. Facing the front of the bulge was the Second Army under General von Weichs, which was to hold back any forward movement of the Russians. The two arms of the pincers would be formed by the Ninth Army under General Model, which was to push down from the north towards Kursk. This force contained twenty divisions, of which seven were armoured, two motorized and eleven infantry, with 1,500 tanks and 3,000 guns. The southern arm of the claw was the Fourth Army of General Hoth, with eighteen divisions, of which ten were armoured, one motorized and seven infantry, with 1,700 tanks and 2,000 guns. In addition air cover was to be provided by Three Air Corps of Field Marshal Richthofen's Fourth Air Fleet. In overall command was Field Marshal von Manstein.

As early as 10 March Hitler had flown to Zaporozhe in the Ukraine to brief von Manstein on the new offensive, which had the codename Operation Zitadelle. At the end of June all the senior commanders were flown to Munich, where Hitler declared in a stage-managed performance in front of them and other leaders that 'this would be a victory to light up the world.' Operation Zitadelle was to start on 5 July.

In total the battle involved more troops than D-Day, more planes than the Battle of Britain and more tanks than El-Alamein. As far as Hitler was concerned they were 500,000 of the best fighting troops left in Germany, together with the very latest equipment, including the new Tiger tanks. However, within two days of the start of the battle it was clear that there were problems with the German advance. After four days the bulge had only been dented by ten miles in the north and thirty miles in the south, and the tips of the two German pincers were still a hundred miles apart. The losses on both sides were enormous, and it was now obvious that this time the German forces had come up against well-prepared Russian defences, and this was not going to be a repeat of earlier victories.

On 12 July the main Russian counter-attack started when it became clear that the German offensive had run out of steam. Orel was recaptured on 4 August and Kharkov on 23 August, starting a momentum that would carry the Russian armies to Berlin. Operation Zitadelle cost the German forces heavy losses: 70,000 killed and wounded, and 3,000 tanks, 1,000 guns, 1,300 aircraft and over 5,000 other vehicles destroyed. These were losses that would be difficult and in some cases impossible to replace.

This, then, was the overall military situation known to Hitler and a few others, in the summer of 1943. The outcome of the war was not yet a foregone conclusion, but now was the time to 'raid' the weapons bank.

But another player now appears on the scene. In early April 1943 Reichsführer Heinrich Himmler, Head of the SS and all Security Services in Germany, visited Peenemünde, the first of several visits in 1943. Dornberger later claimed that little advance notice had been given for this visit, and it was certainly different from the usual VIP organized tours. Himmler was on a fact-finding mission, because certainly he would be one of those who knew what the true military facts were, and this was the beginning of a slow but steady takeover by the SS of all four weapons projects and, eventually, even the jet aircraft programme.

Of the four 'vengeance' weapons, the V2 was the first to receive Hitler's attention, in light of the changing military situation. On 7 July 1943, barely two days after the start of Operation Zitadelle, Dornberger and von Braun, together with the films, models and displays of the V2 and its various developments, were summoned to Hitler's Rastenburg HQ in East Prussia. After watching the complete presentation, including film of several V2 launches, Hitler told Dornberger that if the rocket had been available in 1939, the war would never have started.

Hitler ordered immediate changes to the V2 production programme, increasing the original Degenkolb figure of 900 per month to 2,000 per month by December 1943, with additional production facilities being built in the Demag works at Falkensee. Karl Saur, one of Speer's department heads and an old Nazi Party confidant, was given the task of coordinating the new production organization. Dornberger was promoted on the spot to Major General and von Braun received the title 'Professor'. They returned to Peenemünde with a new air of urgency, emphasized also by the new priority rating for V2 development work, DE (Dringende Entwicklung), the highest possible.

One day later, on 8 July, Speer and Degenkolb arrived at Rastenburg to hear about the changes to the V2 project direct from Hitler. At this meeting it appears that Speer's comments may have prevailed regarding the sudden increase in V2 production. Neither Dornberger nor von Braun was likely to have expressed any reservations at the new figures when they came directly from Hitler, but Albert Speer was different, and the improvements he was already making in armaments production in the face of Allied bombing ensured that Hitler respected his views. Hence the following day, the production figures were revised again, and the 900 target was moved to October, with 1,300 by December, with a gradual increase to 1,800 by April 1944. Saur now had the unenviable task of organizing the multitude of sub-contractors involved in the V2 project, as well as ensuring that there was sufficient liquid oxygen and alcohol to actually fuel those produced. Certain items had to be made by single specialized firms, and hence all the V2 warheads were made by Domitz at Geestlach, near Hamburg, and all the vehicles and handling equipment, including the Meillerwagen (used for site transport and V2 erection prior to launch), Vidalwagen (used for general V2 site movements) and the Strabo crane, were made by J. Gollnow-u-Sohn of Stettin in railway tunnels on the banks of the River Ahr at Dernau, north-west of Koblenz. But all the changes being organized were thrown into disarray on the night of 17 August 1943, when 597 heavy bombers of the RAF bombed Peenemünde for the first time. Allied intelligence reports and photo-reconnaissance had finally confirmed beyond any doubt that new rocket and pilotless weapons were being developed and tested at Peenemünde. Although the aiming point for the main attack was misplaced and most of the damage was done to the civilian accommodation, including that used by the foreign workers, some of the facilities were damaged and two of the senior rocket scientists, Dr Thiel and Dr Walter, were killed. The raid on Peenemünde had been preceded by raids on Friedrichshafen and Wiener-Neustadt, which effectively put an end to mass production plans for these two sites. The pre-production building at Peenemünde, originally intended for mass production of the V2, was undamaged, and it was from here that the first operational examples of the V2 were built for the training units. One of the directives stemming from the re-organized production figures was that only essential modifications were now to be incorporated into the V2, including those intended to assist mass production. Test launches in the summer of 1943 were taking place at around 25 per month, and the most serious problem was still the break-up of the rocket a few thousand feet above the target area, something that was partially solved by insulating the fuel tanks with glass-fibre; but only when the whole of the external structure around the mid-section of the rocket was provided with stiffening was the problem finally eliminated.

The bombing of Peenemünde and the other production sites provided the opportunity that Himmler was looking for, and only two days after the air raid he flew to Rastenburg to discuss the whole V2 project. It was not difficult to convince Hitler that other changes were needed: the Allied bombers rarely paid only one visit to a target, and there was the real possibility that Peenemünde would very quickly be turned into a ruin. Himmler hardly needed to point out the obvious.

Two major changes came from these discussion between Hitler and Himmler. Himmler proposed that a new launch and testing site should be set up at an SS training ground at Blizna in Poland, between Cracow and Lvov, known as Heidelager to the SS. Here, surrounded by pine forests and sufficiently remote from Allied bombers, all future launches, training and development could be carried out in safety, with security provided by the SS.

In addition production would be moved to some abandoned mine workings, then used for the storage of strategic chemicals, at Kohnstein near Nordhausen in the Hartz mountains. Enlargement of the tunnels would provide ample production space for the V2 plus any other armaments in a secure bomb-proof environment. The SS would provide the labour to enlarge the tunnels, since the Buchenwald concentration camp was nearby, and once again, security would be provided by the SS, who were already responsible for civil administration in the area via SS Standartenführer (Colonel) Dr Wagner. Needless to say, Hitler approved Himmler's recommendations, and by 22 August 1943, following meetings between Hitler, Speer, Saur and Himmler, the necessary orders were put into place. The SS now had a major executive role in almost all aspects of the V2 project, and although the SS themselves had not the expertise to provide a technical input to these activities, this was only the beginning.

The person chosen by Himmler to provide this executive role was one of the rapidly rising stars of the SS organization, SS Brigadeführer und General der Waffen SS Dr Ing. Hans Kammler. This name now runs with an ever-increasing frequency through the story until the very end, and beyond, since he disappeared at the end of the war and his true fate is still a mystery. By May 1945 Kammler was the secret weapons supremo, and no one in the Third Reich knew more about the development and use of these weapons than he did.

Kammler was never in the limelight, staying a very shadowy figure, but he got things done, on time and with an efficiency that cut through problems like a knife through butter. There is only one wartime photograph of Kammler, but what we do know is that he was born on 26 August 1901 at Stettin and his father's name was Franz. He was trained as a civil engineer and was married with five children. His residence as on 1 September 1939 is given as Berlin-Lichterfelde Ost, Salzungerpfad 4. The SS had one of their main barracks and administration centres at Lichterfelde, a southern suburb of Berlin, and this was also the home of Baron Manfred von Ardenne, who appears as one of the nuclear personalities later in the book.

Kammler's qualifications are given as Doctor Engineer, Director of Construction and his last rank as General der Waffen SS. His last reported sighting was in April 1945 at Ebensee, Styria in Austria. The SS had two distinct sides and Kammler's qualifications need further explanation. Firstly, the SS controlled all the security services within the Third Reich which came under the general title of the SD (Sicherheitsdienst), or Security Service, and this included the SIPO (Security Police), the Kriminalpolizei (KRIPO), the RSHA (Reichssicherheitshauptamt) Reich Central Security Office, and the normal civil police force, the SCHUPOS. After 1936 this also included the Gestapo (Geheime Staatspolizei) Secret State Police, originally formed by Goering but combined with the SD on 26 June 1936 under the overall leadership of Heydrich, and after his death under Kaltenbrunner. It was the SD that led the extermination groups in Russia and other occupied territories, the civilian-clothed Gestapo who arrived at 4 o'clock in the morning, and the Amtsgruppe DD of the Reich Administration and Economic Main Office (WVHA) of the SS that ran the concentration camps. This was the more public face of the SS under its leader Heinrich Himmler, but the other side was in some respects more dangerous than the first. Himmler also recruited intellectuals, highly qualified young men from the universities and colleges who were looking for something different from the usual industrial and college careers. One of the main offices of the SS was the Wirstchafts und Vernwaltungshauptamt (WVHA) headed by SS-General Oswald Pohl. For the ambitious young engineer, physicist, lawyer or doctor the WVHA offered a career which included the possibility of rapid promotion in an ever-expanding organization. Professor Werner Osenberg, an SS officer, had been coordinating scientific research for the Reich Research Council since 1943, and it was branches of the WVHA that accommodated the majority of these enthusiastic intellectuals, including Dr Hans Kammler. Kammler's early career in the SS is sketchy, but it is believed he worked in Russia before the 1941 invasion, and there is also some evidence that he assisted the Luftwaffe in their construction programme as new airfields and research establishments were built across Europe. The concentration camps were able to use Kammler's expertise, and in particular a request from the commandant of Auschwitz, Rudolf Hess, for 'improvements' to the gas chambers resulted in Kammler's modifications, more than doubling the flow of victims. One of Kammler's last major projects before weapons work became his main concern was the obliteration of the Warsaw ghetto after the uprising which had been savagely crushed by the SS. Kammler was able to send a report on 10 June 1944 to Himmler stating that the ghetto had been erased, and he included a list of all the most valuable materials and pieces of equipment that had been seized during the operation.

[handwritten margin note: Rudolf Höss]

But now we are in the summer of 1943, and apart from the various other projects being built under the supervision of the WVHA, including the huge underground 'city' in the Jonastal region of Thuringia in southern Germany, which was intended to be the new HQ of Hitler and other leaders of the Third Reich when bombing made Berlin untenable, Kammler was the obvious candidate to supervise the Nordhausen project.

Initially 15,000 workers were brought in, the majority from the nearby Buchenwald and a new camp, Dora, built adjacent to the main tunnel entrance. Work carried on twenty-four hours a day, seven days a week, and to become sick was a death sentence. Even before Dora and its crematorium had been finished thousands had already died, and even Willy Messerschmitt estimated that the death rate at Nordhausen was 17,000 a year. Eventually the workforce totalled 32,000, housed in 31 sub-camps of the main Dora camp. When finished the tunnels stretched for 22 miles, and apart from the V2, the V1 was built there, together with a Junkers aero–engine assembly plant, and submarine and aircraft components. V1 and V2 production started at Nordhausen in January 1944, and the total V2 output up to the end of February was around 140 rockets. This output gradually rose until it reached 300 by April and 600 in August, a figure which stabilized in this region: figures for October and November were 650, December 618, January 1945 700, 615 for February and 490 for March. In September and October 1943 the first 400 V2s went to the Blizna range in Poland for use as test and training firings. V1 production at Nordhausen is more difficult to assess, since V1s were also being produced at Fiesler's Stettin plant and the Volkswagen plant, despite the bombing and possible other locations: because the V1 was of relatively simple construction it lent itself to improvised production in smaller units. In 1943 total V1 construction was around 2,500, of which virtually all were pre-production units used for testing. In 1944 the average monthly production was maintained at around 2,500 units, apart from a sudden drop in March to 500, and this was probably due to the switch of production to Nordhausen. Both Dornberger and von Braun were occupied with getting Nordhausen, or Mittelwerk, as it was known at Peenemünde, ready for V2 production, as were other senior members of the Peenemünde team. After the war all these people denied that there had been any harsh treatment of prisoners, and

Dornberger in his book *V2* only refers to Mittelwerk as 'a new emergency factory under construction'. Very few documents from Nordhausen survived, but among them are the minutes of a V2 meeting on 6 May 1944, when it was agreed to obtain another 1,800 workers from occupied countries. The meeting was chaired by George Rickhey, General Manager at Nordhausen, who was prosecuted by the US Army and acquitted after the war. Among those present and on the top of the distribution list for the minutes of the meeting was Dornberger; fourteenth was von Braun, fifty-first was Dr Steinhoff and eleven below him was Arthur Rudolph, Production Director at Nordhausen. Part of the Nordhausen telephone directory has also survived, and this shows that both Dornberger and von Braun were near the top of the list. In 1978 President Carter established the Office of Special Investigations (OSI) to investigate Nazi war criminals living in the USA. One of its young lawyers, Eli Rosenbaum, read *Dora: A Survivor's Story of the Third Reich's Hell-hole Death Camp* by one of Nordhausen's French survivors, Jean Michel. This eventually led to the removal of restrictions on access to the US files on Nordhausen and an investigation into the German rocket and medical experts who had moved to the USA after the war, including members of the Peenemünde team. When Rosenbaum's investigations started in 1979, von Braun had recently died from cancer, but Rudolph was questioned about his involvement at Nordhausen. On 13 October 1982, before any further action could be taken, he relinquished his American citizenship and returned to Germany. It was Rudolph who was Production Director for the US Saturn-Apollo moon-landing project, which put Armstrong and Aldrin on the moon on 20/21 July 1969. Dornberger never joined the rest of the Peenemünde team in America, although he held various consultancy posts with US companies and visited the USA several times.

In 1942 Dornberger had formed a special army unit to train other army units in the handling, servicing and launching of the V2. This group, Lehr und Versuchs Batterie 444, had been operating at Zinnowitz, ten miles south of Peenemünde. With Blizna now taking over the testing, launch and training role, Batterie 444, together with three new launch units, Batteries 485, 836 and 191 Motorized, were moved to Blizna, where, although Dornberger was theoretically in charge, the SS were providing an ever-increasing input to the operation and also formed their own launch unit, SS-Werfer Batterie 500. By the end of 1943, V1 launches were also taking place at Blizna, and both V2s and V1s were using live warheads during training.

Launches of the Rheinböte had continued throughout 1943 and into 1944 with very little enthusiasm from Albert Speer regarding resources, but development continued since, among others, Kammler was in favour of the project and four-stage test firings showed ranges of 120–150 miles. Total production of the four-stage rocket had only reached 100 by the end of 1944, but this was to be increased by an additional 200 in January 1945.

The HDP was also progressing with test firings, using full-size bore and barrel lengths, from the two ranges Hillersleben and Misdroy, using the definitive shell design which had shown that the system worked. The main concern now was that the test firings up to January 1944 had been with unrepresentative explosive charges, and hence the design muzzle exit velocity required for the shells to reach London from northern France had still to be achieved. Discussions between Hitler, Speer and Saur on 25 January 1944 confirmed the continued acceptance of the project, and the monthly output of shells was increased from a projected 2,500 to 10,000.

Further intrusions by the SS in the V2 project occurred on 15 March 1944, when von Braun and two of his senior engineers, Riedel and Gottrup, were arrested under Himmler's direct orders. Although von Braun was a major in the SS and had been a member since 1 May 1940, it was apparently his refusal to join the SS weapons organization that had prompted Himmler to order the arrests. Not until Speer's intervention a few days later were the three released, but it was a warning of things to come.

Of the four weapons, the first to be used operationally was the V1. Originally the start date for the V1 offensive from sites in northern France had been scheduled for 15 February 1944, but bombing of the original production facilities had delayed production so much that Hitler cancelled the start until at least May, by which time Nordhausen would be operational. Colonel Wachtel, commander of the operational launch organization, had left Zinnowitz in October 1943 with a large part of Flak Regiment 155 (W), to prepare the sites in France for the original offensive start date, and although the move was premature, the extra time was spent ensuring that the sites that were finished and undamaged by Allied bombing were fully operational. The reliability and accuracy of the V1 had improved, mainly due to the fact that over 350 test vehicles were used in the development programme, using both ramp and air launches.

If progress with the V1 was satisfactory, the HDP was now encountering serious problems.

Final testing at Misdroy with a maximum of 32 side-branch charges had produced a maximum muzzle velocity of 3,600 ft/sec, comparable with conventional artillery, and only the 11 in (28 cm) Krupp K5 railroad gun had exceeded this figure. With a barrel length of 420 ft, the HDP needed a muzzle velocity of at least 5,000 ft/sec if the shells were to reach London. When the side-barrel charges were increased to increase the shell velocity, two problems immediately revealed themselves. Firstly, isolated sections of the main barrel started failing under the increased explosive pressure due to faults in the steel. More seriously, as the shell velocity increased, so did the problem of shell instability, and eventually complete stability was lost when the shells 'toppled'. It was obvious that insufficient high-speed aerodynamic testing had been carried out, and when the University of Göttingen was consulted on the problem their response was that it was probably too late to change the shell design and that the only possible short-term solution was to reduce the shell weight.

The Heereswaffenamt (HWA) was now advising cancellation of the project, but Hitler was convinced it could be made to work, although Saur did manage to convince him that the shell production figures should be halved while the problems were investigated.

In the meantime, since 1942 Peenemünde had been carrying out its own research under a contract from Krupp, who were also interested in very-long-range artillery. Krupp had produced a family of 11 in (28 cm) railroad guns, all under the 'Bruno' codename. Different barrel lengths were to used to obtain greater ranges, but eventually problems with rifling and barrel flexing caused Krupp to consider a similar shell design to Rochling's. Two barrels were reamed-out to 12.2 in (31 cm) and the rifling removed. Peenemünde supplied a shell design similar to the HDP shell, 71 in (1.8 m) long × 4.7 in (120 mm) diameter, the shell being steadied in the barrel with a sabot-ring which was discarded at the muzzle when four fins deployed, providing spin-stability. This shell was fired as in normal artillery, but the range was only 90 miles maximum, although there were some plans to provide a small solid-fuel rocket motor in the base of the shell to boost the velocity.

On 20 July 1944 an event occurred which dramatically affected the whole V-weapons programme. An attempt was made on Hitler's life at his Rastenburg HQ. Unfortunately for the conspirators, the hot weather meant that the military conference for that day had been moved from its usual bunker location to a wooden building among the pine trees. With some of the windows open, the blast effect of the bomb, hidden in a briefcase under the conference table, was greatly reduced, helped by the solid structure of the table. At precisely 12.50 p.m., as General Heusinger was giving his report on the Russian front, the bomb exploded, killing a stenographer, Berger, outright. General Gunther Korten, Luftwaffe Chief of Staff, General Rudolf Schmundt, the Chief Adjutant of the Armed Forces, and Colonel Heinz Brandt died of their injuries. Others were wounded, some seriously, but Hitler escaped relatively lightly. His hair was singed, his right arm and leg affected by the blast and his eardrums damaged. The revenge of the SS for this failed plot was quick and ruthless. Those of the conspirators who did not commit suicide or were shot immediately after the explosion were soon rounded up by the Gestapo and in some cases put before the Volksgericht (People's Court) as a token gesture, but most ended up hanged at Plotzensee Prison in Berlin. Colonel Stauffenberg, who actually placed the bomb, was shot at the War Ministry in Bendlerstrasse, a few hours after the bomb went off, when it was realized that Hitler had survived. The net of the SS spread far and wide as confessions were extracted from conspirators, and Field Marshal Rommel was implicated in the plot, not as an active member but because he knew about the plot and had said nothing. He was given an ultimatum on 14 October 1944 and chose poison.

If action against the bomb-plot conspirators was swift, it was even faster regarding the V-weapons programme. One of the conspirators was General Friedrich Fromm, C-in-C of the Reserve Army, but more importantly for Himmler, he was also chief of the Heereswaffenamt, the Army Weapons Office, which controlled all the army's rocket and missile projects, including the V2, Rheinböte and HDP. The V1 at that time was still under the control of the Luftwaffe. On the same day as the bomb, Hitler appointed Himmler as Fromm's successor.

On 6 August, Kammler was promoted to SS-Gruppenführer (Lieutenant-General), and on the same day Hitler appointed him as Plenipotentiary (General Commissioner) for all aspects of the Army's weapons projects, including the V2, Rheinböte and HDP. Complaints from Speer, Dornberger and von Braun that their authority was being usurped were wasted, and even an attempt to turn Peenemünde into a limited company was an immediate failure.

The original V-weapon operational plans from the French sites were that an experienced artillery officer, Lieutenant-General Erich Heinemann, was to be in overall control, with Major-General Richard Metz having responsibility for the V2. Although V1 launches had been carried out since 12 June 1944, with the Allied advance into France there was a gradual decrease in the number of V1 sites available, and no operational launches of the V2, Rheinböte or HDP had taken place up to August 1944.

Kammler and his staff had moved to Brussels on 30 August 1944 to start his Behelfmassiger Schnelleinsatz A-4 (Immediate Improved Operation A-4), also codenamed Operation Pinguin, and on the 31st, at a military conference at which both Heinemann and Metz were present, the Army was discredited after the 20 July bomb plot. SS investigations were still in progress, and Kammler stated that the 15th Army Corps was no longer in charge of V-weapons field operations, whereupon both Heinemann and Metz disappeared from the V-weapons programme. The SS, and in particular Kammler, were now virtually in sole command of all long-range weapons.

With the first V2 rocket soon to be launched from Holland on 8 September 1944, the situation regarding all four weapons was as follows.

V2

Due to the Russian advances into Poland, the Blizna site was abandoned in July 1944 and launches transferred to Tuchel Heath (Heidekraut), south-west of Danzig.

The ongoing problem with mid-air structural failure was finally solved by adding reinforcing ribs (stringers), or 'Korsett', externally around the whole fuel tankage area. This, together with detailed strengthening of the guidance and control section, produced the desired result. The extra weight reduced the range slightly, but this could be countered by a reduction in the warhead weight.

By 1944, two different V2 projects were on the drawing board, using trains as a mobile launch system and using U-boats to tow a V2 container across the Atlantic to bombard New York. Three V2 trains were actually completed by 1945, and PRO file ADM 223/702 provides some information on their eventual fate. The trains were intended to transport everything needed for a V2 launch, and each was in two parts. The first carried the personnel, living quarters, laboratories, and workshops, and the second the rockets, vehicles and fuel. Total number of personnel was 100 plus six rockets and the necessary fuel, but no radar-tracking equipment was included, nor were there provisions for oxygen production.

At the end of 1942 the prototype train was ready for testing at Peenemünde, and the operating procedure was that the train would be driven into a suitable tunnel, only emerging when the V2 was ready to be elevated into the launch position. According to Dornberger, development of the trains had been suspended, but Kammler ordered work to be resumed at the end of 1944 for reasons unknown to Dornberger.

At the end of the war, one of the trains vanished, but two were captured by the Russians and these were rebuilt by ex-Peenemünde personnel working from the Thuringia area, then part of East Germany. They were given the title, or codename, of FMS, Fahrbare Meteorologische Station (mobile meteorological station), and the first train left Bleicherode in December 1946, followed by the second in January 1947, but their final fate is unknown.

The U-boat scheme was more unusual and consisted of a submersible container looking not unlike a U-boat, but minus conning tower and with a blunt bow and large stabilizing fins at the stern. The container held one fully assembled V2 with all the necessary fuel and accommodation for the launch team. The idea put forward by Engineer Lafferenz in 1943 was that three containers would be towed by a U-boat, and such was the interest in extending the range of the V2 that the project was taken up by Peenemünde in 1944. It appears that at least one container was completed and towing trials had commenced when the war ended. The semi-submerged containers would have been towed across the Atlantic to the launch area, rotated into the vertical position and the V2 launched. The practicality of such a scheme is doubtful due to the length of time needed to tow the containers across the Atlantic and the question of being able to launch the rocket from potentially rough seas.

V1

Various minor modifications were being incorporated into the V1 to improve its range and speed, but the basic design remained unchanged throughout the offensive. Fuel tankage was increased from 150 to 226 gallons, with a corresponding reduction in warhead weight from 1,830 to 1,188 lb, and the range was increased to 220 miles. Despite the Allied landings in France, the advance along the 'rocket coast' was initially slow due to German resistance around Caen. Not until 31 August was Amiens captured, followed by Brussels on 3 September, and Boulogne and Calais on 6 September; by the 9th the whole of the Pas de Calais was in Allied hands, together with the last of the French sites. Before FR155 (W) moved from France, Colonel Wachtel had reached a maximum launch rate of 200 per day from the 50–60 launch sites still operational, of which about 160–170 were reaching southern England. In the eleven weeks of the offensive almost 9,000 V1s were launched against England, including air launches, the last from France on 5 September 1944. After the stabilization of the front in Holland a series of new V1 launch sites were built in western Holland, usually in industrial areas. Typically sites were built in the oil refinery at Rotterdam/Pernis, in the sugar refinery at Puttershoek and in the Lever Brothers soap factory west of Rotterdam, with one in the glue works south of Delft. Launches against the UK started from these new sites on 3 March 1945 and lasted for four weeks, in which time 275 V1s were launched. Operational air-launches of the V1 had started on

16 September 1944, KG 3 having available an initial total of 75 He111s, and a spasmodic air-launched offensive started which lasted until January 1945. A total of 1,300 were air-launched, but attrition from Allied fighters and other problems resulted in total aircraft losses of 77, and the air campaign was not considered a success. Typically, on Christmas Eve 1944, fifty He111s launched their V1s against Manchester from the North Sea. Only 31 actually crossed the coastline and only one V1 came down within the city boundaries, the remainder falling between ten and twenty miles from the target.

Rheinböte

After 20 July 1944 the Rheinböte had also come under Kammler's control, and at a demonstration on 16 November 1944 at the Leba range, at which Kammler, Dornberger and weapons experts from the HWA and SS were present, three out of the four launches were successful; according to Dornberger, the main problem was the size of the warhead, which had an offensive weight of 55 lb. Kammler insisted that the project should proceed, and production figures of 500 rockets per month were put to Rheinmetall-Borsig. By the end of December, 115 of the largest version, the four-stage Rh-Z-61/9, were available. Field operations were to be under Kammler's control, using Artillery Battery 709.

Plans for providing special launch equipment unique to the Rheinböte were abandoned, and a modified V2 Meillerwagen was used. Unfortunately, launching the 42 ft rocket at an inclined angle required a rigid launch platform if it was to produce an accurate trajectory, and using the Meillerwagen was an unsatisfactory solution.

Kammler issued operational orders to Art. Abt. 709 on 24 December 1944. Launch teams were to operate close to the V2 teams in Holland, and initially twenty-five rockets were available, the target being Antwerp, a range of 100 miles. The Rheinböte offensive ended in the middle of January when supplies of rockets were exhausted and a total of sixty rockets had been fired, mainly against Antwerp, which was being used as the main Allied supply port.

HDP

Kammler had also taken control of the HDP project, and following demonstrations at Misdroy on 29 November and 22 December 1944, using a shortened barrel of 197 ft and production versions of the shell, it was decided that an effort would be made to get the weapon operational, although by this time the original firing site against London, at Mimoyecques, near Calais, had been in Allied hands since September. A possible site was found near Trier, just over the German border on the banks of the River Ruwer, and Art. Abt. HAA 705 started the erection of two of the shortened-barrel versions, the target being the southeast border with France, from Luxembourg to Strasbourg. On 30 December 1944 both HDP weapons started firing at Allied troops in the Luxembourg area, and by 13 January just over a hundred shells had been fired. Kammler in the meantime had instructed Rochling to manufacture two more barrels by the end of June for use against French border targets from inside Germany, but the deteriorating military situation ensured that, although produced, these two additional barrels were never installed at a site. The end for the HDP finally came on 12 February 1945, when Kammler finally agreed that no more ammunition would be manufactured, and the last shells were fired on 22 February. It was to be another fifty-six years before the weapon reappeared in a modern guise when Saddam Hussein of Iraq employed Canadian weapons expert Dr Gerald Bull to design for him a new, simpler version of the HDP, nicknamed the 'super-gun'.

The V2 carried on from various sites in Holland until the 27 March 1945, by which time launch batteries 444, 485, 836 and SS battery 500 had launched nearly three thousand rockets against targets in Belgium, France, Holland and England. The main targets were Antwerp (1,600) and London (1,346), although nineteen were aimed at Paris and forty at Norwich during this period.

At the end of March the various launch teams retreated from Holland, and early in April they were disbanded, the intention being to form them into infantry units.

On 26 January Kammler had received his penultimate order from Hitler, when he was officially made responsible for all V1 and V2 operations. Kammler, now a full general (Obergruppenführer) in the Waffen SS, still had tasks to complete in Germany.

CHAPTER 3

The German Bomb, 1939 to 1945

INTRODUCTION

From 1900 to 1938 the world of nuclear physics was slowly increasing its knowledge in this new branch of science. In England, Ernest Rutherford was carrying out work, first in Manchester and then at Cambridge, which resulted in the classification of radiation into three types, alpha, beta and gamma, and the discovery of the atomic nucleus in 1906. Marie Curie in France was working on radioactivity, resulting in the discovery of radium and polonium. Born in Poland, she was awarded a Nobel Prize in 1911 and pioneered the use of gamma and X-rays in medicine, especially in the First World War. Her daughter Irene carried on the family tradition with her husband Frederic Joliot, and they were awarded the Nobel Prize for Chemistry in 1935.

Neils Bohr in Sweden was also working on the nuclear model of the atom, for which he was awarded the Nobel Prize in 1922, and at the beginning of the 1930s the pace began to speed up. Chadwick in England discovered the neutron (Nobel Prize 1935), and in Italy (Fermi), the USA (Urey), Russia and Japan, scientists of all disciplines were unravelling the secrets of the atom, but it was in Germany that the next major piece of the jigsaw was discovered.

Lenard, von Laue, Planck and Stark had been Nobel Prize winners for physics in 1905, 1914, 1918 and 1919, and in 1932 Werner Heisenberg, Professor of Physics at Leipzig, joined this élite group in Germany. However, as 1938 came to a close, a small group of workers at the Kaiser Wilhelm Institute for Chemistry in Berlin were experimenting with microscopic amounts of the new uranium isotope U.235. With very rudimentary laboratory-produced equipment, the leader of the group, Otto Hahn, and his assistants, Fritz Strassman and Lise Meitner, had been bombarding the nucleus of U.235 with neutrons from a neutron source using the radium isotope Ra.226. To Hahn's surprise, instead of producing an element close to uranium and radium in the periodic table of atomic numbers, U=92 and Ra=88, a new element was produced which was related to barium, atomic number 56. The results were checked and double-checked to see if there had been a mistake, but there was no mistake, they had produced an isotope of barium. Neils Bohr in Sweden had put forward the 'droplet' idea in 1937, that if a nucleus is bombarded by a neutron and absorbs the neutron then two things can happen. If the combined nucleus has little energy, the droplet will extend and then return to its original shape. If the combined nucleus has the 'critical energy', the droplet will extend into a dumbell shape and then split into two almost equal fragments:

the splitting-up into the two fragments is 'fission'. In either case the energy of the bombarding neutron leaves the compound nucleus in an 'excited' state, and the new compound nucleus can emit its excess energy as gamma radiation, forming a new element which is an isotope of the original nucleus but one unit higher in mass number. This non-fission type of neutron absorption or 'capture' results in the new isotope decaying, or disintegrating, until a stable configuration of protons and neutrons is reached in the nucleus. The bomb material plutonium Pu.239 is produced when uranium U.238 captures a neutron and decays eventually to Pu.239.

If the excited compound nucleus has enough energy, the 'critical energy' from the absorbed neutron, for fission to take place, the two fission fragments formed are the main source of the energy produced in fission, approximately 84 per cent. The remainder comes from instant gamma rays, 3.5 per cent, the energy of neutrons produced by fission, 2.5 per cent, beta particles from the fission fragments and other decay products, 3.5 per cent, gamma rays from fission fragments and decay products, 3 per cent and finally neutrino energy, 3.5 per cent. The fission products go through an average of four decay stages until a stable configuration is reached, stable meaning that the new isotope has a very long radioactive half-life. As a general rule, the shorter the half-life, the more radioactive energy the nuclide has, and hence nuclides with very long half-lives emit very little radioactivity and are comparatively safe to handle.

Hahn had produced 'fission', but on such a small scale that the resulting energy was minute. However, once the results of the experiment were confirmed, the news spread around the world like wildfire. Early in 1939 other physicists, including Frederic Joliot-Curie and his two assistants, Lew Kowarski and Fritz von Halban, in Paris and two groups in America, including Fermi and Szilard, extended the scope of Hahn's work and showed that not only were two fission fragments expelled, but at the moment of fission, which took place in a fraction of a micro-second, neutrons were also produced. This result was as amazing as Hahn's, since their experiments showed that although only one neutron was required to start the fission process, once fission occurred something like 2.5 neutrons were also produced with the fission fragments. Since there are billions of nuclei in a small amount of U.235, it followed that if every neutron in fission produced 2.5 neutrons, there would be a massive neutron multiplication and production of energy in a very short period of time. This was the 'chain reaction' that would eventually lead to nuclear power and nuclear weapons.

But in the summer of 1939, little had been proved and no one had produced a chain reaction or had any idea of how to control it once it started. However, this was 1939, and around the world the talk was not of peace but of war.

A quick calculation by the physicists showed that if a kilogram (2.2 lb) of pure U.235 was able to fission completely it would produce a similar amount of energy to 2,500 tons of coal or 20,000 tons of TNT. The potential advantages were obvious, not for industry, but for use as a weapon of war, and from the very start this new source of power was given a label as a weapon. In Germany the munitions factories were turning out ever more tanks, guns, aircraft and warships. The Army Weapons Office, the HWA, was not only directing and financing most of this work, it was also providing the money for the rocket work of Dornberger and his team at Peenemünde.

In January 1939, physicist Enrico Fermi and his family arrived in New York, having fled Fascist Italy. On 18 March he gave a brief presentation to the US Navy on the possibility of producing a nuclear explosive, but at the time such an idea was not taken too seriously by the military minds. Nevertheless, by April 1939 it had been confirmed that fission did produce around 2.5 neutrons and these neutrons were available to produce further fissions; in theory a chain reaction was possible. In Germany at this time, physicist William Hanle gave a lecture at Göttingen in which he suggested that the energy from a graphite-uranium reactor could be harnessed for commercial purposes, and a report on this lecture was forwarded to Abraham Esau, Head of Physics at the Reich Research Council. An ex-student of Otto Hahn's, Nicholas Riehle, now working for the Auer metal company, which was later to provide both uranium and thorium for German nuclear work, wrote to the HWA, acquainting them of the military potential of the new discovery. More significantly, Paul Harteck, Professor of Chemistry at Hamburg University, wrote to the War Ministry on 24 April 1939. In his letter he pointed out that nuclear fission had the potential to provide explosives with unimaginable force, and hence the country that possessed such material would have a dominant position throughout the world. Despite Harteck's claims after the war that the main purpose of the letter was to obtain funds for nuclear research, the tone of his letter to the War Ministry implies a real interest in developing nuclear weapons in the interests of Germany.

On 24 April 1939 Hitler gave his last peacetime speech in the Reichstag, in reply to a telegram from Roosevelt, who had asked for assurances that both he and Mussolini had no military intentions towards thirty-one countries listed, including Poland, France and Great Britain. This speech, described by William Shirer as Hitler's masterpiece, poured scorn on Roosevelt's attempt to blame Germany for the present insecurity in the world. Hitler stated before an enthusiastic audience that Germany was only seeking to regain its rightful position in the world, denied for so long by the 448 articles of the Versailles Treaty, and Germany had no interest in other countries. This speech, full of sarcasm and innuendo, was received with rapturous applause, but it only served to increase the concerns in Europe and the USA. France in particular was now engaged in a frantic effort to extend, enlarge and modernize the Maginot Line, especially after being told at the end of 1936 by the Belgian Prime Minister that in the event of war with Germany, Belgium would declare itself neutral. This left a gap in the defences of nearly 200 miles from the last of the original Maginot fortifications, Ferme Chappy, near the Belgium–Luxembourg border, to the Channel coast.

In Germany the task of reviewing the sudden arrival of nuclear fission as a potential weapon was given to Professor-General Erich Schumann, Head of Research at the HWA. As Schumann was not a nuclear physicist he enlisted the advice of Kurt Diebner, who was working on uranium research at the Army's Kummersdorf firing range, also the original home of the Peenemünde team, and Abraham Esau, Head of Physics at the Reich Research Council. The result of these discussions was that a series of meetings took place from April to October 1939 at which all the senior physicists and other scientists, including Harteck, were invited to determine the way ahead. It was unlikely that any of those present had much in the way of inhibitions towards any possible military applications of nuclear power. We know of Harteck's letter, and that Heisenberg, among other German physicists, had visited the USA, Heisenberg as late as June/July 1939, to discuss nuclear work with physicists now working in America, some of whom had left Germany and Italy due to the political/military situation that was developing in Hitler's Third Reich. Heisenberg himself was asked why he did not move to America, but his reply was that he wanted to take his chance with the 'new' Germany. The problem in Germany was that, if you were prepared to ignore the military preparations and the treatment of the Jews, the German economy was booming and 'the people had never had it so good'.

In America on 2 August 1939, Albert Einstein, sent his famous letter to President Roosevelt in which he mentioned that the discovery of fission had led to the possibility of producing an extremely powerful bomb. Even at this time no one, not even Einstein, knew how the bomb was going to be made, and how or if it could be controlled. In his letter Einstein mentioned that the bomb might have to be carried by a ship and it would be too heavy to be carried by aircraft.

The effect of Einstein's letter was a polite 'thank you', and in particular the military showed little interest. If little response came from the military and political leaders, scientists in the UK and America were now looking at some of the basic problems in determining if a nuclear explosion was possible. At one of the scientific meetings in Germany on 16 September 1939, the general consensus was if it was possible to make a bomb, it must be done. Hans Geiger, whose name is linked with the radiation monitor from work he did with Rutherford in Manchester, was present at this meeting, and he agreed that if it was at all possible, the work should be done.

At the HWA, Erich Schumann decided that packages of nuclear research would be distributed among the various leading organizations in the field of nuclear science, the objective being that within a short period of time it should be possible to use the results of this work to judge which was the best way forward. The work was distributed as follows: University of Leipzig (Heisenberg and Dopple), Army Research Centre Gottow (Diebner and Bagge), University of Hamburg (Harteck), Kaiser Wilhelm Institute for Medical Research Heidelberg (Bothe), KWI for Physics, Dahlem, Berlin (von Weizsacker, Wirtz, Diebner, Bopp). The focal point for this work would be the KWI in Dahlem.

As the work now involved the military and therefore was State Secret, the resident Director there, Peter Debye, a Dutchman, was asked to accept German citizenship or resign. He declined to become German and went to America, as many of his co-workers had done. As an interim measure, Diebner was appointed in his place. The two main areas of nuclear work in Germany were to be the construction of a reactor and isotope separation. What scanty knowledge existed in late 1939 on reactor design was hardly enough to write on the back of an envelope. What was known was that at their 'birth' in the fission process all neutrons were 'fast' neutrons, but with a suitable moderator, which slowed them down by scattering collisions without them being absorbed, these 'slow' neutrons would fission more readily with U.235 than with fast neutrons. The main ingredient of natural uranium was U.238, 99.3 per cent, whereas U.235 only comprised 0.7 per cent, but U.238 would only fission by means of fast neutrons, and the probability of this happening was very small. Ideally, if you had a uranium fuel where the percentage of U.235 had been increased to around 3 or 4 per cent, the chances of achieving fission would be much greater. The problem was separating U.235 from uranium to enrich the fuel with extra U.235. This separation of U.235 had only been done with microscopic amounts in the laboratory, using a cyclotron, a method completely unsuitable for producing kilograms of U.235.

Could natural uranium be used as the fuel? Quite possibly, but several tons would be needed to ensure there was enough U.235 in the total mass of uranium to achieve the critical mass, and since U.238 captured neutrons, removing them from the process, the moderator used would have to be very efficient at producing scattering collisions and slowing neutrons down. Finally, if a reactor could be constructed in which fission occurred, how would the fission process be controlled? There were physicists who believed that any large-scale fission process, as in a reactor, would be uncontrollable and explode like a bomb.

Information was also needed on the interaction of alpha, beta and gamma radiation on materials. The Curies in Paris had done a lot of work with radium isotopes and their products, but as Hahn had shown, fission produced a completely new family of radioactive nuclides.

In 1940, these were some of the problems that existed, not only in Germany, but in any country where research was being carried out on nuclear weapons and reactors, and this included America, Great Britain, France and Japan.

In France, however, on 21 June 1940 it was all over as far as serious nuclear research was concerned, when Hitler and his generals arrived at Compiegne to formally witness the capitulation of that country. Frederic Joliot-Curie stayed in Paris for the remainder of the war, but his two main assistants, von Halban and Kowarski, fled to England with their supply of heavy water, and the bulk of their uranium was secretly buried in Morocco.

In Germany, Werner Heisenberg's work on reactor design was completed, and work by Bothe on using graphite as a moderator had shown that it absorbed too many neutrons during the scattering process. Therefore, the emphasis shifted to an alternative, heavy water, which is composed of deuterium, the hydrogen isotope which has a mass twice that of the constituent of ordinary water, hydrogen and oxygen. Although small amounts of heavy water were available in Germany, the conquest of Norway in 1940 produced another source. Norsk-Hydro had a plant for producing hydrogen using electrolysis from the ample supplies of hydro-electricity at Rjukan. One of the by-products was heavy water, and from late 1940 production was increased to five tons per year using additional equipment designed by Harteck, and the whole plant was put under the control of I.G. Farben. With heavy water now accepted as the best candidate for the moderator, work on graphite was centred on it being used as a reflector in the reactor, to bounce any escaping neutrons back into the fuel.

The use of heavy water as a moderator was not only because of its availability, but also because heavy water is vastly superior as a moderator in comparison to graphite. Moderators of heavy water can slow neutrons down to become thermal neutrons after only 25 collisions with the nuclei of heavy hydrogen, whereas it takes one neutron something like 115 collisions with the carbon nuclei in graphite before they become thermal neutrons. Heavy water also absorbs fewer neutrons than graphite, and as the moderator tends to remain cool there is little need for the control system to adjust the reactor core activity.

By 1941, Heisenberg had become the self-appointed leader of the nuclear community in Germany, and by the end of 1941, with all the various packages of work returned to the HWA, Schumann decided that nuclear work should be classified only as work important to the war effort. This was typical of one of the consequences of the success of the German armed forces by the summer of 1941, and was similar to the attitude of the HWA to the work at Peenemünde when Dornberger found the priority ratings reduced and the very real possibility that work on the V2 might be cancelled.

Heisenberg's favoured reactor design at this time was for layers of natural uranium sandwiched between layers of heavy water; between each sandwich would be a layer of carbon, and the whole would be surrounded by a neutron reflector of carbon. Control would be by a neutron-absorbing poison such as cadmium, boron or silver.

In the USA in early 1941, the Manhattan Project to build a nuclear weapon was already under way. In March the first microscopic amounts of the new element plutonium had been produced in the laboratory, using a cyclotron. A few days later it was confirmed that when bombarded with slow neutrons from a neutron source, it fissioned as readily as U.235 and produced more energy. In the two years since 1939 the US political and military leaders had accepted that nuclear energy could be turned into a decisive weapon, and they had been apprised by the experts as to the best way forward to separate U.235 from natural uranium in order to provide an enriched fuel (3 per cent) for a reactor or for a bomb (70–90 per cent). The most promising methods of U.235 separation were centrifuge, gaseous diffusion and electromagnetic. To obtain Pu.239 for a bomb the options were a nuclear reactor with enriched fuel, either graphite or light-water moderated, or using natural uranium fuel with heavy water as the moderator. The Americans pressed on with a single-minded objectiveness, concentrating on what was the most promising method of separation, gaseous diffusion. In the meantime Enrico Fermi and his colleagues were building a nuclear pile in a sports ground in Chicago, using six tons of uranium metal, 40 tons of uranium oxide, and a graphite reflector one foot thick around the uranium, with the fission process controlled by neutron-absorbing strips of cadmium and using forced-air cooling. CP-1, as it was known, went critical on 2 December 1942, proving that a controlled, self-sustaining nuclear reaction was possible. The thermal power of CP-1 was only 200 watts, and at this power output it would have taken thousands of years to produce enough Pu.239 for a bomb, but most importantly it confirmed that a reactor could be made to work and be controlled without exploding like a bomb.

In Germany in 1941, no reactor was working, but von Weizsacker had written a paper in which he put forward the theory that there could be another fissionable element with a higher atomic number than uranium, and that it could be produced in a uranium reactor following neutron capture by U.238 and its subsequent decay. In this paper the new element was described as a potential explosive. In the two years plus since Paul Harteck had sent his letter to the War Ministry, very little real progress appeared to have been made under the self-appointed leadership of Heisenberg. Harteck was now considering building his own reactor based on the principle that a reactor was possible in which virtually no thermal power was produced, but which would still produce irradiated material and radioactive isotopes, plus the new element referred to by von Weizsacker. Hateck's reactor would be moderated at a very low temperature using solid carbon dioxide (dry ice) at $-80°C$, which was relatively cheap and easily obtainable. Harteck had contacts with I.G. Farben, and he had already been told that 15 tons of carbon dioxide would be available. Obtaining the required amount of uranium oxide proved more difficult, and in this respect Heisenberg was unhelpful. Eventually, late in 1940, Harteck's first reactor experiment, using 500 lb of uranium oxide, was completed without criticality being reached. But the uranium situation had suddenly improved following the German occupation of Belgium. For years the Union Minière company had been mining uranium in the Belgian Congo, and at their refining and storage plant at Oolen, in Belgium, the Germans discovered 1,000 tons of mixed uranium products which they had not had time to ship to the USA, and one train-load was also discovered abandoned near Le Havre. Harteck now planned a much larger reactor experiment, using 20 tons of uranium and 30 tons of dry ice, figures which would have approached those of the first US reactor, CP-1. However, Harteck's proposed experiment was critized by Heisenberg, who was of the opinion that it was too large and a more gradual approach should be made, otherwise it would be a waste of valuable resources. In the face of this criticism, Harteck's plan was abandoned. By early 1942, still no major nuclear advances had been made in Germany, and the attitude at the Heereswaffenamp (HWA) who were 'driving' the process forward appears to have been similar to their attitude to Peenemünde: by all means carry on with your work, but there is no urgency in the matter. Certainly, despite what appeared to be minor set-backs in Russia during the first winter of the offensive, there appeared to be no reason to change the opinion that the German forces would control the major part of Russia by the end of 1942.

Some changes were taking place in Germany which had some effect on the nuclear work. The Reich Research Council was transferred to Herman Goering's empire, and Albert Speer began to take an interest in nuclear research in his new role of Minister of Armaments, following Fritz Todt's death. Speer arranged a conference on 4 June 1942 at which all the leading nuclear figures were asked to provide an up-to-date report on their work and the possibility of building a reactor and nuclear weapon. Military and political leaders were present and Heisenberg was the main speaker. He repeated many of the points he had made at an early conference, before a less distinguished audience, at the House of German

Research in Berlin. Among the items mentioned by Heisenberg were the advantages of using a nuclear reactor in a submarine, since it consumed no oxygen, and the new element with an atomic number of 94 (now known as plutonium) which could also be a powerful explosive like U.235. The various reactor experiments were also mentioned, using the layer arrangement and one using spherical lumps of uranium, built at Leipzig in 1941.

After the conference Speer asked Heisenberg how long it might take to build an atomic bomb and how much money would it take. The reply was at least two years, depending on the effort applied. But the amount of money mentioned by Heisenberg, a few million marks, surprised Speer, since the projects he had inherited from Todt usually involved hundreds of millions of marks. Another player also now appears on the nuclear scene, Dr William Ohnesorge, Minister for Posts and an old confidant of Hitler's and Party Member, one of the very few government ministers to survive to the end of the war. Ohnesorge had contacts with a scientific entrepreneur, Baron Manfred von Ardenne, who had supplied electrical equipment to the Post Office, and in wartime the Post Office had developed many technical interests having little connection with delivering the mail. In the grounds of his home in the Berlin suburb of Lichterfelde-Ost (also Kammler's home address), Ardenne had built an extensive laboratory complex with an underground bunker, and by 1941 he had several physicists working for him on contracts from the Post Office. One of these physicists was Fritz Houtermans, something of a rebel in the scientific community. Houtermans had never belonged to the established 'nuclear club', but had always worked on the fringes. In the 1930s he had spent some time at Cambridge, and then moved to Russia, where he was arrested as a German spy. Released after the signing of the Russian–German pact in August 1939, he returned to Germany and was sent back to Russia after the German invasion to report on Russian scientific work. He finally ended up back in Germany in late 1941, and looking for a new job, he was taken on by Ardenne, whose approach to scientific research probably appealed to Houtermans. One of his first tasks was to revisit some of the earlier work carried out by Harteck and Weizsacker, including the low-temperature reactor idea and the new element, plutonium. Heisenberg had visited Ardenne's laboratory on 28 November 1941, together with Weizsacker, and a few days later Otto Hahn also paid a visit. By this time Ardenne's nuclear interests included isotope separation, and despite claims by Heisenberg after the war that Ardenne was doing nothing of real value, it is more than likely, as we shall see later, that this was not the case.

Early in 1942 Heisenberg had been appointed to the top physics post in Germany, Director of the Kaiser Wilhelm Institute for Physics in Berlin, a post which also included a professorship at Berlin University, and this appointment was seen as confirming Heisenberg's position as the leader of the nuclear community in Germany. At the start of 1943, things were beginning to change, as in other weapons projects. In the first instance the Allied bombing affected nuclear research earlier than projects like the V2, since much of the work was in laboratories and establishments in and around Berlin, and Berlin was now a regular bombing target. The first to move some of his work was Heisenberg, who started transferring equipment and staff in the middle of 1943 to Haigerloch, near Hechingen in south-west Germany, and Otto Hahn and his team moved to the nearby Tailfingen. The scientific authorities in the Third Reich must by now have begun to question the lack of progress towards building a working reactor and a bomb. Some of this concern is shown by the removal of Abraham Esau as Head of Physics at the Reich Research Council, and his replacement with a recognized physicist, Walter Gerlach. Gerlach, Professor of Physics at Munich since 1929, had been involved in some important physics experiments in the 1920s, and hence was a much better person than Esau to assess and help direct the work on reactors and weapons.

Diebner, still working directly for the Army at Gottow on reactor experiments, was also on the move from the Berlin area. Later in 1943 Diebner and his team moved to Stadtilm, where he continued his experiments in some requisitioned school buildings.

Until the end of the war, the 'official' history of nuclear work in Germany has little to say involving real progress towards building a working reactor and a bomb. Bothe was working with graphite as a moderator and reflector at Heidelberg, as the original experiments with carbon had been shown to be flawed, and hence work on graphite had been resumed some time earlier. In 1944, Heisenberg was travelling around Europe, giving lectures and attending conferences in Holland, Switzerland, Poland, Denmark and Strasbourg, where Weizsacker was now Professor of Physics at the University. Some nuclear work was still being carried on in Berlin, where a bunker had been built in the grounds of the KWI, and this was untouched by the bombing. Harteck was still involved with low-temperature reactor experiments and organizing the production of heavy water, but the last shipment to Germany was in February 1944, and this was lost when the ferry it was on was sunk while crossing Lake Tinnsjo in Norway.

Erich Schumann, Head of Research at the HWA, and his deputy, Bieder, had visited Frederic Joliot-Curie at the Collège de France in Paris soon after the French capitulation in June 1940.

Joliot-Curie had a small cyclotron in Paris, and this was used by visiting German physicists on non-military work during the war. According to Joliot-Curie, these visitors were Diebner, Gentner, Hartvig (astrophysicist), Bagge (colleague of Heisenberg's and interested in cosmic radiation), Maurer, Riezler and Rackwitz (technician). Bothe was an occasional visitor, Abraham Esau visited in 1943 and Weizsacker gave a lecture in Paris in 1942.

As the Allied armies advanced into Europe after the D-Day landings, an American scientific mission followed immediately behind the troops. Their task was to seize as much information as possible on German scientific work, and this included rockets, nuclear physics and medicine. The organization ALSOS, founded by General Groves, Head of the Manhattan Project, interviewed Joliot-Curie in Paris before going on to Belgium, Italy and eventually Germany. What Joliot-Curie did not tell ALSOS, and he may not have been aware of the fact, was that the German military counter-intelligence organization, the Abwehr, had installed a fake scientific company, Cellastic, in a building off the Champs-

Elysées, whose task was to spy on the French nuclear workers, including Joliot-Curie. Sympathetic physicists, some from occupied countries, were used to monitor the work in Paris, the information being passed on to Berlin.

The scientific head of ALSOS was physicist Dr Samuel Goudsmit, a Dutchman who had taken American citizenship before the war, leaving his parents in Holland. Being Jews they were victims of the Holocaust. This tragedy affected Goudsmit's relationship with the German physicists after the war, including Heisenberg, whom he had known before 1939. In the last few weeks of the war in Europe, Goudsmit and ALSOS were responsible for locating and detaining not only the Peenemünde team, but the leading nuclear scientists also, including Heisenberg, Hahn, Harteck, Weizsacker and Diebner. Once located, they were subjected to imprisonment of a sort, since they were not free to go back to their families, being moved between France and Belgium, and finally to Farm Hall near Cambridge in southern England, where they were subjected to 'house arrest' for six months.

THE FARM HALL TAPES, FRITZ HOUTERMANS AND PROFESSOR BLACKETT

Between May and June 1945, ten of the most senior German physicists were kept under house arrest, Operation Epsilon, at Farm Hall, a safe house which had been used by British Intelligence during the war for agent training and other clandestine activities. One useful feature of the accommodation was that the rooms were fitted with hidden microphones, and this equipment allowed conversations to be recorded. The ten were, in alphabetical order:

Erich Bagge (1905–) student with Heisenberg at Leipzig, doctorate in physics 1938, in 1939 joined the HWA working for Diebner. In 1941 he moved to the KWI and worked on isotope separation under Heisenberg until 1945.

Kurt Diebner (1905–64) studied physics at Halle, doctorate in physics 1931, in 1934 joined the German Bureau of Standards and moved to the HWA, where he worked on nuclear reactors and weapons at Gottow, and later Stadtilm, until 1945. From 1939 until 1942 he was also Director of the KWI for Physics following the resignation of Peter Debye.

Walter Gerlach (1889–1979) studied physics at Tübingen up to the First World War, doctorate in 1911. Served in the German Army and then taught at Frankfurt University from 1920–4. 1924–9 professor at Tübingen. 1929–57 professor at University of Munich. 1944–5, Head of Nuclear Research at the Reich Research Council.

Otto Hahn (1879–1968) studied chemistry at Marburg and Munich, lecturer at Marburg 1901–4, doctorate in 1911. Carried out research in London, Montreal and Berlin 1901–28. 1928–45 Head of the KWI for Chemistry. Nobel Prize in 1945 for his discovery of nuclear fission.

Paul Harteck (1902–85) student in chemistry at Berlin University to 1926, doctorate in 1926. 1926–33, at the KWI for Chemistry in Berlin. Professor of Physical Chemistry at Hamburg, 1934–51.

Werner Heisenber (1901–76) doctorate in physics from Göttingen 1923. Nobel Prize in Physics 1933. 1927–42, Professor of Theoretical Physics at Leipzig. 1942–5, Head of the KWI for Physics, Berlin.

Horst Korsching (1912–) doctorate in physics from Berlin 1938. 1939–45, worked for Diebner, and later Heisenberg, at the KWI on isotope separation.

Max von Laue (1879–1960) doctorate in physics from Berlin 1903. Nobel Prize for Physics 1914. 1914–19, Professor of Physics at Frankfurt. 1919–43, Professor at Berlin. Deputy Director of KWI for Physics until 1945.

Carl Friedrich von Weizsacker (1912–) doctorate in physics from Leipzig 1933. Worked with Heisenberg until 1936. 1936–42, KWI for Physics in Berlin. 1942–4, Professor at Strasbourg under German occupation. 1944–5, returned to the KWI, Berlin, working with Heisenberg. His father was a member of the Foreign Ministry in Berlin under von Ribbentrop.

Karl Wirtz (1910–) doctorate in physics from Breslau in 1934. 1935–7, research in chemistry at Leipzig. 1937–42 at the KWI for Physics, Berlin.

The conversations of the ten detainees were recorded for the full six months they were at Farm Hall, but it has been estimated that only ten per cent of the recorded conversations were actually retained to form what is now known as 'the Farm Hall tapes'. The primitive recording discs were wiped clean after each recording, re-varnished and used again, hence there is no complete record of all the conversations. Despite this, the tapes were classified as secret until 1991. Two copies are now available on microfilm at the Public Record Office, Kew (file WP 208/5019). Since 1991, the Farm Hall tapes have been used by many historians wishing to add weight to the argument that Germany did not have a nuclear weapon of any sort, did not construct a working reactor and that the most senior nuclear physicists, and in particular Heisenberg, did not understand some of the basic mechanics of reactors and bombs. There are several reasons why the tapes have to be viewed with some scepticism if they are to be taken as a real and full record of their nuclear apprehension and work during the war, especially as regards their discussions after hearing of the bombs dropped on Hiroshima and Nagasaki. These reasons are:

1. The tapes are not a complete record of the conversations, and these are now lost for ever as the discs were re-used several times.
2. The recorded conversations were subject to the limitations of the equipment available at the time, and this equipment was crude by today's standards.

3. Much of the subject matter recorded was highly specialized technical material, and the actual task of producing translated paper copies of this material is a potential source of error.
4. Perhaps the most serious problem about the veracity of the tapes is the question: did the ten know that their conversations were being recorded?

This question is dismissed very quickly by the historians or not even considered worthy of mentioning, but we have to consider the following facts.

The ten had just spent six years in Hitler's wartime Third Reich. Even before the war started, the SS under Himmler had organized the internal security of Germany in such a fashion that almost any dissension would be detected by the SD and Gestapo. If the SD was the active intelligence branch formed to protect the integrity of the State, the Gestapo was largely the unseen part of the security organization, and contrary to many beliefs the Gestapo had relatively few operatives, especially in Germany itself. It relied on information supplied by work colleagues, neighbours and friends, and even relations, to provide the initial information on any subversive activities. No Gestapo records survived the war intact, but in 1998 a complete set of Gestapo wartime files were found in the town of Würzburg, which is mid-way between Frankfurt and Nuremberg. In the Second World War, the Würzburg area had a population of slightly under one million, and just twenty-eight Gestapo officials were responsible for State security. American Professor Robert Gellately is currently working through the thousands of documents, many of which are hand-written letters to Gestapo HQ in Würzburg, in which thousands of citizens were reported by neighbours, etc. for having said or done something which might be inferred as being against the State.

This then was the atmosphere that all ten detainees had worked in for over six years, and Heisenberg had actually experienced the attentions of the SS from a much earlier date. In 1937 Nobel Prize winners Johannes Stark and Philipp Lenard had denounced physicists like Heisenberg as following a branch of science related to the Jewish influences of Einstein and others, while they themselves believed in what was described as a 'Deutsche Physik'. This attack on Heisenberg attracted the attention of the SS, and if it had not been for the personal intervention of Himmler, who had a distant family connection with Heisenberg, and other members of the scientific community, the consequences could have been serious for him. As it was, Heisenberg was interviewed by Heinrich Müller, later to head the Gestapo, in Berlin, and probably as a result of this affair, in 1939 he lost the opportunity to take up the prestigious vacant post of Professor of Physics at Munich. Thus by 1940 at the very latest, the whole group of ten would have been very much aware of how the security of the State was being managed. Being men of the world and much travelled, in many cases multi-lingual, they would have realized that the German security service was not unique: as every schoolboy knew from his secret agent spy stories, hidden microphones were all part of the game.

At the very start of the recordings there is a superb example of how the ten were going to, as it were, put the listeners at their ease. On 6 July 1945, only three days after their arrival at Farm Hall, the following conversation was recorded, though the precise size of the group present was not stated.

Diebner says, 'I wonder whether there are microphones installed here?'
Heisenberg, 'Microphones installed? [laughter]. Oh no, they're not as cute as all
that. I don't think they have the real Gestapo methods, they're a bit old-
fashioned in that respect.'

This, then, set the scene for what was to follow over the next few months. The
detainees had 'met' their unseen listeners and put them at their ease. The author
would certainly recommend anyone interested to spend an afternoon at the Public
Record Office, Kew, viewing the tapes. The detainees deserved 'Oscars' at least
for their acting performances and scripts.

The transcription of the tapes occupies several hundred pages, a good deal of
which is related to everyday concerns of the group, such as how long they were
going to be detained, and what was happening to their families and homes in
Germany. But it is the scientific information which has been used to support
other evidence that none of the group really understood how to build a working
reactor or a nuclear weapon. In particular, it is the recorded words of Heisenberg
which have been used to show that the 'leaders' of the nuclear physicists in
Germany were technically backward when compared to their American and
British counterparts. There are two main areas which have been used to illustrate
this apparent lack of knowledge. Firstly there is the weight of the critical mass of
fissile material, and secondly what is required to make a bomb.

The critical mass of fissile material is related to how far a neutron would have
to travel in the material before it collides with a nucleus and hence enables the
fission process to proceed. This distance is known as the 'mean free path', and for
natural uranium with very little fissionable U.235, the distance is quite large.
Hence a reactor using natural uranium has a large mass of uranium, and this is
made worse because neutrons are also lost to the fission process through leakage
from the material surface of such a large mass and through capture by U.238. In
pure U.235, however, the mean free path is quite small, about 2 in (50 mm), and
hence the diameter of the lump of U.235 need only be slightly larger than this to
obtain an explosive chain reaction. A critical mass of 220 lb (100 kg) would only
be about 6 in (150 mm) diameter.

Heisenberg's original estimate for the weight of U.235 required was several
tons, and this figure was repeated in the early recordings at Farm Hall, but was
eventually reduced on the 6/7 August 1945 recordings to around one ton. The
uranium bomb dropped on Hiroshima used about 130 lb (60 kg) of fissile
material.

However, in February 1945 a report was sent to the Heereswaffenamt in which
a figure of 10–100 kg (22–220 lb) was mentioned as the material required for a
bomb. The author of the report is unknown, and no substantiation was provided
for the figures, but it is very likely that Heisenberg was involved in the writing of
the report.

On 14 August 1945, after the bombs had been dropped on Hiroshima and
Nagasaki, Heisenberg gave a lecture to the other detainees in which he provided
figures which resulted in approximately the same critical masses as used in the US

bombs. This is a remarkable recovery in comprehension from several tons, to one ton, and finally producing the correct amount of U.235 or its plutonium equivalent. Not only that, but he produced the idea of firing one piece of non-critical material into another mass of non-critical material at high speed using a gun barrel, the two masses being compressed very quickly to form the critical mass. This was precisely the method used for the Hiroshima bomb, and yet the details were still secret.

He also went on to explain why slow neutrons cannot be used in a bomb because the bomb material would vaporize before all the U.235 could be fissioned, reducing the explosive effect. Slow (thermal) neutrons travel at speeds of a rifle bullet, whereas fast neutrons travel at speeds thousands of times greater than a rifle bullet. Hence, if they are used, there is more chance of complete fission of all the bomb material before it is vaporized by the explosion, especially if a 'tamper' is used, which surrounds the fissile material with a dense, solid layer to contain the explosion long enough to achieve the maximum use of the fissile material. Heisenberg also discussed cross-sections, which are an essential part of the mechanics of fission, and other processes, such as scattering, absorption and capture. It is clear from this lecture that he understood concepts of which he was supposed to be ignorant, in particular the reasons for using fast neutrons in a bomb and needing to assemble the fissionable material quickly. This is a remarkable turn-around, especially since all the newspaper reports on the US bombs, which had been read by the detainees, gave no technical details.

On 11 August, thorium and its isotope Th.230, also known as ionium, were discussed. Ionium, Th.230, is a stable radioactive isotope of thorium with a half-life of 80,000 years, and it is used for dating ocean sediments in a similar fashion to how carbon-14 is used.

Ionium is produced as a decay product of the uranium radioactive series, one of a series of three (uranium, thorium, actinium) naturally occurring and one artificial (neptunium) unstable radioactive nuclei chains that disintegrate by alpha or beta decay until a stable nucleus is formed. Th.230 is produced from the decay of U.234, and its 'daughter' is radium 226, as used originally by Madame Curie for medical purposes and with beryllium as a neutron source. But ionium does not fission in the 'bomb' sense.

On 11 August, however, Hahn, Gerlach and Bagge, a Nobel Prize winner, a senior nuclear physicist professor and a senior nuclear physicist, had an in-depth discussion about using ionium in a bomb, which was technically inept. No mention was made during this discussion that thorium Th.232 is similar to U.238 in that they both readily capture slow neutrons, followed by beta decay to a highly fissionable isotope, Pu.239 in the case of U.238 and U.233 in the case of Th.232.

Why was the obvious mistake made regarding ionium, and why wasn't the more obvious connection made with thorium and the production of U.233, which could be used in a bomb?

Gerlach also went on to mention that others were involved in the ionium project, including an Austrian physicist called Stetter, and the SS, and that an Indian physicist had been sent to him in 1944/5 to work on ionium, but that Gerlach suspected that he was a Japanese spy!

From what we know of the nuclear properties of thorium and its isotope U.233, in the space of a few words, Gerlach managed to raise dozens of questions relating to the work on thorium and the involvement of the SS and Japan. This is an example of what appears to have been an organized effort by the detainees to 'play-act' for reasons discussed later. What we now have is another reason why the thorium episode is undoubtedly a red herring, and it involves Fritz Houtermans.

Fritz Houtermans was detained by the ALSOS Mission, who incidentally had Army uniforms and ranks, round about the same time as the group of ten. Manfred von Ardenne, for whom Houtermans had worked, had gone to work for the Russians, as had the Minister for Posts, Wilhelm Ohnesorge, whose Deutschen Reichspost had been involved in nuclear research and had provided contracts to Ardenne. Hence, if Houtermans had been working on anything related to nuclear weapons via the Ardenne–Ohnesorge chain, then he was free to say more or less what he liked about his wartime work since his bosses were now working for the new 'enemy'.

On 3 September 1945, Houtermans gave a document to his American captors (Figure 1). This was only a few days after the Farm Hall conversations on the use of thorium on 11 August, which demonstrated an apparently abysmal knowledge of the fission properties of thorium. What the Houtermans document shows is that not only did Houtermans know that U.233 was fissionable, he knew how to obtain it from Th.232; and the other technical details reveal a level of knowledge that implies that if he had not been directly involved in such work, he knew the people who were, and yet Houtermans was not supposed to be at the forefront of the German nuclear effort. Uranium U.233 which is obtained, not from uranium, but as a decay product of the thorium isotope Th.232, involving an identical process to the production of the bomb material Pu.239. If thorium Th.232, like U.238 in uranium, is bombarded by thermal neutrons in a reactor, because Th.232 and U.238 do not fission by slow neutrons like U.235, both Th.232 and U.238 capture neutrons, and then after three stages of beta decay they become the stable elements U.233 and Pu.239.

This decay process is for U.238:

U.238 > U.239 (half-life 23 minutes) > Np.239 (half-life 2.4 days) > Pu.239 (half-life 24,400 yrs)

and for Th.232:

Th.232 > Th.233 (half-life 23 minutes) > Pa.233 (half-life 27 days) > U.233 (half-life 160,00 yrs)

The increase in mass numbers in both cases illustrates the neutron capture process, which means that because of the extra neutron, the new compound nuclei are isotopes of the original materials but with one unit higher in mass number, 238 to 239. (Np is neptunium and Pa is proactinium.)

The discovery of plutonium Pu.239 in 1941 was considered to be a major scientific discovery, although wartime restrictions in the USA meant it was not

How to use Thorium for nuclear energy from fission.

Take pure thorium or thoriumoxide, mix to it some U 235 or U 239 separated
from U238. The amount of U235 or 239 necessary will presumably be lower than
0.7%, because resonance capture in Th seems to be stronger than in U238. By
neutron capture Th233 is formed. The mixture should be such that in heavy
water, possibly also in metallic beryllium, or even BeO, or in graphite the
chain reaction is just started, retarded only by resonance capture of Th232.
It may be that the chain reaction will work only at low temperatures, if the
width of the Th-resonance capture is given by Doppler-broadening. This will be
true especially, the heavier the material is for slowing down the neutrons, i.e
for graphite. It might be necessary to cool away even at low temperatures the
energy released by the chain reaction, but any neutron lost will form an atom
of Th 233, which decays with T= 23 min to Pa 233, a body known to emit β-rays
also and to decay into U 233. U 233 seems to have rather a long half life,
and may be α-active. But from general considerations similar to those of
Bohr-Wheeler, I should be rather think that U 233 has a fission treshold low
enough that thermal neutrons will be able to make thermofission. Since you
get weighable quantities of neutrons from the chain reaction in the separeted
isotope U235 or 239 you will thus be able to enrich either U 233 to such an
extent, that the chain reaction will start at normal temperatures or else to
separete U 233 chemicall from the thorium mixture and use it as U235 or 239
as fuel for the machine.

September 3rd, 1945.   F.G. Houtermans

P.S. by Gerard P. Kuiper, Frankfurt-Hochst, 7 Sept., 1945.

This is Prof. Houtermans' prediction of how the Russians will make the atomic
bomb. No copy of it has been made; this is the original. If any "profit"
or "credit" will result from his proposal its author requests that the
benefits will go to his wife, Mrs. Houtermans, Physics Department,
Radcliffe College, Cambridge, Mass.

                                    Gerard P. Kuiper

                                    Alsos Mission

Figure 1. Houtermans' thorium to U.233 document.

publicized at the time. Up to the discovery of Pu.239, which involved four of the USA's top scientists, Seaborg, Segre, Kennedy and Lawrence, uranium U.235 was the only known nucleus that would fission by neutrons of all energies.

But here we have Houtermans, without any other names mentioned and who was never quite on the same 'level' as Hahn, Heisenberg, etc., calmly handing the Americans the equivalent of discovering Pu.239. Not only that, his knowledge implied that he knew, as might be expected, a great deal about the process. For instance, he knew that resonance neutron capture by Th.232 is higher than that of U.238, hence more fissile U.233 will be produced from Th.232 than Pu.239 from U.238.

He knew that one of the intermediate decay products, Pa.233, has a half-life of 23 minutes and decays to U.233. The fact that Pa.233 has a half-life of only 23 minutes complicates the research and analysis problems, since this means that firstly Pa.233 is highly radioactive because of its short half-life, and that any analysis work has to be carried out within a very short timescale. He also appreciated that U.233 has a long half-life and he was correct when he said it might be an alpha emitter. He also mentioned that resonance capture of neutrons might be a problem. Resonance capture is increased as the fuel temperature rises, because the resonance absorption peaks broaden (the Doppler effect), removing activity from the system because fewer neutrons are available for fission; hence the fission process may work better at lower temperatures.

From Bohr and Wheeler came the theory that all heavy nuclei should be fissionable by fast neutrons and that heavy nuclei with an even atomic number but an odd number of neutrons should fission by neutrons of all energies. Hence, uranium has an atomic number of 92, i.e. 92 protons, and U.233 and U.235 have 92 protons and 141 and 143 neutrons respectively, while the equivalent for Pu.239 is 94 and 145.

The last part of the Houtermans report on how to use the U.233 is merely stating the obvious.

Both U.233 and Pu.239 are fissionable by either fast or slow neutrons, and U.233, like Pu.239, is a very powerful bomb material, even more so than U.235. The drawback with Pu.239 and hence U.233 is that to produce them you have to have a reactor in order to have an adequate supply of neutrons to start the capture and decay process, or a powerful neutron source, but the big advantage is that you do not necessarily need enriched uranium for a reactor, since it will work using natural uranium oxide or uranium metal, which does away with the very complicated business of separating U.235 from U.238.

The $64,000 question, though, is: how did Houtermans get hold of the information about thorium when those classed as his scientific superiors, Hahn, Gerlach and Bagge, were still talking on 'student'-level terms about the same subject at Farm Hall?

The thorium affair has another strange twist. When the Allies entered Brussels on 3 September 1944, Samuel Goudsmit of ALSOS went immediately to the offices of the Union Minière, which had mined uranium in the Belgian Congo before the war. Although most of the files and paperwork had been destroyed by the retreating Germans, Goudsmit found the remains of some correspondence with the German metal-refining company, Auer. It had been an Auer physicist who had written to the War Ministry back in 1939 to acquaint them of the military possibilities of the fission process. The scraps of correspondence linked an Auer chemist called Jansen to the French thorium supplies and also to the Belgian town of Eupen.

Eupen had just been captured by the Allies, and Goudsmit and his team, hot on the trail, visited the address mentioned only minutes after the Allied troops arrived. Here they found Jansen, who was visiting a girl-friend before returning to Germany and had been caught out by the speed of the Allied advance. Under interrogation Jansen revealed that he had been one of those responsible for transporting the entire French stock of thorium to Germany only weeks earlier, and his recent travels had also included Hetchingen, the town adjacent to Haigerloch, where the Heisenberg nuclear work had been transferred to avoid the Allied bombing. Jansen's reason for visiting Hetchingen, he claimed, was to visit his mother, but most bizarre of all, he told ALSOS that Auer wanted the thorium to make toothpaste that would whiten teeth better than anything available at the time, and the company wanted to 'corner the market' after the war. Even more incredible is that Goudsmit accepted Jansen's story, and he was released, and apparently ALSOS made no further enquiries regarding the thorium question.

So, we have Nobel Prize winner Hahn and others discussing rudimentary nuclear properties of thorium, with no mention of the bomb material U.233 derived from thorium, and at the same time Houtermans is giving the Americans a report which 'discovers' the thorium version of Pu.239, U.233, and which shows them how it can be used to make a bomb. Plus the fact that Germany had seized all the French thorium supplies to make 'extra-white toothpaste'. Unbelievable!

We now come to another part of the Farm Hall saga, the involvement of British physicist Professor Blackett.

Firstly a few details of the Professor's background. In the 1920s and 1930s, Patrick Blackett was a member of a very select club. After serving in the Royal Navy in the First World War, he went to Cambridge and carried out research with Ernest Rutherford, the 'father' of the atom, obtaining the first photographs of the transmutation of an atom. Other research at Cambridge involved cosmic rays, and in 1937 he became Professor of Physics at Manchester University, which at the time was second only to Cambridge in the importance of its nuclear research, attracting visiting researchers from around the world, including Germany and America.

Before the Second World War he travelled around Europe attending the frequent physics seminars and conferences, which were really 'get-togethers' for members of the exclusive 'nuclear club'. Blackett met and was on friendly terms with Bohr in Denmark, Max von Laue, Heisenberg, Szilard, Houtermans, Weisskopf and others, and in fact Heisenberg had stayed at Blackett's house. In April 1945, shortly after he was 'captured', Houtermans wrote a personal letter to Blackett expressing his relief that the war was over and mentioning that he and

Heisenberg had often discussed him (Blackett). Houtermans asked Goudsmit if he could get the letter to Blackett somehow, but apparently the letter was found in Goudsmit's files after he died, 35 years later. In 1933 Blackett became a Fellow of the Royal Society, the top scientific honour in Britain, and in 1948 he was awarded the Nobel Prize for Physics.

This sets the scene for Blackett's involvement in the Farm Hall story. Politically he could be described as a Socialist intellectual, and in 1945, when a new Labour Government was formed after the defeat of Winston Churchill and the Tories, he was asked by the new administration to investigate how the various military scientific organizations could be adapted to the post-war era. He already had some experience of politics and science, as at the end of the war he had been a member of the Advisory Committee on Atomic Energy, and one of his first tasks in his new job was to reorganize Scientific Intelligence into an independent operation from the three branches of the Armed Forces into which it had been integrated during the war. Hence, by later in 1945, Professor Blackett was not only an internationally known nuclear physicist, but well acquainted with the world of Intelligence and how it operated, including the methods used to obtain information; 'bugged' conversations were one of the most obvious. So, to return to Farm Hall, we do not have to look very far to see the first mention of Blackett, in, for instance, Bernstein's book on the Farm Hall tapes. It appears inside the front cover as part of a quotation from a letter from Heisenberg to Blackett written on 18 September 1945 from Farm Hall.

During their six-month detention at Farm Hall, the group of ten had very few visitors, one of the main reasons being that their actual whereabouts was secret and few people actually knew where they were being held. They had only three scientific visitors, Sir Charles Darwin, Sir Charles Frank and Professor Blackett. Professor Blackett arrived at Farm Hall on 8 September and stayed until after lunch on Sunday 9 September, so there was ample time to discuss anything relating to pre-war, wartime and the immediate post-war situation, and it must be remembered that all the ten knew Blackett either personally or by reputation.

So what do we find when we read the recorded conversations, that lasted several hours? Immediately apparent is the almost complete lack of any sort of scientific discussion especially relating to the group's work in Germany during the war, and yet Blackett must have been very interested in finding out what had happened in Germany first-hand, from people who had been almost working colleagues a few years previously. Also, newspapers were full of articles on the atomic bombs dropped on Japan, and these newspapers were read by the group, but once again there is no discussion between Blackett and the 'ten' about possibly the most important nuclear event of the century.

What we do have are several pages of mediocre conversations about what was happening in Germany now the war was over, what sort of nuclear work the ten might get involved in after their release, the future of German science and the possibility of any messages being given to their families.

The impression given by the conversations is that everyone was on their best behaviour to say nothing that could affect their future activities in Germany or their families, and most importantly that nothing was mentioned that connected any of the ten with a German nuclear weapon of any description. Blackett himself asked no questions that might have proved embarrassing to answer by the ten regarding their wartime nuclear work, and yet Diebner had been working for the Army on nuclear weapons since the start of the war. It was all very sanitary. After Blackett's visit, Heisenberg wrote to him on 18 September outlining the general aspects of the nuclear work the ten had been carrying out in Germany during the war, and again there was not the slightest mention of nuclear weapons, even when referring to Diebner and the work at Stadtilm.

In 1948 Professor Blackett published a book, *Military and Political Consequences of Atomic Energy*. This book was obviously written between 1945 and 1948, and so it included many of his thoughts and ideas which had developed during the war and immediately after it. The book looks at the war in Europe and Japan, the atomic bomb as a weapon, future technical developments regarding weapons and their delivery, the possible use of nuclear weapons by America and Russia, methods of controlling nuclear weapons and the future of atomic energy. There are several remarkable features of this book which are relevant to the present story. One of these is the speed at which the use of radioactive material as a weapon is put forward as being more effective than atomic bombs. On page 5 of the Introduction is the first mention of the use of radioactive material, and he quotes a statement by Senator McMahon to the US Senate in 1947.

'It would not be necessary for an enemy to destroy our cities or to destroy us. By the use of radioactive particles or death-dust in a combination with disease germs, every living thing in our cities could be annihilated and the cities themselves left standing and empty of resistance to an invader.'

The advantages of using radioactive material as a weapon in preference to an atomic bomb is repeated in numerous instances throughout the book, it is a persistent theme. One quotation involves Dr Oppenheimer, scientific head of the US Manhattan Project, in which he states that air attacks by the USA could eradicate more than forty million people in the USSR. As Blackett pointed out, the experience of Hiroshima and Nagasaki had shown that one atomic bomb killed on average 40,000 people. Hence forty million killed in the USSR would require 1,000 bombs of the present destructive power actually delivered to their targets, and even years afterwards this was a colossal number of bombs. Blackett goes on to argue that Dr Oppenheimer must have been thinking in terms of radioactive material weapons. Later in the Oppenheimer article, it is stated that Russia might use a bacterial weapon in retaliation (it was believed that Russia did not have an atomic bomb in 1948), and hence 'Americans might die of the plague while Russians die from radioactivity', not, as Blackett points out, from atomic bombs.

The use of pilotless aircraft and rockets as carriers for nuclear weapons are also referred to, and both the V1 and V2 are mentioned several times. This is based on the premise that the performance of manned bombers will eventually reach a limit and air defences will improve to such an extent that the ability to attack enemy targets with aircraft will become impractical.

What Professor Blackett is outlining in his 1948 book is basically the same line of thinking as was being pursued in Germany in the Second World War. The statistics against dropping atomic bombs are obvious, as is the ease with which radioactive material can be produced. The message from Blackett is, if you must produce nuclear weapons, then the most efficient are ones containing radioactive material. Of course, Blackett was writing about atomic bombs as they existed in the 1940s and the foreseeable future, not about developments in thermo-nuclear hydrogen bombs and the miniaturization that now provides dozens of warheads in one ballistic missile, and it is the 1940s that now concern us.

Blackett's book and his forthright analysis of nuclear weapons is in complete contrast to the mild-mannered 'tea-party' conversations at Farm Hall, and there is no doubt in the author's mind that Blackett knew, as did the ten, that their conversations were being recorded. The ten were allowed strolls around the gardens, and it is unlikely that these were 'bugged', in which case it was probably on one of these strolls that Blackett discussed what they were going to talk about, and after all, he was now in Intelligence himself.

There are two other items that Blackett discusses in his book which are highly relevant to this story. It is almost as if Blackett is leaving clues for some future investigator to follow, but because of his own work and responsibilities, he could not refer to them directly, and his post-war task of reorganizing Scientific Intelligence meant he had access to secret material which could have included reports on German secret weapons.

The first is the Allied bombing of the Skoda factory at Pilsen, near Prague, on 25 April 1945.

The American and Russian forces were approaching the area from West and East, and on 9 May 1945 Prague was captured virtually undamaged. So why destroy the largest industrial centre in Czechoslovakia when it would have been invaluable for the rebuilding of the country after the war, even if it was in Russian hands? Blackett has no answer to this question, but we now know that there was another reason, and that it was related to the SS and Kammler's secret weapons that were being developed at Skoda. Secondly, Blackett is puzzled by the urgency with which the American atomic bombs were dropped on Japan, and if indeed they needed to use them at all. The first uranium U.235 bomb on Hiroshima, using the gun-method to assemble the critical mass quickly, had never been tested before as a complete weapon system. The plutonium Pu.239 bomb dropped on Nagasaki had been tested, but only once, and that was a ground-based test at Alamogordo, New Mexico, on 16 July 1945. The US seaborne invasion of the main Japanese islands was not planned to take place until November 1945 at the earliest. Since 1945, US bombers were virtually free to bomb any targets in Japan as and when they wished. A large area of Tokyo had already been destroyed by fire-bombing with B-29 Superfortresses, and with regard to strategic materials, Japan's stocks of oil, petrol and metals were almost exhausted.

Blackett does not believe the 'official' story that the bombs were dropped to save lives, although, of course, the saving of lives had to be considered, but that if the conventional bombing raids had continued for only a few more weeks, Japan's main industrial and populated areas would have been a wasteland. The only other possible alternative was that the USA was concerned that Russia might try to extend its sphere of influence into Japan. Manchuria and Korea were probably lost causes as far as future Russian influence was concerned, but Japan must be kept in the 'West' at all costs. With this concern in mind, it meant that the war against Japan must be finished as quickly as possible, since Russia had already cancelled the Russian-Japanese Neutrality Pact on 5 April 1945, leaving itself free to take any action against Japan, but the Russian forces had still not crossed the Manchurian border into Japanese-controlled territory. If Japan surrendered quickly, US forces could be in Tokyo before Russian forces had time to overrun Manchuria and North Korea. It was a reasonable argument, but Russia did not declare war on Japan until 9 August 1945, hours after the dropping of the second atomic bomb. If the bombs had not been dropped, Russia might not have taken this action for some considerable time.

Both the Skoda bombing and the dropping of the atomic bombs on Japan are referred to later.

THE BETATRON PARTICLE ACCELERATOR

The betatron is one member of a family of nuclear research tools known as particle accelerators. A nuclear reaction is initiated when two nuclear particles collide with each other, but all nuclear particles except neutrons contain positive charges. Hence, if two positively charged particles hit each other they will be repelled, since it is a basic fact that two positive electric charges repel each other, and this force becomes stronger the closer the two particles get to each other. The way to get round this repulsive force is to give the colliding particle a very high velocity so that by shear speed and momentum it overcomes the force trying to repel it. This is why particle accelerators were invented. They include the Van de Graaff cyclotron and various versions of it, including the synchrotron and linear accelerators.

For the purposes of investigating the disintegration (decay) of nuclei of any element into radioactive isotopes and artificial radioactivity by the bombardment of materials with high-energy particles, particle accelerators in general, including the betatron, have been largely superseded as a research tool by the vast number of reactors that have been built since the Second World War around the world. In 1950 there were only six working reactors around the world, but by 1954 there were over thirty and by 1969 this had grown to more than 400. When materials were placed within the reactor core, they could be subjected to the effect of high-energy particles, including neutrons, without the need for separate research equipment. However, in the 1940s particle accelerators were one of the few means available, if there was no convenient reactor at hand, of reproducing some of the effects of high-energy particles. The betatron accelerates electrons, and the energy of these electrons can vary from 2 MeV in the early models to 100 MeV in later versions, and finally up to 300 MeV for the betatron-synchrotron. These high-energy electrons produce X-ray and gamma-ray photons, and hence, if the energy is high enough, material subjected to this high-energy photon bombardment produces photo–electric disintegration and emits neutrons, the gamma–neutron reaction. This is the reverse of the neutron capture process, in which the nucleus captures a neutron and then disintegrates by beta decay, and at the same time emits gamma radiation. Other reactions produced by this bombardment include the gamma–proton, gamma–deuteron, gamma–triton (tritium) and gamma–alpha reactions.

The brief physical details of the betatron are shown in Figure 2. Basically a doughnut-shaped vacuum tube is placed between two large solid magnets like a sandwich. The charged particles circulate through the tube thousands of times, each rotation increasing slightly the energy of the particle. When the particles have reached their desired energy, a capacitor is discharged through two coils, one above and one below the circular path of the tube, producing a sudden increase in the magnetic flux, which destroys the stability of the electron. The electron then moves outwards to a larger radius until it strikes the target material, producing a beam of secondary photons. One of the problems of the betatron, especially the higher-energy versions, is the radiation produced from the electromagnetic waves which can be observed as visible light, very often in shades of blue. This radiation is obviously a health hazard, and normally shielding would have to be provided while it was operating.

From the various reactions mentioned above, the betatron is capable of providing alpha, beta and gamma radiation plus neutrons, all of these emissions being dependent on the energy available from the bombarding electron compared to the 'binding energy' of the particle to be ejected. For example, if a piece of iron was the target material, it is known that the 'threshold binding energy' for iron is 14 MeV, and hence, if the photon energy exceeded 14 MeV, the iron would start disintegrating (decaying), with an increasing beta ray emission as the energy of the bombarding particles increased, until a stable nucleus was formed.

A betatron with tube and magnets only five feet in diameter could bombard a piece of iron weighing one pound in ten minutes, and so there is the potential to produce a large amount of radioactive material in a relatively short period of time. The fact that beryllium becomes a powerful neutron source when subjected to alpha particles leads to the possibility of producing neutron sources. Beryllium has a photoelectric threshold of 1.6 MeV, and so if the bombarding electrons have an energy greater than 1.6 MeV, the beryllium will disintegrate with the emission of neutrons.

According to the history of nuclear science, the first successful betatron was designed and built by D.W. Kerst in America in 1940, based on theoretical work done by R. Serber.

If this piece of history were found to be not quite true, and in fact the first betatron was built in Germany at the same time or before the one by Kerst, the situation could have existed in Germany where equipment was available for producing radioactive material and powerful neutron sources from 1940 onwards. If this was so, the ability to produce a nuclear weapon based on radioactive material, as mentioned in numerous occasions in Professor Blackett's book, was also possible, and this may well have removed some of the pressure to build a working reactor or such work may have concentrated on the use of thorium.

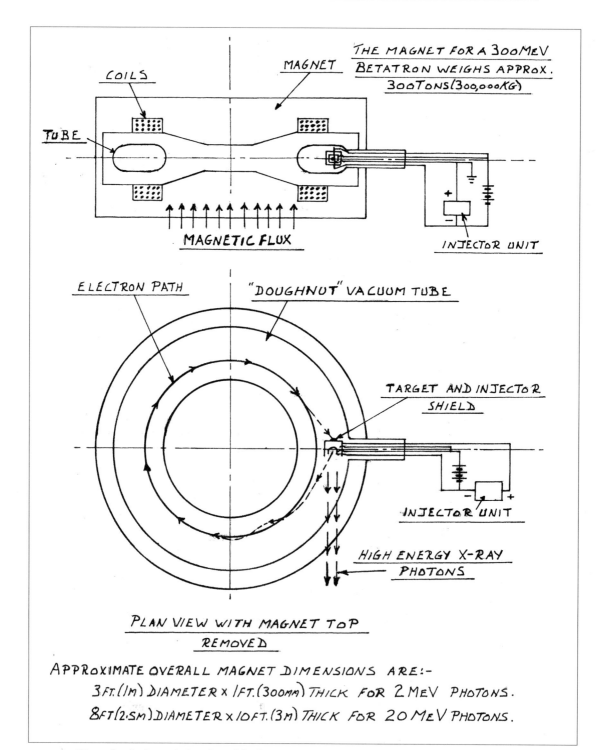

Figure 2. A schematic drawing of the Betatron particle (electron) accelerator.

THE STADTILM OPERATION

Stadtilm had been the centre of Diebner's nuclear work for the Heereswaffenamt since some time in 1944, when his operation was moved there to escape the Allied bombing. The choice of Stadtilm could not have been an accident, and this can be clearly seen from its relationship to other locations from where rocket and other secret work was being organized. Hence Stadtilm is only thirty miles south of Nordhausen and Bad Sachsa, to where the V2 work was moved from Peenemünde, and it is in the centre of the triangle of huge underground bunkers to where the administration of the Third Reich and other activities were to be moved from Berlin, the largest of these being at Ohrdruf and Crawinkel.

Heisenberg and his team had moved to Haigerloch, south of Stuttgart and 200 miles from Stadtilm, so we can deduce from this separation that the two groups were not involved to any degree towards the end of the war.

On 21 April 1945 the ALSOS Mission reached Haigerloch and seized Heisenberg's uncompleted reactor experiment, and on 26 April the ALSOS group reached Stadtilm. At both locations they found that most of the equipment had disappeared, including the most important materials, such as heavy water and uranium, and this applied particularly to Stadtilm. Although 1,000 tons of uranium ore was found by the Americans near Stassfurt, about 45 miles north-east of Nordhausen, no trace was ever found of the heavy water and other nuclear materials from Stadtilm and Haigerloch. They disappeared like Kammler into thin air. In 1945 a ton of heavy water was worth around $300,000, and between the two sites they had at least five tons, and possibly as much as fifteen tons, quite a useful find! What they did find at Stadtilm was some documentation and a few scientists, including physicist Dr Berkei and Dr Stuhlinger, a V2 propellant expert and a senior member of the Peenemünde team. Although ALSOS did not find very much at Stadtilm, it was enough for them to radio back to Goudsmit in Paris that they had found a goldmine and a physicist who would tell them everything. Among the things that Berkei did tell them was that all the equipment had been removed by the Gestapo some days earlier. What Berkei probably meant was that the SS were the removal men, as nuclear weapons were not the Gestapo's field of operation. What other communications passed between Stadtilm and the ALSOS leadership is not known, but on 30 April, less than a week after their arrival at Stadtilm, they received an order from Washington (Figure 3). In this order they were instructed to stop any further analysis of the Stadtilm documents and forward the captured TA documents to Washington for final analysis. TA stood for Tube Alloys, the codename for US and British nuclear work. What ALSOS found at Stadtilm could not have been very much, but it was enough for them to produce the list in Figure 3. This list contains two very important items, Nos 8 and 14, Betatron and Target Material. We know what the betatron could do, and 'target material' is the material being bombarded, but this is the first and only indication in the history of German nuclear work that such a device existed and was being used at a nuclear weapons establishment. Why was ALSOS ordered to stop further analysis of the documentation on 30 April and send it to Washington, which meant General Groves and the Manhattan Project, in what

SECRET

HEADQUARTERS   Copy No. 1 of 5 copies
EUROPEAN THEATRE OF OPERATIONS
UNITED STATES ARMY
ALSOS MISSION
APO 887

30 April 1945

SUBJECT: Stadtilm Operation

I. Instructions have been received to forward all captured TA documents to Washington for final analysis. No further analysis of Stadtilm documents will, therefore, be made by the Alsos Mission.

II. For the benefit of Washington personnel who will study the documents, the following summary is given of classification already started on this side:

(a) The material consists of unfiled papers, mainly technical data and reports, and of correspondence files and folders. Each of these file folders has been numbered on the back. Many of them have been read and an index of the important material made on separate cards.

(b) Now folders with the following general subject titles have been set up:

1. Organization
2. Financial
3. Pile experiments
4. Heavy Water
5. Uranium
6. Ultra centrifuge
7. Isotope Separation   Other
8. Betatron
9. Medical
10. Miscellaneous
11. KWI for Chemistry
12. Personnel
13. Instruments & Measurements
14. Target Data
15. Non-TA General Intelligence

(c) Some of the original files   been stripped of important material which has been put in the above folders according to subject. Cards for these folders which have been   but not yet classified are included in the envelope marked "Folders   done." Folders for cards appear in neither envelope have not yet been read.

F.   WARDENBURG
Expert Consultant

End   **SECRET**

Figure 3. Message from Washington to ALSOS, Stadtilm, ordering the return of all documentation.

appears to be some haste? If Germany had been operating a betatron for some time, so what? The war was virtually over and there was certainly no time left to use a weapon containing radioactive material in Europe, it was too late.

But the Second World War was not over yet, for on the other side of the world Japan was threatening to fight to the last man.

The date is critical, on 1 and 16 April 1945, German U-boats U-873 and U-234 left Kristiansand in Norway on the final leg of their journey to Japan. Both U-boats had very special nuclear cargoes, especially U-234. From the ULTRA decoded messages it was probably known there was a special nuclear cargo on board U-234, the only thing lacking being the detail, and now, at Stadtilm, some of the details had been found.

Needless to say, there was no mention at Farm Hall by Diebner or any of the other members of the group that a betatron had been operating at Stadtilm, or of the nuclear cargoes going to Japan.

NUCLEAR MATERIALS, TRANSPORT TO JAPAN, THE CODES AND ULTRA

In the world of nuclear weapons and reactors there are some materials that are so special that they might almost be described as having 'magic' nuclear properties. Some of them have other uses apart from nuclear, but when they are intended for the same organization in Japan, the implication is clear. Without these special materials, nuclear weapons and reactors would still work, but even in 1999 they would be less efficient, and in the 1940s these materials were essential if rapid progress was to be made.

All the following materials were on a series of nuclear 'shopping lists' sent from Tokyo to Berlin and intercepted by the Allied code-breakers.

The first 'magic' material is beryllium, a metal which appears in every nuclear book published. A quarter of the weight of steel, it is very hard and brittle and extremely toxic if the dust or fumes are inhaled into the lungs: death can follow in a matter of days after a large dose into the body. It is very expensive and in the 1940s it was also very rare. In Hansen's definitive book, *US Nuclear Weapons*, he says that the USA would have liked to use more beryllium in its weapons programme, but its scarcity in the USA meant that not until 1946 was Los Alamos able to use beryllium on a large scale in its nuclear weapons and reactor work. We now know where the US beryllium came from in 1945/6, but more of that later.

Beryllium is a very unpleasant and expensive metal, but it has three 'magical' nuclear properties which make it unique. Firstly it has a very low absorption cross-section of thermal (slow) neutrons, and secondly it has a very high neutron-scattering cross-section, which results in beryllium being very good at slowing down fast neutrons without absorbing them. It can also bounce neutrons back into the fission process without them being lost to the system, hence it is a good moderator and reflector. Finally, if beryllium is mixed with an alpha particle emitter such as radium or polonium, or bombarded with high-energy particles, it becomes a very powerful neutron source, ejecting millions of neutrons per second, enabling it to be used to initiate criticality in reactors and act as a sort of 'spark-plug' for nuclear weapons. In fact Enrico Fermi used a beryllium neutron source to trigger the first reactor in the USA at Chicago in 1942.

A nuclear weapon core when surrounded by a reflector of beryllium has a lower critical mass than any similar weapon, and it can also be used as a tamper in nuclear weapons, to contain the fission explosion until as much material as possible has fissioned.

These nuclear properties mean that it is still used in nuclear weapons, but its toxicity and expense have resulted in limited modern reactor use. In the 1940s, particularly in the USA, it was thought that beryllium alloyed with iron, nickel, etc., would produce some revolutionary new lightweight materials, but problems with fabrication – it is impossible to produce crack-free welds – meant that its only commercial use was alloyed with copper for springs, bushes, etc. Even this usage was eventually restricted for toxicity reasons.

There is one further nuclear property of beryllium which is worth a mention: when beryllium is struck by a high-energy neutron from a fusion (hydrogen bomb) weapon, it emits two neutrons of its own, which boosts the fusion process; and since a small amount of fusion occurs in a fission explosion, this property can also be used to improve the yield of a fission weapon.

The first reference to beryllium in the German nuclear weapons/reactor programme came in Heisenberg's lecture in the House of German Research (Haus der Deutschen Forschung) on 26 February 1942, in which he says, referring to work on materials to use as moderators, that 'thorough investigations are being carried out on suitable substances such as beryllium and carbon'. But if beryllium did not figure prominently in the 'official' publicized German nuclear work, it was certainly being produced on a massive scale in Germany.

The second material is zirconium, once again, like beryllium, a very low absorber of neutrons with a very low thermal neutron absorption cross-section. Unlike beryllium, however, it is not toxic and it has excellent structural properties, which include high strength at elevated temperatures and resistance to corrosion; it also withstands damage from neutron bombardment and does not form highly radioactive isotopes or become a neutron source.

These properties mean that it has a universal use, even today, as a material for the fuel tubes in nuclear reactors. Virtually every water-cooled nuclear power station operating today uses zirconium alloyed with small amounts of tin, iron, chrome and nickel, as Zircalloy fuel tubes, including Sizewell 'B' PWR in the UK. Zirconium hydride can also be mixed with uranium fuel in a reactor, and this results in a fuel which also contains a moderator, the result being a reactor which is more stable to operate, the fuel and moderator temperature following each other with little delay.

Zirconium was difficult to obtain on a large scale until the early 1940s, when Justin Kroll in Luxembourg developed the Kroll Process, Luxembourg, of course, being within the sphere of German influence in the Second World War. One other property related to zirconium is that it also contains hafnium, which has almost the opposite nuclear properties to zirconium in that it is a very efficient absorber of thermal and high-energy neutrons, which together with its good mechanical properties makes it an ideal but expensive material for reactor control rods.

Hence all traces of hafnium must be removed from the zirconium if it is to be used for reactor fuel tubes. Once again it was Herr Kroll who devised the process for producing hafnium and removing it from zirconium.

Zirconium can be used as an alloying agent with steel, and as an abrasive, but there are cheaper and easier ways of achieving the same results in these cases.

The third material is thallium, another toxic metal, highly poisonous and at one time used as a rat poison, but it was too dangerous, as all the soluble thallium compounds are toxic. If it has a very limited commercial use, it does have one nuclear use, which once again makes it unique in this field. Thallium can be used in infra-red lenses and photoelectric cells, but this application also has a nuclear use. The scintillation counter was and still is a more accurate and efficient means of detecting alpha, beta and gamma radiation than any other instrument, including the Geiger counter. In the scintillation counter the radiation produces a pulse of fluorescent light which is recorded on a sensitive photoelectric cell, and an essential part of this instrument is a crystal, the most sensitive and effective for radiation of all energies being those which are 'doped' with thallium.

Fourth is lithium, a metal used in many applications, but on the particular ULTRA message in question it is ordered by the same department as was using the zirconium, neon, high-frequency insulation and the 'core clamps'.

If lithium 6, one of the natural isotopes of lithium, is bombarded with slow neutrons, which can be from either a reactor or a neutron source, it produces helium and tritium. Tritium is one of the fuel elements of the boosted-fission weapons and the fusion (hydrogen) bomb.

Finally the last of the 'true' nuclear materials are the borons, borax and boric acid. Both borax and boric acid are derived from the same basic mineral, kernite. Borax is used in glass and ceramic manufacture, and boric acid is used as an antiseptic, fireproofing agent and as a preservative. Boron, however, also has a very important nuclear property that is still being utilized today. It is a very high absorber of neutrons of all energies, and it has a very high neutron–absorption cross-section. So high, in fact, that it is still used in water-cooled and moderated (PWR) nuclear power stations as the final resort to shut down a reactor if the control rods fail to operate, diluted boric acid being injected into the coolant system. It can also be used in the actual control rods, but its mechanical properties mean that this usage is restricted to smaller, non-commercial reactors. In the 1940s, it was a very important nuclear control and shut-down material, especially since it was readily available, as Italy had a natural source of boric acid.

Germany was short of very few strategic materials during the war, as the chemical industry had organized the manufacture of ersatz versions of petrol, oil, rubber and nitrates, but there were still a few items that were in short supply. These included natural rubber, tungsten (Wolfram), tin, quinine and opium for the medical industry. As far as Japan was concerned, it was short of certain chemicals such as strontium (used in flares and tracer bullets), mercury, lead, aluminium, special alloy steels, optical glass, machine tools, bearings and a whole host of electrical and electronic equipment in the world of transmission and detection. Before Japan entered the war these materials were sent by surface ships, known in Japan as 'Yanagi' ships. Even though Germany was at war with Great Britain and France, these Yanagi ships were allowed to transport material between Germany and Japan since a state of war did not exist at the time with Japan. After Pearl Harbor and the declaration of war with Japan, these ships became blockade runners, and one or two German freighters were also used for the same purpose. By 1944, none of the surface ships were completing their voyages, and several valuable cargoes were lost when the ships had to be scuttled when caught by Allied warships.

The successful location of these ships in the vast areas of the oceans was due mainly to the breaking of some of the Japanese codes used between their embassies in Europe, especially Berlin, and Tokyo. The British breaking of the German Enigma code has been much publicized, but it must be remembered that Enigma-type machines had been around for years before the war, being used in many commercial enterprises around the world, and there were thousands in the German armed forces. What was just as important, especially to this story, was the breaking of the Japanese codes used in their embassies. There were basically three main code systems used by the Japanese, two from their embassies and the naval code. From 1937 onwards, all the diplomatic traffic was sent by an alphabetical typewriter known as the Type B machine, the 97-Shiki O-bun Injiki. US code-breakers called this Purple, and it was broken in 1941 by the USA. The machine was similar to switching machines used by the Western Union company in the USA in its telephone exchanges. Two Purple machines were among other code-breaking equipment sent by the USA to England in January 1941. From late 1940, the Japanese Naval Attachés used a machine similar to Enigma, the 97-Shiki Injiki san Gata, known in the USA as Coral. The Coral code was not broken until 1943. The Japanese Navy used another code system which used two books and hence was known as a book code. From 1931 to 1939 they used the Blue Book, and from 1939 Kaigun Ango-sho D or Navy Code D. The system worked basically by having one book which contained 33,333 words and phrases, each of which was given a five-figure number. Another 'additive book' contained lists of random five-figure number groups. Each table page was numbered, as were the columns down and across, and by a combination of both books any message could be sent as a series of random numbers. The additive tables were changed every six months and came in books of 100 pages of numbers. This was a good system as long as the books did not fall into enemy hands and the operators did not use repetitive groups of numbers when sending messages. The British code-breakers at Bletchley Park had broken the IJN book code, known as JN-25, by 1939, unknown to the USA, and therefore they should have been able to intercept any IJN operational orders from this time, including Pearl Harbor, but that is another story.

However, from 1943 onwards both British and US Intelligence was able to decode Japanese Diplomatic and Naval Attaché traffic from their embassies around the world. These messages contained no operational orders, which were transmitted solely by the IJN book code. The British called these decoded messages ULTRA and the Americans Magic.

With the increasing problem of the surface ships being intercepted, submarine transport had been used from 1942 onwards, and the Japanese I-30 had arrived in Lorient on 5 August 1942, the journey taking about three months from Penang, Singapore.

By 1944 the submarine transport arrangements were well organized from the German side, since they had more boats available, and a German report dated 5 January 1944 provides some interesting details of the arrangements. It states that in 1944 nineteen submarines, including one ex-Italian and one IJN boat, were dispatched to the Far East, and of these eight reached their destination, six were missing and five were *en route*. The return trips involved twelve boats, including two IJN and one ex-Italian boat, of which four, including one IJN and the Italian boat, were missing and five had to return to port. The three boats that arrived carried in total 266 tons of tin; 124 tons of rubber; 40 tons of Wolfram; 2.5 tons of quinine; 2.2 tons of opium.

The ports of departure/arrival in the Far East were either Djakarta in Java or Penang, Singapore, with the occasional boat such as U-511, with Admiral Nomura on board, reaching Kure in Japan in August 1943. What is not mentioned in the German report are the various other materials which were transported between the two countries. There was a regular flow of gold from Japan to Germany, and some of the details of this traffic, together with the nuclear materials, are now known from copies of ULTRA messages found in the Public Record Office, Kew. Japanese submarine I-29 (codename Matsu) arrived at Lorient on 11 March 1944 with two tons of gold, and I-52 (Momi) also had two tons of gold on board when it was sunk off the Azores in July 1944.

Regarding the nuclear materials, the beryllium cargo had a very chequered career. ULTRA message 1201 dated 22 November 1944 from Berlin to Tokyo shows that loading list Item 14024, 2,590.16 kg (2.5 tons) of beryllium alloy intended to be loaded on I-52 (codename now Gimmatsu), which had been sunk near the Azores, was presumed lost on its way back to Germany. Cargo from Lorient had been sent back to Germany due to the Allied advances into Normandy after D-day. However, it appears the beryllium was not 'lost', as ULTRA message 1809 of 15 April 1945 from Berlin to Tokyo gives the loading list for U-873 (codename Anton-1), which sailed for Japan from Kiel at the end of March 1945. U-873 left Kristiansand, Norway, on 1 April 1945 for Japan and surrendered to the US Navy in mid-Atlantic on 11 May 1945. The story of U-873 and its commander, Friedrich Steinhoff, brother of the Peenemünde Steinhoff, is related later. However, Item 12720 on page 4 of U-873's loading list is '1,402 bars of beryllium alloy'. It is to be presumed that this is the same cargo of beryllium that supposedly went missing from Lorient to Germany. If it is not, then Germany was producing a massive amount of the material.

We now have two crucial questions. How was Germany able to have enough beryllium to be able to send 2.5 tons of it to Japan when from Hansen's book it is clear that the USA, engaged on a massive nuclear weapons and reactor programme, had hardly any? Secondly, what did Japan want with this massive cargo of beryllium? There can really only be one answer, that both countries were also engaged on nuclear weapons and reactor programmes far greater than has been revealed to date. But U–873 also had another nuclear material on the loading list: on page 3 is Item 02169, 100 kg (220 lb) of thallium metal.

What about zirconium? ULTRA message 1443 dated 16 January 1945 from Tokyo to Berlin (Figure 4) is an order list for various equipment and material, and on pages 1 and 2 it states,

For Department No. 3:
1. Diamond dies (diameter between 0.02 and 0.08 mm, as large a quantity as possible of all kinds.
2. Metallic zirconium [500 kg of a standard of 99.5% or over].
3. Metallic lithium, 500 kg.
4. Neon gas (as much as possible).
5. Insulating material for ultra-high frequencies.
6. 2,000 or more [Haspekerne, ? clamp cores].

Diamond dies (Item 1) are used for producing very fine wire, the wire being drawn through holes in the diamonds. Note the small hole diameters, 0.02 to 0.08 mm (0.0008 to 0.0032 in). The instrumentation used in nuclear reactors is a critical part of the whole system. Accurate measurements are especially required of neutron flux and fuel temperature at various stages of operating and shut-down conditions, since these show how much fission activity there is in the core, which is necessary to be able to control the reactor safely. This instrumentation requires a considerable amount of fine wiring which has not been contaminated by lead solder, etc., hence it is drawn through dies, and diamonds maintain their accuracy over extended usage.

Item 2 is the zirconium, and the interesting point here is that the purity is specified. All zirconium originally contains hafnium, and because hafnium is a very powerful absorber of thermal neutrons it has to be removed. When zirconium is used for fuel tubes, ideally the hafnium content should not exceed 0.01 per cent, and here we have Dept No. 3 specifying the purity of the zirconium. Zirconium, like beryllium, is not used in its pure state, but as an alloy, and if Japan was intending to obtain twice the above amount, half a ton, this would provide a considerable amount of nuclear structural material.

Item 3 on the list is metallic lithium, whose nuclear use has already been discussed, and Item 4 is neon gas. Neon has an obvious use in neon lighting tubes, but it also has a nuclear use, and large amounts of neon gas are used in high-energy research. The neon is used in spark chambers to detect the movement of nuclear particles, their paths being shown as a trail of sparks which result from the ionization of the neon as the particles pass through the chamber. Neon can also be used in radiation detectors such as the Geiger counter.

NAVAL SECTION   ULTRA/ZIP/SJA/1443

JNA 20   C/S 114/1/2/3   NEW/535

TOO 161920 January 1945

From : TOKYO

Action: BERLIN

Action: BWG [Chief Technical Superintendent].

From : CJR [Naval Technical Directorate].

Your secret telegram No. 848 [SJA/1358: enquires what cargo is to

be shipped in submarines proceeding to the Far East].

It is desired to obtain the following material urgently by means of

the German transport submarines proceeding to Japan.

2. For Department No.3:

1) Diamond dies (diameter between 0.02 and 0.08 mm., as large

a quantity as possible of all kinds).

2) Metallic zirconium (500 kg of a standard of 99.5 per cent or

over).

3) Metallic lithium, 500 kg.

4) Neon gas (as much as possible).

5) Insulating material for ultra high frequencies, 10 kg of each

kind.

6) 2,000 or more [HASPEKERNE, ? clamp cores].

3. For Department No.5:

1) As many BOSCH fuel pumps models 10 and 6 as possible.

2) 1 polarizing microscope.

3) 10 cam shaft grinders.

4) 10 MAAG gear wheel grinders.

Figure 4. Nuclear materials to Japan. (Note: Depts 1 and 2 deleted from ULTRA by author.)

Item 5 is high-frequency insulating material, and high frequencies are associated with nuclear fission. Specialized insulation is always provided for all the main reactor parts, including the actual vessel containing the nuclear core, and hence the order for insulation.

Item 6 is not a material but a finished product, and here the translator has got things the wrong way round. This is understandable if you are not technical and translating Japanese into English. The word should be *Kernehaspe*. *Kern* does not appear very often in modern German technical dictionaries, but if you go back to the 1950s, *Kern(e)* was the German word for nuclear or core, hence *Kernbrennstoff* is nuclear fuel, *Kernpfropfen* is core plug, *Kernreacktor* is nuclear reactor, *Kernwaffe* is nuclear weapon, etc. *Kernehaspe* can be translated as 'core clamp', and what is interesting is that the order asks for 2,000 or more. In a reactor there are several areas where thousands of clamps are used, and these include the fuel rods/tubes, the control rods and their mechanisms and the insulation. A reactor of 300 kw might have 200–1,000 fuel tubes, while a large PWR of 1,000 MW would have 50,000. The significance of the 'core clamps' will be discussed later.

The final item being transported by submarine is boron, and here there were two orders placed for borax/boric acid. On 18 January 1944, ULTRA message 1309 shows that 60 tons of borax and 20 tons of boric acid were ordered from Italy for onward transport to the Yokosuka Naval Dockyard, Japan. The purchase was confirmed on 22 February 1944 in ULTRA 882. The Yokosuka Naval Base was the largest naval base adjacent to Tokyo, and much of it was buried in tunnels underground. The connection between Yokosuka and Japan's nuclear work is dealt with in a later section.

On 18 April 1945, ULTRA message 1860 states that 15 tons of borax were transported to Sweden for onward transport by surface ship to Japan. It is unlikely that this cargo ever reached Japan.

The PRO file at Kew contains twenty volumes of ULTRA messages sent by the Naval Attaché between the Japanese embassy in Berlin and Tokyo, with some later ones sent from Geneva and Stockholm. The dates start in 1943 and end in 1945, with the occasional item from 1941/2. The files contain the loading lists for two of the last German submarines to leave Kiel for the Far East, U-864 (codename Caesar), a Type-IXD2, and U-873 (Anton-1), a Type-IXD2. U-864 left Kiel in December 1944 for Bergen and departed Bergen in February, and according to ULTRA it was sunk on 9 February 1945 by HM Submarine *Venturer*, off Bergen. U-873 left Kiel at the end of March and surrendered to the US Navy on 11 May 1945. In the loading lists for both U-873 and U-864, some items are described by name, while others just have reference numbers. It is quite possible that some of the material on U-864 was nuclear, and the description on page 1 of the loading list – 'CASPAR 63: total 69 packages' – is intriguing. Caspar was one of the three wise men who travelled to Bethlehem bearing gifts of great value for the infant Jesus. What indeed were the 69 packages if they also were of 'great value'?

It is believed that only two other U-boats sailed for the Far East from Germany in 1945. These were U-234, a Type-XB converted minelayer, and U-534, a Type-

IXC/40. There are no loading lists for either of these boats in the PRO files, but it is apparent that U–534 contained no significant war material. U–543 was sunk on 5 May 1945 by the RAF off the coast of Denmark, and it was salvaged on 23 August 1993 through the efforts of a Danish entrepreneur, Mr Carsten Rees. It was known beforehand that no crew members were on board and hence it was not classed as a war grave. No significant war material was found on the boat when it was raised, but it is clear from the amount of wine, beer and spirits found on board that it was intended to carry some special passengers from Norway to the Far East.

Since 30 May 1996 the boat has been on display at Birkenhead, and guided tours are arranged of the interior throughout the year. The boat has been lifted onto the dockside, the silt, etc., removed from the inside, and apart from the bomb damage to the stern, it is almost as it left Kiel in 1945. The author would definitely recommend a visit, since U–534, like other boats bound for Japan, was a Type-IXC/40, one of the smaller ocean-going U-boats in the German Navy. Seeing first-hand a U-boat interior is quite an experience, regardless of its connection with this story. On the tours the boat is entered via the forward torpedo hatch on the deck, and you slowly move aft, clambering through the watertight doors. Among the more vivid recollections of the visit is the area in the forward torpedo room, with its four tubes. Up to twenty-five men lived here for over three months on the Far East trips, sleeping among the twelve torpedoes. On the starboard side against the bulkhead is one of the two 'heads', complete with washbasin. The tiny galley has two hot-plates and oven, the ceramic tiles still on the floor and the full-size fridge opposite, complete with ice trays. Next are the radio and sonar rooms on the starboard side, and across from them the captain's cabin. Then comes the control room with its periscope, which is being restored to working order, and the mass of control valves, Osram light bulbs still in their sockets and under the floor the Varta batteries. One of the batteries was returned to Varta in Germany and they filled it with fresh acid, charged it up and it worked perfectly, after fifty years under the sea! Next is the engine room, the MAN diesels either side of the walkway, and hanging above the engines are some spares, piston rings, a piston with its liner, push-rods, all still covered in grease and gaskets in their original wrappers. Above the engines are the two handwheels that closed valves in the exhausts when the boat dived, an operation that was carried out with some haste. Further on are the two electric motors with their clutches for disengaging the drive from the diesels. Next the compressor room, on the starboard side the main vertical compressor, and opposite, the back-up, a horizontal vane-type. Finally the aft torpedo room with the second 'head' on the starboard side, and the torpedo loading hatch, home for up to fifteen men and six torpedoes, on the starboard side a small lathe and bench for doing running repairs, now blown into the walkway by the force of the explosions on the starboard side in the stern, the cracked plates that caused U–534 to sink still visible. In the two aft torpedo tubes they found two of the latest T11 acoustic homing torpedoes, and the MoD were so keen to see these that they were unloaded and sent to the Royal Navy, more or less as they were found, complete with charges. U–534 was fitted with a permanently erected snorkel at the U-boat base in Bordeaux just before it was occupied by the Allied forces, and it was attacked several times by the RAF before safely leaving the port.

ULTRA message No. 1461 from Berlin to Tokyo, dated 30 December 1944, refers to cargo still to be transported to Japan from Bordeaux and states that 'according to later reports from the Germans, three German submarines, which were being equipped in the port at the time, left hurriedly for Japan, taking with them a considerable amount of mercury, lead and optical glass from the goods left behind as ballast.' One of these U-boats may have been U-534, which, instead of heading for the Far East, returned to Germany.

The most important boat to leave Kiel in 1945 for Japan was U-234, a transport boat converted from a Type-XB minelayer (Figure 5). U-234 left Kiel on 25 March 1945. The first leg of the journey, like many before, was to the Norwegian port and U-boat base of Kristiansand.

Here last checks were usually carried out, supplies taken on, fuel topped up and the final passengers embarked, including General Ulrich Kessler of the Luftwaffe. The complete passenger list was Oberst Fritz von Sandrath, Luftwaffe air-defence specialist; Leutnant Erich Menzel, Luftwaffe radar specialist and aide

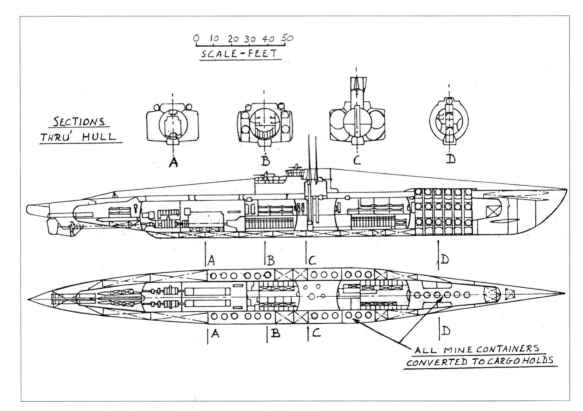

Figure 5. U-boat type XB minelayer, such as U-234.

to Kessler; Fregattenkapitan Gerdhard Falck, naval architect with responsibility for lead containers; Korvettenkapitan Dr Ing. Heinz Schlicke, radar and electronic specialist; Kapitanleutnant Heinrich Hellendorn, naval anti-aircraft gunnery specialist; Kapitanleutnant Richard Bulla, air–sea cooperation specialist; Oberstleutnant Geshwaderichter Kay Nieschling, military judge appointed to investigate the Sorge spy affair in Tokyo; August Bringewald, Messerschmitt Me163 and Me262 design engineer; Franz Ruf, Messerschmitt procurement specialist for Me163 and Me262.

Two Japanese officers were also on board, Colonel Genzo Shosi, Japanese Army Air Force, and Captain Hideo Tomonaga, submarine designer.

The fact that U-234 carried a nuclear cargo was admitted by the USA after the submarine arrived at the naval base of Portsmouth, New Hampshire, on 19 May 1945, following its surrender to US Navy destroyer *Sutton* on 13 May 1945. Since we now know that British and US intelligence were decoding the Japanese Naval Attaché messages between Berlin and Tokyo and that this traffic included the loading lists for the submarines travelling between the two countries, it is virtually certain that such a loading list was decoded for U-234, despite there being no record in the PRO files. The timing of the transmission of the U-boat loading lists is important because from this date Allied Intelligence would have been aware, with reasonable accuracy, what each boat was carrying, and if there was anything special on board.

The list for U-864 was transmitted from Berlin to Tokyo at 10 a.m. on 28 February 1945, and the boat left Bergen for Penang early in February, being sunk on 9 February 1945. The U-873 list was transmitted at 5.40 a.m. on 15 April 1945, and the boat left Kristiansand for Japan on 1 April 1945. It is most likely, therefore, that the list for U-234 was sent out from Berlin before the end of April, probably between 10 and 20 April. Hence, by the 20th at the latest, Allied intelligence would have decoded U-234's loading list and been aware that it had a special cargo, even if it was not spelt out in so many words. They may have used a coded description that implied the cargo was nuclear. It is extremely unlikely that the nuclear material was mentioned by name, even if, as the US authorities claimed after the war, the cargo was uranium oxide.

Appendices A and B are technical details of U-234 and its preparation for the Japan voyage, and details of the cargo as released by the US authorities after it was unloaded at Portsmouth, New Hampshire. These will be discussed later, but some of the points of interest referring to U-234 include its conversion into a transport at Germania Werft, Kiel. Despite the rapidly deteriorating military situation in September 1944, the starboard propeller was replaced because it was too noisy at 100 rpm, a possibly vital change if the U-boat was being hunted when submerged and the enemy was listening for the slightest sound of disturbed water. One of the more obvious points about the US cargo list for U-234 is the uranium oxide: Japan was not desperate for a few kilos of uranium oxide, and in this state it emitted virtually no radiation, but it was transported in special containers in U-234, whereas Union Minière stored such material in wooden barrels. The other items are the 106 kg (233 lb) of thallium and the fuses (for munitions). The nuclear use of thallium in radiation detectors has already been mentioned, and sending a box of fuses to Japan does not seem to have any special significance, although it is known that German fuses were probably the best in the Second World War. Regardless of this, there still does not seem to be much point in using valuable cargo space for something as ordinary as a few fuses which were only going to be used to detonate bombs or shells. But vital components of the plutonium implosion type of nuclear weapon as used at Nagasaki were very reliable and fast-operating fuses which imploded the nuclear material, compressing the fissile material very quickly into a critical mass, speed being essential if the maximum amount of material was to fission before it evaporated in the heat of the nuclear explosion. A number of fast-operating fuses were placed with conventional explosives around the circumference of the plutonium Pu.239 in the Nagasaki bomb, and hence this may have been the reason for having such items among the cargo of U-234.

In addition, proximity fuses are an essential part of the detonation system for air-dropped nuclear weapons. To ensure the maximum heat and blast effects, the weapon must be exploded above ground, which is how the Hiroshima and Nagasaki bombs were used. This will also be discussed later.

CHAPTER 4

The Storage, Servicing and Launch Sites for the V1, V2, Rheinböte and HDP

INTRODUCTION

Any weapon system needs facilities for storing it when not in use, for servicing it and preparing it for launch, and firing or launching the weapon at the target regardless of the type of warhead. The V1, V2, Rheinböte and HDP were no exception. In northern France, stretching from the Pas de Calais to the Cherbourg Peninsula, a huge system of sites was built for this purpose, sites that could be used to launch the weapons with either a conventional warhead or a nuclear or chemical one as required. Two main factors determined what was provided for the weapons during the construction phase between 1943 and 1945, regardless of the role of the weapon. In 1942, when the design of many of the sites was started, the prospect of any serious threat from Allied bombing to the building and operation of the sites looked remote, but the possibility existed. From 1943 onwards the threat from Allied bombing was increasing as every month went by, and hence the site system evolved to take this changing threat situation into consideration.

There are major problems in determining operational details of the larger sites for several reasons:

1. Original German drawings have survived for only two of the sites, the V2 bunkers at Watten and Wizernes.
2. None of the sites was completely finished, that is with equipment installed, due to Allied bombing.
3. Shortly after capture by Allied forces, some of the sites were partially demolished in case German forces reoccupied them in the event of Allied military reverses.
4. After the war the areas of the sites dangerous to the public were filled in with earth and rubble.

Hence what documentation there is available tends to be concerned with communications with the contractors, the Organisation Todt (OT), who built all the sites, about matters dealing with building progress, materials required and the effects of Allied bombing on the particular project. There is very little documentation which gives any direct indication that the sites might be intended for special purposes, and so the picture has to be put together from the site remains in France and what we know of the weapons themselves.

The SS connection is present at the very beginning of the foundation of the OT. Dr Fritz Todt, although appearing as a rather benign figure in photographs, was in fact a close member of Himmler's inner circle, having been on Himmler's staff since the very early days of the SS in 1931, with the rank of Standartenführer (Colonel), and he had been a member of the Nazi Party since 1923. Although Todt was killed in an air crash on 8 February 1942, and the OT became part of Albert Speer's empire, it is unlikely that Speer introduced any major changes to the operational regime of the OT, leaving the SS connections intact, something that was to prove valuable from 1943 onwards.

THE V1 SITES

The V1 had the most comprehensive site system of all three weapons, since it was the only one of the four that became operational in France. Due to this it is worthwhile looking briefly at all the V1 sites, regardless of their operational role, since this best illustrates the differences between those sites intended for the conventional high-explosive V1 as used against London and other cities shortly after D-Day, and those with the capability to store, service and install unconventional warheads, either nuclear or chemical. For the conventional role the original V1 campaign was designed to operate from a system of missile storage sites, eight in number, plus approximately 120 launching sites, the great majority of the launch sites being in the Pas de Calais, that is between Calais and the River Somme.

The eight storage sites, all above ground, were:

1. Pas de Calais to the Somme: Renescure, Sautricourt, Domleger.
2. Somme to the Seine: Neuville-au-Bois, St Martin l'Hortier, Biennais.
3. Normandy: Beauvais.
4. Cherbourg Peninsula: Valognes.

The majority of the V1 storage buildings are of brick construction with wooden doors, and located as they are, on open field sites, offer very little protection from air attack. Warheads were intended to be stored in the open between earth walls. From these arrangements it is clear that they were designed before the Allied bombing campaign became a serious threat.

Of these eight sites, all were finished except St Martin l'Hortier. The total storage capacity of these storage sites was around 1,800 V1s. The launching sites were provided with a little more protection, but even this was not intended for heavy bombing raids. The most prominent feature of these original launching sites from the air were the three V1 storage buildings, which resembled giant skis laid on their side, and hence they became known as 'ski sites'. One of these launch sites was at Hardinvast near Cherbourg, where total storage capacity was about twenty-five V1s. In some instances the site location used natural camouflage. At Eclimeux, near Hesdin in the Pas de Calais, for example, the launch ramp starts in the centre of the village and ends at the cemetery, all other buildings being built into the village layout. At other locations there is a complete disregard for camouflage, and near Frevent the site is built on the highest piece of ground for miles, the buildings standing out like a beacon. Many of these sites used French construction workers and contractors supervised by the OT, and a fairly leisurely construction programme was followed, with each site taking about three months to complete. The majority of the launch ramps were 150 ft long, the steel structure being enclosed within blast walls. As Allied Intelligence began to comprehend what the sites were for and establish a link between the storage and launch sites, the actual site layout began to change to counter the Allied bombing raids. The ski storage buildings were sometimes located several miles from the launch site; the launch ramp, which had been identified very early on by Allied Intelligence as being similar to those at Peenemünde, was reduced in length to 70 ft and not assembled until the site was ready for use; and security generally was tightened-up, especially during construction. Following the bombing of selected storage sites by the Allies, these sites were more or less abandoned, and three new sites were built using existing caves and tunnels. These new sites were at Nucourt and St Leu d'Esserent, originally mushroom-growing caves north of Paris, and Rilly-la-Montagne, a railway tunnel seven miles west of Rheims. These new storage sites added considerably to the transportation between sites, at least sixty miles, which meant that transfer from storage to launch site usually took place at night. This was the organization originally planned and built for the conventional V1.

For V1s with a nuclear or chemical warhead, five bunker sites were planned, and these were:

1. Siracourt, three miles from St Pol, and
2. Lottinghen, fifteen miles west of St Omer; both in the Pas de Calais.
3. Couville.
4. Tamerville and
5. Brécourt; all on the Cherbourg Peninsula.

Some of these sites had a multiple V1/V2/Rb role, and some were converted to a dual role as the campaign progressed. This changing situation was due partly to the Allied bombing and partly to the takeover of the site construction programme by the SS in mid-1943. The programme for building these sites was approved by Hitler on 28 June 1943, and by August work had started at all five sites. The most advanced were Siracourt and Couville, whereas at Lottinghen and Tamerville only the rail link had been started. Brécourt is a special case, since it was not a 'green field' site but already had the underground workings built as part of the French oil storage depot.

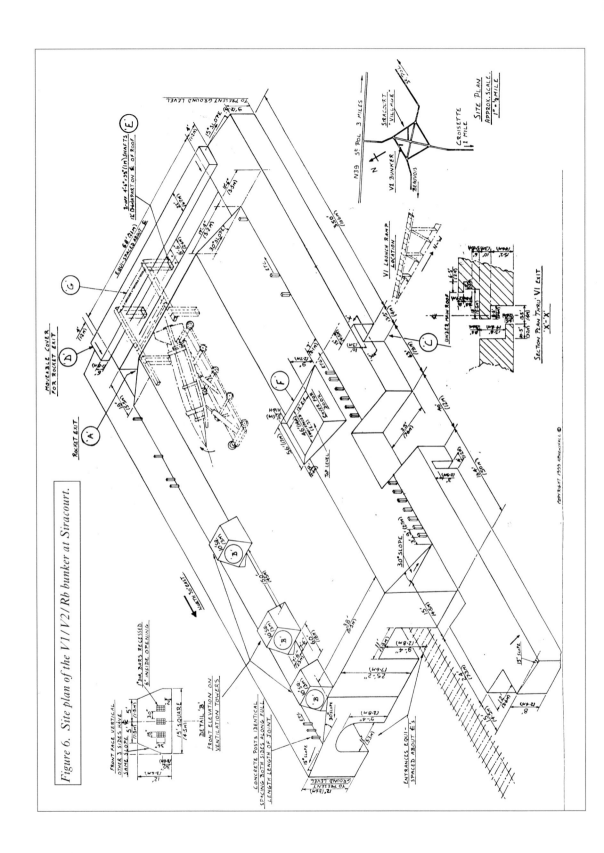

Figure 6. Site plan of the V1/V2/Rb bunker at Siracourt.

1. Siracourt (German site name Wasserwerk Saint Pol)

Figure 6 shows the V1/V2/Rb bunker at Siracourt. Construction of the bunker was based on a system used at several sites, and was called 'Erdschalung' (Earth shuttering) by the OT. The foundations and supporting walls were built first, and the ground in between was left in place. This was then used as a support during the construction of the roof, and as soon as the roof was finished the earth was excavated from underneath, leaving the finished structure. The material was reinforced concrete, maximum roof and wall thicknesses were 16.5 ft (5 m) and 21.9 ft (6.6 m) respectively, and the size and number of the steel reinforcing bars exceeded that used on normal civil structures. A standard gauge loop line was laid from the nearby St Pol–Doullens main line, and this entered at the north end of the bunker. Very little attempt was made to provide camouflage for Siracourt, and this would have been difficult as the site is located on elevated ground devoid of trees, etc. Despite this, the main structure was finished before the Allied bombing started in the summer of 1944, resulting in work being abandoned before all the earth was removed from the interior.

Siracourt is an example of how the role of the bunker was changed to suit the changing military situation. Originally intended for the V1, the bunker would have provided protection for several missiles, their warheads, fuel and HTP. The V1 would have emerged from exit 'C', which originally would have been about 22 ft wide, suitable for a V1 with wings fitted, the wingspan varying from 16 ft to 17.5 ft, depending on model and range. There are the remains of the foundation blocks for the launch ramp supports a few yards from the exit, launch direction being north-west. The tapered addition to the roof, 'F', above the exit 'C' was intended to accommodate the mechanism for a sliding bomb-proof door, moving in a slot 8 ft (2.4 m) wide and protecting the interior. This feature was abandoned, and exit 'C' was built with a width of 13.5 ft and a dog-leg section added, as a simpler form of blast protection for the interior. The final width of 'C' means that a V1 with wings fitted could not pass through this exit, and it would have been a very tight fit for the fuselage alone. At the south end of the bunker a new section was added, 48.5 ft long, for the full width of the roof. This was equipped with an opening slot, 'A', 18 ft wide and 68 ft long, extending to the floor of the bunker, although the slot is now blocked with rubble. There are two smaller slots, 'E', either side of the roof centre-line, intended for lifting gear 'G'. Resting on the rear of the extension, adjacent to the slot, is a massive concrete block, 'D', 6 ft thick × 22 ft wide and 74 ft long. This block is not a fixed part of the extension, and as it overlaps the slot by four feet at either end and is four feet wider, its original purpose was most likely to act as a protective cover for the slot, sliding over it on concealed runners.

What appears to have happened at Siracourt is that early in 1944, following the repeated bombing of the V2 bunkers at Watten and Wizernes, it was accepted that these sites were unlikely to ever be available for their original purpose. At this time, Siracourt was relatively undamaged, and hence its use as a V1 bunker was scrapped and it was modified as above, to accommodate the V2. The new extension with the slot 18 ft wide × 68 ft long was wide enough for a V2 with fins

MA/Paris/732

Military Attache's Office
British Embassy
Paris

30 June 1951

The Director of Military Intelligence
The War Office (M.I.10(a))
Whitehall, S.W.1

"CROSSBOW SITES"

I enclose for your information the first draft of the joint
report on the "Crossbow Sites". It has not yet been agreed by the
other members of the commission, but as we all agreed verbally about
it, the final version should not be greatly different.

I also enclose some new photographs of WIZERNES which may be
clearer than those I sent you last year as it was a brighter day.

It was very much drier than the last time I visited these
places and that we were able to get into the workings at Wizernes and
under the concrete roof at SIRACOURT, so that I now know more about
them than I did last year. I would like to be sure that everyone at
home is quite clear about the state of completion of these places.
There are some rather fanciful sketches in the report of the Sanders
mission which may give a false impression.

At SIRACOURT the concrete structure has been completed but
no more than perhaps a third of the soil has been excavated from
underneath it. Masterson found it difficult to conceive of this as
an assembly and launching site for V.1's, as he would have expected
separate but adjacent storage for hydrogen peroxide. One curious
feature of this building is that at present no complete V.1 could
pass through the ramp entrance. Some 20-30 feet inside this entrance
there is an emplacement which may have been intended for bomb-proof
doors like those at Watten (the bulge giving head room for these
shows very clearly on my old photo 7). Between this emplacement
and the entrance there are two massive cubes of concrete, one behind
the other but staggered. The outermost shows clearly in S.3 while
the other can just be made out in the gloom inside, reaching across
from the right hand side of the hole to about level with the edge
of the left hand block. The gap between these blocks is only about
six feet, at right angles to the entrance. The blocks extend from
ground level to roof, joining on to the roof and to the left and
right hand walls of the entrance respectively.

On my first visit I thought that these blocks had been made
by the French, to block the entrance. The French representative
believes them to have been put there by us for the same purpose.
It is difficult to decide from the appearance of the concrete whether
they were made as part of the structure or not. I am now of the
opinion that the Germans, as a result of damage to the roof of the
western wing, which shows in S.3, may have abandoned the idea of
using the ramp entrance and put these blocks in as supports.
Certainly the roof around the inner block looks as though there may
have been a small penetration almost exactly above it.

The French representative had a tale, alleged to have come
from the local inhabitants, that in 1946 a party of British Sappers
and German prisoners came and, with hollow charges used to make holes
for larger camouflet charges, pierced the roof in several places and
then patched the holes with cement. There are certainly patches in
the roof, which I had previously assumed were German repairs to bomb
holes which had not penetrated, but in that part of the roof which
we could get under nothing showed. It should be possible to check
on this story.

Figure 7. British report on 'Crossbow Sites', 1951.

fitted, maximum width 13 ft, and long enough for the fully assembled rocket, 45 ft. The V2 would then be launched from the roof using a Meillerwagen, the rows of concrete posts either side of the roof providing supports for camouflage netting when launches were not taking place.

Siracourt was inspected by a second British mission in 1951, and one page from their report is included in Figure 7. Even in 1951 there was still some confusion about the purpose of Siracourt, but there is agreement that the original exit was now too narrow for a V1, although no comments are made about the reason for the extension and slot at the south end of the bunker.

In recent times the earth blocking the entrances has been removed and parts of the interior are now accessible, although this is restricted by the amount of soil still under the roof, which is probably as the Germans left it in 1944. From 31 January 1944 until 6 July 1944, the total weight of bombs dropped on Siracourt was 5,070 tons. This included sixteen 12,000 lb Tall Boy bombs dropped on 25 June, of which four fell in the site area, with two actually hitting the bunker.

2. Lottinghen (German site name Wasserwerk Desvres)

Lottinghen is about thirty miles from Siracourt, and it was intended to provide a similar V1 facility. The site access road is about one mile out of the village on the

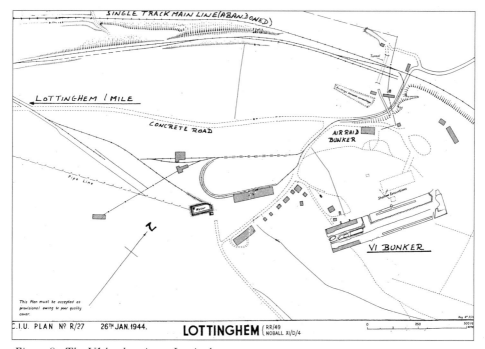

Figure 8. The V1 bunker site at Lottinghen.

edge of Les Grands Bois, and since it was heavily bombed in 1943/4, the trees have now almost completely obliterated the remains, only the overgrown bomb craters giving an indication of the severity of the bombing. The site was adjacent to the Boulogne–St Omer single-track branch line (now abandoned), and a loop and sidings were taken off this line to supply the site. The auxiliary buildings and supply arrangements were well established, but the main construction of the bunker only progressed to the supporting walls of the 'Erdschalung' system before Allied bombing forced work to be abandoned in 1944. The west supporting wall shows evidence of an exit similar to that at Siracourt, enabling V1s to be launched from a ramp at right angles to the wall in a north-west direction. Figure 8 shows the layout of the site, based on a drawing at the PRO, Kew.

The overall dimensions and layout of the bunker are similar to Siracourt, although Figure 8 does not show any signs of rail access for V1 supplies directly into the bunker, as at Siracourt, although this may be due to the incomplete state of the main structure. There is also no sign of an extension at one end of the bunker, and once again this is probably due to the less advanced state of construction. The total weight of bombs dropped on the site between February and April 1944 was 605 tons, and this was sufficient to result in construction being abandoned.

3. Couville (German site name Wasserwerk Cherbourg)

Like Siracourt and Lottinghen, there is evidence that Couville was originally intended as a V1 bunker, since it appears as one of eight 'Wasserwerk' planned for the V1 and discussed at Luftwaffe meetings chaired by the Secretary of State for Air, Field Marshal Milch.

Couville is a small village, half a mile from the station on the main line from Paris to Cherbourg and six miles inland from Cherbourg. Work started in July 1943 with the laying of a standard gauge loop line from the main line, together with 35 track sidings adjacent to the main line, which gives some indication of the amount of rail traffic expected to use the site. Work at Couville advanced quickly, and by October the rail link had been built, together with the supporting walls of the main bunker and a number of smaller buildings. Unfortunately, Allied bombing started on 11 November 1943 and carried on every few days until 21 January 1944, followed by the last raid on 12 May 1944. Just under 500 tons of bombs were dropped on the site, and this was enough to destroy most of the buildings and the rail link, leaving virtually nothing but the partially completed supporting walls of the bunker. These walls, 28 ft apart and 4.5 ft thick, with a total length of over 500 ft, have little in common with either Siracourt or Lottinghen, the 28 ft internal width allowing for the storage of a V1 with wings fitted but very little capacity for movement of any sort. After the first heavy bombing raid in November 1943, construction was virtually abandoned, but some work continued, to give the illusion that it was intended to complete the site, and a large Luftwaffe AA battery was moved into the area to complete the ruse. The decision to leave the site uncompleted was most likely connected with the takeover by the SS and Kammler of the site construction programme from October/November 1943.

4. Tamerville (German site name Wasserwerk Valognes)

Tamerville is about two miles from Valognes, eight miles inland from Cherbourg, and features in the early Luftwaffe-Milch meetings as one of the planned 'Waterworks' sites. Work at the site never progressed further than preparing the ground for the rail link off the same main line as Couville, but on the other side of the tracks. Tamerville was most likely another 'casualty' of the SS takeover, and since it was obvious that the Allied bombing was going to intensify, not decrease, and since construction had not even started, it was quickly deleted from the list.

5. Brécourt (German site name Wasserwerk No. 2 and Olkeller Cherbourg)

Brécourt, almost on the coast and three miles west of Cherbourg, was a multi-purpose site capable of launching the V1, V2 and Rheinböte. As its use as a V1 site was dropped in favour of its other uses, this site will be covered in the V2 and Rheinböte section.

THE V2 AND ITS LARGER DEVELOPMENTS

The original plan for the V2 and its larger developments was for two large bunker sites in the Pas de Calais and two more on the Cherbourg Peninsula. All four would be capable of storing from thirty to a hundred V2s, and would have their own liquid oxygen plants and storage for alcohol, HTP and catalyst. They would be completely bomb-proof and able to provide a complete servicing, fuelling and arming service regardless of the type of warhead, conventional or nuclear/chemical. The four sites were Watten, site name Kraftwerk Nordwest, and Wizernes, site name Schotterwerk Nordwest, both in the Pas de Calais; and Sottevast, site name Reservelager West-Bauvorhaben 51, and Brécourt, site name Olkeller Cherbourg, both near Cherbourg.

In addition, some modifications were made to a partially completed French coastal defence site, Castel-Vendon, a few miles along the coast from Brécourt. In addition to the four bunker sites, a system of semi-protected open sites was planned, possibly four in number, and about fifty open, unprotected launch sites. All these sites would be supplied with rockets from eleven underground storage sites, utilizing existing caves and tunnels. Three of these sites were located almost 200 miles from the coast, Hollogne near Liège, Tavannes near Verdun and Savonnières near St Dizier, and the remainder were within fifty to a hundred miles of the coast. Liquid oxygen production and storage was one of the main problems, due to its low-temperature storage requirements, since it boils-off at −182°C and has to be stored at a minimum of −200°C. Production was to be based at Wittringen in the Saar, Liège, Euville, Origny and Rouen, with storage at Rinxent, near Boulogne, and Caumont. All the large bunker sites were to have their own production and storage arrangements, as were the smaller semi-protected sites. Alcohol was less of a problem: one main storage depot was to be provided at Tourcoing, which is part of the Lille–Roubaix–Tourcoing industrial triangle, with nine smaller field storage sites close to the launch points. Seventy per cent of all V2 activity was to take place between Calais and the Somme, with the remainder from Caen to Cherbourg.

In the days up to the summer of 1942, when Germany either occupied, controlled or had as allies most of Europe and a sizeable part of Russia, this organization must have looked perfectly feasible. Indeed, for a weapon as revolutionary as the V2, a considerable amount of thought must have gone into the facilities required for its operational use against Britain initially and America in the future. Up to 1942, no V2 had travelled more than a few hundred yards from assembly to the launch pad, as Peenemünde was a self-contained manufacturing, testing, assembly and launch establishment. Now, this rocket with its hundreds of valves, switches, relays, transducers, etc. was to travel several hundred miles by rail to its storage/launch point. This needed some very careful planning for it to be a success, and if nuclear weapons were to be included, this was an extra complication.

Although the four bunker sites are of most interest as bases for a nuclear campaign, it is not inconceivable that, if required, the smaller semi-protected sites could also have been used for this purpose. Three of these smaller sites are therefore described first, covering the arrival of the rocket from Germany, its storage and testing and its temporary storage adjacent to the launch site.

(i) Villiers-Adam (German site name Mery s./Oise)

The Villiers-Adam site is on the edge of the Forêt de l'Isle-Adam, a mile from the village, which is only twelve miles north-west of Paris, and there is a rail loop off the main Paris line within a mile of the site. The area is well known for its limestone caves used for mushroom growing, and one such location was chosen for the site (Figure 9). When the rockets arrived from Germany they were put immediately into storage in the caves. When required, they were removed and broken down into sections in preparation for testing in the service buildings, as shown in the figure. These structures are still in excellent condition, the only parts missing being the large wooden doors at either end. The concrete plinths, complete with mounting bolts for the rocket sections, are still in place, as is the twin-track narrow gauge railway in front of the test buildings.

The V2 could be broken down into the following sections, moving down from the nose:

Warhead/nose section: 5 ft 11 in long, weight 2,150 lb complete with 1,650 lb Amatol high-explosive filling, or appropriate ballast if used in a nuclear role. The warhead would travel independently regardless of its type, and be stored at the same location as the rocket, but in a separate area. No servicing of the HE warhead was required other than attachment of the detonators and arming just prior to launch.

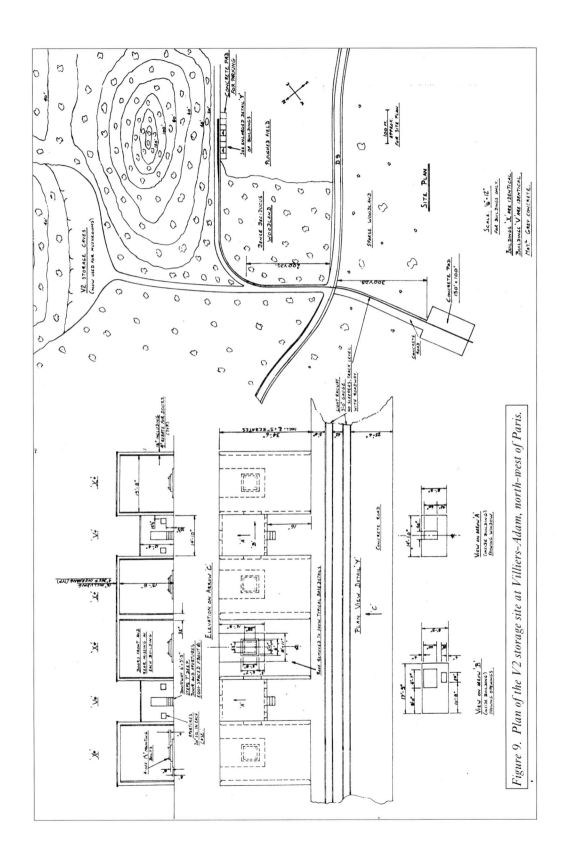

Figure 9. Plan of the V2 storage site at Villiers-Adam, north-west of Paris.

Instrument and control section: 4 ft 8 in long, weight 975 lb including structure weight of 325 lb. The overall weight of this section varied slightly depending on the type of equipment installed.

Centre section fuel storage: 20 ft 3 in long, weight empty 1,795 lb of which 1,185 lb was structure.

Motor compartment: 14 ft 8 in long, weight 4,000 lb, of which 1,595 lb was structure, 890 lb HTP turbine/fuel pumps and HTP/catalyst, 1,035 lb for the rocket motor, 480 lb for the four graphite internal control vanes and associated control gear.

Before leaving Germany it would have been considered pointless carrying out integrated functional checks on the missile systems in their fully assembled state, since over a journey of several hundred miles, any number of faults could develop. The layout of the service/test buildings are interesting, as can be seen from Figure 9. Between each test bay is a smaller building which would have contained the instrumentation and personnel carrying out the test procedures, allowing each of these sections to work on two rocket sections at a time.

Using procedures from Peenemünde, each section of the rocket would have been checked, and typically this would have included the following operations.

The centre fuel section would have had the tanks and other piping pressurized to check for leakage. No leaks could be tolerated due to the volatile nature of the fuel.

An operational check would have been made on any valves, relays, etc. in the motor section, together with another pressure check on the HTP/catalyst storage tanks. The rocket used numerous valves of various types (solenoid, pressure-reducing, non-return, safety, vent, and distribution), and they all required checking. Operation was either electrical or pneumatic, and the faulty operation of these valves had caused many of the launch failures at Peenemünde.

The main problem was the high level of vibration as the main thrust of the motor built up on the launch pad. To guard against accidental operation of valves and relays during this period, they were given a high operational resistance, to open or close. This required careful adjustment if the valve or relay was not to remain open or closed when the signal was given.

A leak and operational check would also be made on the nitrogen system used to pressurize the HTP and catalyst tanks to 350 lb/in². This nitrogen was also supplied to the fuel tanks at 20 lb/in² via a reducing valve in order to prime the the fuel pumps, and later in flight, to pressurize the alcohol tank.

As a general rule, all rocket testing is carried out with the sections in the vertical position, as at launch. The V2 in particular used a gravity feed system from the fuel tanks to the motor after the main fuel valves were opened, and this was ignited by a pyrotechnic torch or similar. Not until an observer was satisfied that this fuel had ignited were the turbine driven fuel pumps started via the external power supply on the pad. The most complicated and time-consuming testing would be that involving the control and instrumentation (C&I). The C&I

bay would probably be mounted on a swivelling table that allowed simulation of the initial trajectory. The guidance system of the V2 was designed to provide control over the three basic factors that affected its flight path – height, direction and velocity. Being a ballistic missile similar to a long-range artillery shell, changes to its trajectory were limited to the initial part of the flight, and this required accurate control over pitch attitude (the angle of the longitudinal axis of the rocket compared to the horizon), while the rocket began its change from vertical to inclined flight path. To achieve the correct direction, control was based on the difference between a reference axis, usually north, and a very accurate compass bearing of the target. The V2's control system used an auto-pilot similar to the V1's, only more complicated, but basically a combination of gyros, servo motors, associated electrical pick-offs and transducers. To provide the two basic controls of the trajectory, the auto-pilot used a two-degrees-of-freedom vertical gyro for pitch attitude and therefore height control. This gyro had a gimbal whose displacement about each axis was a measure of its own angled deviation from the local vertical axis, which was maintained parallel to gravity by a gravity-sensing device. This provided a constant vertical reference against which any trajectory requirements, such as that specified for the V2, of a gradual inclination from the vertical after lift-off which terminated in an approximate angle of 45° after 52 seconds, could be arranged through a simple clockwork timing mechanism. This gyro was also arranged to provide an indication of roll attitude of the rocket via the outer gimbal axis.

To provide a horizontal alignment of the target on the compass bearing, a two-degrees-of-freedom directional gyro was used. This gyro indicated the motion of the rocket longitudinally from an original compass bearing. This accurate target bearing was established before launch by orientation of the spin axis to a reference, usually North, using several readings from an accurate surveyor's theodolite, and rotating the launch platform to line up the axes, as an accurate plot of the latitude and longitude of the target was essential.

In this case, the outer gimbal of the directional gyro was used to sense changes to the left or right. Electrical pick-offs provided impulses from these gyros which were fed via a system of servo motors to four external tabs on the fins and four graphite rudders in the rocket motor exhaust gases. The graphite rudders provided the main control forces, while the external tabs were used to damp-out any unstable aerodynamic oscillations during flight. The gyro auto-pilot was sometimes supplemented by a beam guidance system, or 'Leitstrahl', which corrected trajectory deviations by radio signals from the ground.

One essential factor in achieving the desired target accuracy was control over the velocity of the rocket, since, when viewed in plan, if the rocket was too fast it overshot, and if it was too slow, it fell short of the target. This meant accurate control was required over the timing of the rocket motor shut-off, in order to guarantee that it was travelling at the correct velocity for the target.

Originally, control of the V2's velocity was by radio signals, using the Würzberg-Riese radar to monitor the flight path. Using the Doppler effect, the velocity of the rocket could be determined from a direct comparison of the returning frequency of the signals bounced off the rocket and back to the Wurzberg. When the velocity reached a figure taken from the trajectory plot corresponding to the required range, a radio signal shut off the fuel pump turbines, stopping the motor, and the unpowered rocket then continued on a true ballistic trajectory. This original system, called 'Radio-Brenschluss', like the Leitstrahl system, had obvious drawbacks, of which the most serious was its reliance on ground control. An elaborate system of electronic filters was therefore built into the equipment to prevent spurious signals, especially from the enemy, affecting the equipment's operation. Also, both ground control systems required the transmission of the signals to be immediately behind and directly in line with the trajectory, otherwise it was inaccurate. This meant that if more than one target was used, a series of transmitting stations had to be arranged in an arc behind the launch point, each one aligned on the bearing of a particular target. This point is also discussed later at the Watten and Prédefin sites. To overcome the radio signal problem, later V2s used a gyro system in the form of a pendulous integrating gyroscope accelerometer, 'I-Gerät'. This was another example of completely new technology being used for the V2. This type of gyroscope uses an intentional imbalance in the gyro rotor. Any horizontal accelerations along the input axis, in this case the rocket's pitch axis, causes motion around the precession axis as a result of the unbalanced mass. The gyro, mounted in gimbals, is part of a servo loop in which motion around the precession axis is detected by a pick-off, and this is fed to a gimbal torquer to produce motion between the gimbal and its case. The torquer, which is a device to move a gimbal axis by applying a torque, postioned along the gyro axis, produces a rotational motion of the gimbal in which the gyro sits; this motion is equivalent to the integral of the rocket's horizontal acceleration, which is the velocity. When this velocity is the same as a prearranged figure, another signal shuts off the motor. Although this device made the V2 independent of ground signals, problems did occur due to errors in the gyroscopes which resulted from deficiencies in design, poor manufacturing standards and insufficient testing. An example of the accuracy required in velocity measurement is illustrated by a modern ICBM with a range of 5,000 miles travelling at 20,000 ft/sec, where a relative error of only 1 ft/sec would produce a target error of more than one mile. The three sets of gyros, vertical, directional and integrating, all attempt to maintain their position fixed in space. In practice, due to various problems, this hypothetical fixed motion in space cannot be maintained, and the gyros deviate from their initial fixed position. The rate of this deviation is called 'drift rate', and depends on natural effects and limitations on the manufacturing accuracy of the gyros. The natural effects can be taken into account, but no amount of testing can remove them. These natural effects result from the fact that the earth is spinning and any long-range missile must adopt a curved trajectory if it is to hit the target. This effect would be maximized if the rocket was launched from the North Pole and aimed at, say, New York. Over a flight lasting one hour, New York would have shifted 900 miles in a clockwise direction. The missile on a straight flight path would hit Chicago instead of New York. This phenomenon is known as the Coriolis effect, after the French engineer and mathematician, Gaspard Gustave de Coriolis.

The drift rates due to design and manufacturing limitations can be checked, as they depend on the physical characteristics of the gyros. These drift errors are caused basically by friction in the bearings and inaccuracies in the balanced mass of the gyro rotor. Another area where testing is required is the caging mechanism by which the spin axis of the gyro rotor is locked prior to launch and uncaged a few seconds before launch. This caging is used to reduce drift errors of the reference axis, and for vertical gyros the process by which the gyro is initially aligned to gravity is called the erection time. On some operational V2s, instrumentation was fitted for transmitting information on such items as temperatures and pressures at various locations using transducers, and on structural movements using strain gauges. A transmitting device was sometimes fitted to give an indication of the impact point. The electrical checks on the V2 would have taken several hours. The drift rates would have been checked for the individual gyros against acceptable figures, rates being in degrees per minute. Also, the vertical repeatability of the vertical gyro is used to check the overall friction, balance and accuracy built into the gyro mechanism. After establishing a vertical reference, the gimbal elements are then displaced and allowed to return to the vertical under the control of the vertical reference mechanism. Any error in failing to reach the vertical is measured in terms of the half-cone angle, which is half the spread between the extreme settling positions. Apart from these tests, each complete gimbal device has routine tests carried out on the pick-off, torquer and motor, covering impedance, output voltage, voltage gradient, torquing rate, starting and running power and run-up time. For the accelerometers the checks cover linearity, threshold acceleration, zero stability and uncertainty and cross-axis error. Any special equipment fitted to a particular rocket would also be checked, as would be the signal reception. This testing programme would include other items, but it does give some indication of the complicated and highly specialized nature of the work necessary to ensure a successful launch and flight. The importance of this testing is illustrated by the target error from launches at the Blizna range in Poland of about half a mile. This compares with about ten miles during the final V2 offensive from Holland, when the V2 was rushed straight to the launch site from Nordhausen, given a 30-minute pre-launch check, and very often launched despite problems being discovered.

An unusual feature of Villiers-Adam is the launch pad connected by the narrow gauge railway from the test buildings, where the rail track is still in place across the main road. Villiers-Adam is at least 75 miles from the coast in a direct line to London. This would reduce the effective range of the V2 considerably, and London would be an extreme-range target for a launch from the site, adding to the inaccuracy of impact. The Villiers-Adam launch pad was probably intended for rockets that had faults that were not serious enough for the V2 to be scrapped, but would have worsened if a journey by road/rail of at least sixty miles was undertaken to the pre-launch storage near the coast.

Following assembly of the three sections, the V2, less warhead, which travelled independently, was then transported to a field storage site adjacent to a number of launch sites. A typical example is Bergueneuse.

(ii) Bergueneuse

Bergueneuse is a tiny village in a hilly area a few miles south-west of Boulogne
and about fifteen miles from the coast. The site is on the outskirts of the village
and there are the remains of quarry workings in the area. Like Villiers-Adam,
there is no sign of bomb damage to either the site or the village. The tunnel used
for rocket storage extends into the hillside. The entrance provided about ten
inches clearance for a V2 with fins fitted, arranged on a trailer at 45°. The main
tunnel opens out to a width of 15 ft, 10.8 ft from the entrance, and this extends
for 150 ft, at which point it reduces in width to 11 ft.

Immediately afterwards the tunnel curves to the right at about 45° and extends
another 300 ft before ending in a rough rock face. Both sides of the tunnel are of
reinforced concrete and the height of the curved roof is 18 ft. There is a 6.7 ft
wide side-tunnel on the left, 45 ft from the entrance, which extends at right-
angles for 30 ft before it also widens out to 15 ft. After a further 60 ft the passage
is blocked by two massive steel doors, completely sealing off the tunnel. This
side-tunnel must have been intended for warhead storage, and the steel doors
would have provided some protection in the event of an explosion. Although
there are no indications of how the rockets were to be moved inside the tunnel,
close to the entrance are several sections of narrow gauge rail track which were
probably used during construction and also intended for internal use.

The next and final stage of the rocket's movement would have been to the
launch site, and Thiennes is featured next.

(iii) Thiennes

Thiennes is a village on the edge of the Forêt de la Nieppe, a heavily wooded area
between Boulogne and Lille. It is encircled by the Canal de la Nieppe, which
feeds into the main canal network into Belgium, Holland and Germany. The main
railway line from Hazebrouk to Belgium passes nearby, and a loop, now
abandoned, was taken off this line to serve the nearby villages of La Motte and
Merville. The forest covers an area of twenty square miles, and all the roads in the
forest are provided with concrete shelters for the troops guarding the site area.
Many of these have suffered bomb damage, and near the actual launch site there
are still craters among the trees. Figure 10 shows the site and despite the craters,
the main building is undamaged and is still complete with wooden shutters over
the air intakes and vents in the oxygen production section. The main building is
about 60 ft into the forest, and beyond this the land is cleared of trees, forming
the launch area. Beyond the launch area are two personnel shelters, each with 4 ft
thick walls and capable of accommodating between twenty and thirty launch and
security staff. The main building has an overall size of 112 ft × 43 ft × 18 ft high,
and is constructed out of concrete blocks, 30 in × 20 in. At the front entrance
facing the launch area is a 9 ft wide recess with a steel-framed observation port
and a doorway into the interior. Unfortunately, not all the interior of the main
building can be inspected, as a doorway through to the end section is blocked.
The first room, 28 ft long, would have contained the test and launch equipment.
The second room, fitted with wooden shutters over air intakes, would have

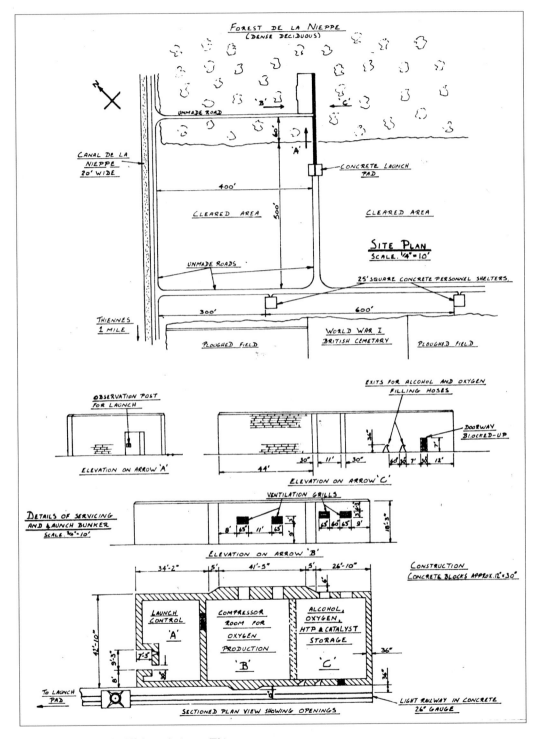

Figure 10. The V2 launch site at Thiennes.

contained the compressors, coolers, filters, etc. for producing the liquid oxygen (LOX) from the outside air, together with nitrogen as a by-product to be used in pre-launch pressure-testing and purging. From the size of the LOX production room, it is estimated that it could house equipment capable of producing about 2 tons of LOX in twenty-four hours. The V2 required 4.9 tons of LOX at launch if maximum range was to be achieved. Because of the large amount lost through evaporation from the –200°C storage temperature, it would have required three days' continuous operation to produce sufficient for one launch, unless this was supplemented by tanker supplies from another production site. It is unlikely, therefore, that a continuous launch programme was envisaged for the site, but rather a period of LOX production followed by the launch of several V2s. The end room contained the storage tanks for the LOX, alcohol, HTP, catalyst and nitrogen; this was probably stored in vessels sunk into the floor, which have since been removed, leaving large holes which have now filled with water, and this probably accounts for the blocking of the access to this area. On the outside south wall of the storage tank section are two staggered, funnel-shaped openings, pointing downwards, and along this wall, set in concrete, is a 26 in gauge rail track. The funnel-shaped openings were intended for the fuel hoses, and the rocket would have been positioned vertically, opposite these openings. The rail track has been removed at the start of the clearing, but it would have continued to the launch pad. At a launch site such as Thiennes, the count-down sequence would have been similar to the following:

–3 hours	Warhead removed from transport and attached to the main body of the rocket in the horizontal position, arming devices added. During this time the rocket would be examined for any obvious signs of damage or sabotage.
–2 hours	Rocket elevated to vertical position and placed on flat rail trolley.
–1.5 hours	Clamps removed from trim tabs, batteries fitted for auxiliary power supplies, fuel tanks pressurized at 30 lb/in^2 to check for leaks and the complete fuel system purged with nitrogen.
–1 hour	Rocket moved along rails to fuel hose positions in south wall and tanks filled in the following order: alcohol 8,750 lb, LOX 11,000 lb, HTP 370 lb, calcium permanganate catalyst 30 lb. The venting system allows 5–10 lb of LOX to evaporate per minute, depending on the ambient temperature. Rocket moved to launch pad and stabilizing legs fitted to trolley, four graphite control vanes fitted to motor exhaust.
–30 min	External power supply connected via umbilical cable to C&I bay, trajectory checked using compass bearings of site and target, gyros set to the required vertical and horizontal reference axes using collimator readings from the launch pad, initial systems checks carried out on guidance, control and motor circuits, warhead armed with detonators already fitted. The launch area is now cleared of all personnel.

−10 min	Final run-through of all system switches, relays and valves in their firing and operational sequence, pressures and temperatures checked.
−3 min	All gyros start running.
−2 min	Final checks completed, LOX vent valve closed, gyros uncaged.
−1 min	Black powder igniter lit under rocket motor, main alcohol and LOX valves opened, allowing 20 lb of fuel per second to flow by gravity into combustion chamber.
−20 sec	Visual observer confirms fuel has ignited, HTP system initiated and turbines start rotating to power fuel pumps and associated systems.
−10 sec	Turbines now running at maximum revolutions, external power supplies switched off, internal batteries switched on, initial thrust stage starts.
−5 sec	Thrust now at 8 tons and all systems working.
Zero	Main thrust stage of 25 tons starts and all systems GO.
+8 sec	External power supply jettisoned, all systems now running on internal power, thrust increases to 25 tons.
+10 sec	Lift-off, trajectory timing sequence starts, rocket vertical axis still at 90°.
+14 sec	Rocket starts inclining from vertical.
+18 sec	Maximum rocket angle of 45° reached.
+24 sec	Speed of sound reached, Mach 1.
+35 sec	Mach 2.0.
+54 sec	HTP turbines stopped, fuel pumps stopped, height 20 miles. Velocity, Mach 5.0. Rocket continues on ballistic trajectory.

Immediately the rocket leaves local air-space, the site is cleared of equipment and returned to its camouflaged state. Local defence measures, fighter cover, etc., are stood-down. All clerical work associated with the launch is completed, files made of launch checks, with results of any problems, readings and observations for return to operational HQ near Paris before being returned to Peenemünde. The local radar tracking station stays in communication with the site until the rocket is out of range at between 24 and 35 seconds after launch, to confirm that the initial trajectory is satisfactory.

Assuming the V2 offensive had gone according to schedule, the above system of sites would have complemented the much larger and more complex sites capable of launching rockets larger than the V2 with secure storage for all types of warhead. These larger sites, four in number, are all unique and diverse, but there is no doubt that one site in particular was planned to be the ultimate rocket base for attacks against Great Britain and America. The site was Watten.

(iv) Watten (Kraftwerk Nordwest)

The location chosen for what was to be the ultimate rocket base was the Forêt d'Eperlecques, three miles from the town of Watten and a few miles inland from

Calais. Watten is on a junction of the main canal network from France and Belgium through to Germany. St Omer, six miles away, was a Luftwaffe base, part of Luftflotte 2 under Field Marshal Kesselring, and provided Me109s, Me110s and Ju87s during the Battle of Britain. It remained a first-line base until the evacuation of France, but unfortunately for Watten, it was unable to provide the air cover required to protect the base from the inevitable attacks by Allied bombers.

The area was inspected in December 1942 by officials from the War Ministry, the OT and from Peenemünde, and the particular location chosen was on the edge of the forest at the base of a low escarpment and close to some granite quarries. Work started in March 1943 and it was planned that the site should be operational by October 1943, which in normal circumstances would have been a very tight schedule. Although the OT were experienced in large construction projects, the timing of the construction programme meant that they were unable to provide the necessary manpower from their normal labour force. The problem was put into the hands of Fritz Saukel, Hitler's organiser of civilian workers in all the Reich's occupied territories. Saukel, who was hanged on 16 October 1946 for war crimes, admitted in the courtroom that of all the millions of foreign workers used by the Third Reich, not more than 200,000 were volunteers. In the first stage, 6,000 were brought to Watten – Russian, Poles, Belgians, Dutch, Czechs and French. They were housed in two camps a mile from the site, and work continued twenty-four hours a day, seven days a week in twelve-hour shifts, and at any one time there were always 3,000 to 4,000 on the site. The 'Sklavenarbeiter' were controlled by a mixture of OT and SS guards, and discipline was strict: to fall ill, like on many other projects, was a death sentence. During the six months the site was under construction, over 35,000 workers passed through the camps. It is not surprising that, as with Nordhausen, Dornberger and von Braun played down their involvement with Watten, giving the impression that neither they nor anyone else at Peenemünde had anything to do with the project. But the fact was that no one in Germany had a better knowledge of the operational requirements of the V2 than the Peenemünde team. Plans for the V2 and its larger developments meant that Watten had to be capable of handling rockets twice the size of the V2 in a bomb-proof environment, and this resulted in some unique construction problems. The primary concern was that the flat roof of the main building presented the worst angle for protection to a bomb falling vertically.

Hitler, with his ability to grasp the most important points of a technical subject, understood the most significant advantages of steel-reinforced concrete. It was cheap, used mainly non-strategic materials and could be made thick enough to withstand the heaviest bombs used or ever likely to be used in the future. Xaver Dorsch of the OT provided figures from tests carried out on captured bunkers and shelters. These tests showed that with the correct thickness of concrete, a building could be constructed which would withstand the heaviest bomb in the Allied armoury, which at the time was the 12,000 lb Tall Boy. The 21 ft (6.4 m) long Tall Boy had an explosive weight of 5,400 lb, the off-set fins in the tail gave it a slow spinning motion to help accuracy, and the streamlined shape was intended to ensure that impact occurred as close to Mach 1 as possible. The only aircraft capable of lifting the Tall Boy was a Lancaster, and this had to be specially modified to take the single suspended weight of the bomb. Dorsch, not unreasonably, believed that this bomb was the maximum weight that anybody was going to build in the Second World War. Actually the RAF's Grand Slam, at 22,000 lb and 25.4 ft (7.7 m) long, was the largest single bomb ever carried in the Second World War, and once again the Lancaster was the only aircraft able to lift it. But in 1943, the biggest bomb was Tall Boy. The magic figure was 18 ft (5.5 m), and Dorsch showed that if the roof of any building where the ultimate protection was required had a roof of this thickness, it would withstand the Tall Boy. From some fairly recently released formulae issued by the American National Defence Research Council, and using the dimensions and impact velocity of the Tall Boy, a figure of 9.9 ft (3 m) is produced for the penetration depth and 18.4 ft (5.6 m) for the scabbing depth. To improve the scabbing protection for buildings such as Watten, standard practice was to build a steel mattress of girders into the underside of the roof, and the ceiling at Watten was provided with this extra protection.

From June to July 1944, four of the bunker sites were subjected to a special bombing campaign using Tall Boys. These sites were Watten, Wizernes, Siracourt and Mimoyecques. In addition, Watten was subjected to a further bombing raid early in 1945 in which the USAF co-operated with the RAF to drop several 'Grand Slam'-type bombs on Watten to test their destructive power. The first part of this special bombing campaign started at Watten on 19 June and 25 July, and a total of 32 Tall Boy bombs were aimed at the bunker, of which only one was actually on target, hitting the main building. The later raid in 1945 also obtained one hit on the main building, above the west entrance, striking the roof at one of its strongest points, the junction between the supporting wall and the roof. The shock-waves from the explosion caused a number of the steel reinforcing bars to be ejected, and 'spalling' occurred, a large piece of concrete being blown off the roof. The Tall Boy hit near the centre of the building on the south side caused the most serious structural damage, although the main integrity of the structure was not affected and it could have been repaired. Again, spalling occurred, and this time the explosion blew a section weighing several tons off the roof onto the ground below, but it was inside that the most serious effects can be seen. The ceiling under the point of impact is badly cracked, and a large piece of concrete has become partially detached, only the anti-scabbing mattress preventing it falling to the floor below. This evidence confirms the figures above, as the ceiling at this point is between 16 and 18 ft thick, which is just below the 'scabbing thickness' of the Tall Boy. This ceiling damage can no longer be seen, because in the 1990s a false ceiling was added to the main building, and this has hidden the effects of the Tall Boy impact.

Once 16–18 ft was established as the required thickness, the problem then was how to construct such a roof nearly 80 ft above the ground.

The finished roof weighed 50,000 tons, and this would have required some very special high-level concrete production and pouring equipment. The problem was solved by the OT in an unusual way. The walls were built up to a height of 15 ft (4.5 m), and then the 16–18 ft (4.8–5.5 m) thick roof was constructed on top

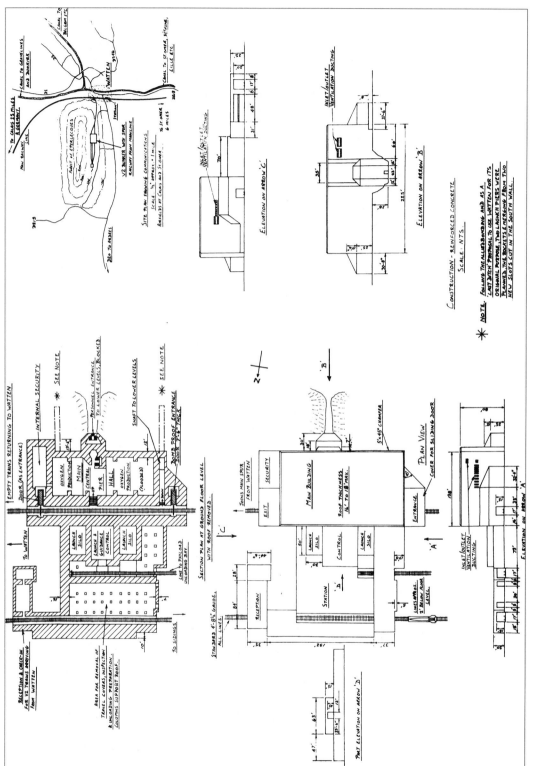

Figure 11. The V2 bunker site at Watten.

of the walls, with few access problems at this height. Providing its own protection, the roof was then slowly raised inches at a time, using hundreds of jacks. The walls were then built up underneath to their full thickness which was a maximum of 18 ft (5.5 m). To transport the vast quantities of cement, sand, gravel, steel and eventually the rockets, a standard gauge railway was run from Watten, with two narrow gauge tracks for the construction traffic running to a siding on the high ground behind the site. Material was loaded into skips at the siding, pushed to the edge of the incline and allowed to run down by gravity, pulling an unloaded wagon back to the top at the same time.

From March until August 1943, work proceeded without hindrance, and enough progress had been made for it to be possible to predict with some certainty that the target date of October 1943 would be achieved. However, on the night of 17 August 1943, Peenemünde was bombed for the first time, and on 27 August Watten suffered the same fate. The raid by 185 B-17 Flying Fortresses of the US 8th Air force was a high-level daylight raid, and hence accuracy was not very good. Although the damage caused by this first raid was not serious, it was only the beginning of a constant bombardment from the air that lasted until August 1944. In total about 4,000 tons of bombs were dropped on the site and its surroundings in twenty-five air-raids. The main building was not seriously damaged, but some of the adjacent buildings were badly affected and after each raid much of the construction equipment and access were destroyed, killing many of the workers. A halt in the bombing between October 1943 and February 1944 gave both sides an opportunity to assess the situation. From the Allied point of view, the bombing results were not conclusive, for the main building was still standing and there had been variable damage to the remaining buildings. Construction had been disrupted, but no one knew what work was going on in the main building. In fact, at this time Allied Intelligence did not know what Watten was intended for, and the only criterion had been that all large concrete structures and developments of any kind in northern France were to be bombed.

On the German side, by October 1943, with the takeover by the SS of the V-weapons site-building programme, it is clear a more realistic approach was being taken as to what part, if any, such sites would have in the V-weapons programme. Obviously, the halt in the bombing was only temporary, and it would resume, probably on an even heavier scale, some time in the near future. Work continued at Watten but at a reduced pace. Figure 11 shows the site and buildings as they were in April 1945, based on plans made by the author. When the bombing resumed in February 1944 there were an increasing number of reports to Allied Intelligence that a large rocket existed, and that like the V1 it originated from Peenemünde. Hence every week from February to May 1944, Watten was subjected to a bombing raid of varying intensity, such that although the main building was still not badly damaged, the site area was completely unusable and all equipment and access was virtually destroyed. In July 1944 an attempt was made to finally destroy the main building using Tall Boy bombs, but only one hit the target, as described earlier. An attempt was also made to demolish the main building using time-expired Flying Fortresses packed with 22,000 lb of high-explosive, the idea being that the crew would pilot them to the target area and set the fuses before baling out, and the final dive on to the target would be radio-controlled from an accompanying aircraft. Project Aphrodite was not a success, and one of the aircraft exploded prematurely over England, killing Joseph P. Kennedy, the brother of the future US President.

Watten is privately owned and open to the public seven days a week in the summer; tours are self-guided and most areas are accessible. Unfortunately, since 1990 the guide book has been amended to make it more 'politically correct', and gone are references to the more unpleasant aspects of Watten and how it was built. In addition, the main building has been altered internally, with the addition of false ceilings and a reduction in the access available compared with 1980. The interior of the main building is still flooded to just below ground level, despite claims that it was to be pumped clear some years ago, and hence the lower levels cannot be reached. At the west entrance of the main building, the bomb-proof door, 7.5 ft (2.3 m) wide, is now operating in its slot, protected above by a concrete canopy similar to that at Siracourt. Although the rail track and door at the east end are flooded, access through the west door can be made to the right, where equipment for LOX production was to be installed, although the plinths and other features have now vanished. Immediately to the right of the west door is a passage which had a vertical shaft at the far end giving access to the lower levels (flooded), and this has also vanished in the modifications of the 1990s. There are similar larger vertical shafts in the rocket-unloading bay (flooded). After the trains were halted in this section, and the bomb-proof doors closed at either end, rockets would be hoisted down to the lower levels for storage, servicing and launch preparation. Trains arriving from Watten would first be stopped in the reception station, where all documentation would be checked, transportation covers removed and an inspection made of the rockets and wagons for any signs of damage, sabotage or irregularities. This would also include a check on radiation levels if nuclear material was included. Any non-essential supplies would be unloaded at this time and stored initially in the covered-over part of the station. This initial check and inspection was an important part of the site organization, as the main building would have been regarded almost like a sterile area in a hospital, in that no 'foreign' material would have been allowed to enter. The possibility of a bomb or radiation leak going down to the lower levels could have been catastrophic.

Once checked, the train moved forward to a siding a few hundred yards west before being reversed back towards the main building. If the train was composed of rockets it entered the main building through the west door, both sliding doors were closed and the rockets were unloaded. Height clearance here is about 60 ft (18 m), and originally the runway beams for the lifting hoists could still be seen above the track, but these are now hidden from view. The rockets were lowered down to the working areas before the east door was opened, and the now empty train returned to Germany via Watten. If the supply train had contained warheads, alcohol or other material, it would have entered the second unloading bay between the station and main building. This is a single-storey structure since only normal headroom would be required. The wagons were unloaded and their contents transferred to the lower levels. LOX would have been produced in the main building. When ready for launch the rockets would be raised almost to the surface at either of the silos via a lift system similar to the Minuteman ICBM silos. After final checks, the count-down would take place and the rocket would be launched from just below ground level, the exhaust being vented at either side. Watten could easily handle rockets twice the size of the V2, with very large rockets transported in sections both to avoid damage and because of limitations on transport arrangements. The actual launch silos have an exit measuring 30 ft (9 m) × 50 ft (15 m), and this would give adequate clearance for much larger rockets than the V2. Recently released archive drawings of the site which appear in the guide book show the launching arrangements as two huge slots cut in the south wall of the main building, the rockets emerging vertically in pairs to be launched about a hundred feet away. Obviously, with two huge slots without doors cut in the south wall, the whole security of the main building would have been compromised, rendering the two sliding doors at either end redundant. There are no signs of any attempt to cut these slots in the wall, which would have been a massive undertaking in the 18 ft thick concrete. The problem with Watten is that once the bombing had reached a certain stage it would have become obvious to the planners of the V-weapons offensive that Watten could never be completed in its original form, and hence other schemes were prepared and drawn-out to show Watten in an alternative role. In the 1980s, reference was also made inside the main building to the Prédefin radar site, and a large diagram showed the physical relationship between Watten, Prédefin and the next site to be covered, Wizernes. Unfortunately, this also has now disappeared from Watten.

(v) Wizernes (Schotterwerk Nordwest)

If Watten was to be the ultimate rocket base, it had a 'sister' only ten miles to the south-west, in a chalk quarry near the small town of Wizernes. Wizernes was designed to the same basic specification as Watten, to provide a bomb-proof environment for storage, servicing and launching rockets, together with LOX production and accommodation for all the necessary personnel. At Watten, no attempt was made to disguise the site, and it stands out, even today, like a huge monument in concrete. At Wizernes, had the site been finished and with the dome covered in soil, it would have looked very little different from just another chalk quarry. Construction started at Wizernes in July 1943, a few months behind Watten, and the method of construction adopted was similar to that at Siracourt, the Erdschalung technique.

In the case of Wizernes the massive hollow-dome roof was built first, supported on the chalk underneath, chalk being the only local material capable of supporting such a weight, around 25,000 tons. The dome has a maximum thickness of at least 16.5 ft (5 m), with an internal diameter of 201 ft (61 m) and an internal height of 48 ft (14.3 m). The material is reinforced concrete, and it was built at the west end of the quarry which had already been excavated to a depth of over 100 ft (30 m). There are very little published data on the effect of missiles striking reinforced concrete at oblique angles, but it can be assumed that the 16.5 ft thickness of the dome at Wizernes would have provided even better protection than the roof at Watten. Under the dome the working area is an octagon with walls 5 ft (1.5 m) thick, extending from ground level to a 6.5 ft (2 m) thick floor under the dome. This gives a total maximum working height of 75 ft (22.7 m), and hence the maximum height of rockets that could be assembled at Wizernes is slightly less than this. From the author's plans (Figure 12), the layout of the site can be seen, together with the complex arrangement of underground workings which were part of the original plans. At the rear of the dome is a personnel exit/entrance, probably intended for emergency use. When the author first visited the site in 1976, the site was abandoned. On the quarry floor were the remains of the standard gauge railway leading into the main tunnel, 'Ida' (original German name), and also at right-angles to the south cliff face, tunnel 'Sophie'. There was an iron grille over the entrance to 'Ida', but access was still possible. However, the water level over the rail track leading into the tunnel was several inches deep, and although equipped with Wellingtons and torch, the author only ventured a few yards into the interior, being concerned that there might be a sudden increase in the depth of water, the condition of the tunnel in 1976 being very poor. Twenty years later, in May 1997, the site was opened to the public after a joint French- and EC-organized project to make the interior safe for visitors as a memorial to what might have been. Visitors enter by the original railway tunnel 'Ida', the damp conditions illustrated by the amount of water flowing in drains either side of the track, though the rails have now been removed and the tunnel skimmed with concrete. Either side of 'Ida' are shorter branch-tunnels intended for storage, one still housing a diesel generator used in the original construction. Partway along 'Ida', headphones are available which trigger multi-language descriptions at various locations as visitors follow the indicated route. A few yards further along 'Ida', the tunnel is blocked and visitors take a branch-tunnel which joins up with 'Mathilde'. Originally an unloading station for rockets and material was planned near the 'Ida-Mathilde' junction, and a narrow gauge railway was to have served the remainder of the tunnel complex before joining the other standard gauge railway at 'Sophie'. After several yards the visitor now turns right off 'Mathilde', although the tunnel has been restored beyond this point, and enters a lift to the original floor, immediately under the dome. This floor now contains a large selection of original Second World War material, and several film shows take place around the floor on the history of the V2 and related topics. The same lift is used for the return, except that exit is made by the opposite door and the route now passes through the partially completed octagon walls, which can be seen disappearing into the dark above. The exit route now rejoins 'Ida' at the 'headphone' office, and visitors leave at the entrance to 'Ida'. At least two hours can be spent on the tour, depending on how much time is spent watching the film presentations and viewing the other exhibits under the dome.

Rockets were intended to be assembled and checked prior to launch inside the octagon under the dome before moving out to one of the two launch piers, 'Gustav' and 'Gretchen'. A British post-war survey of the site indicates that it is possible that the bomb-proof doors for 'Gustav' and 'Gretchen' may have been

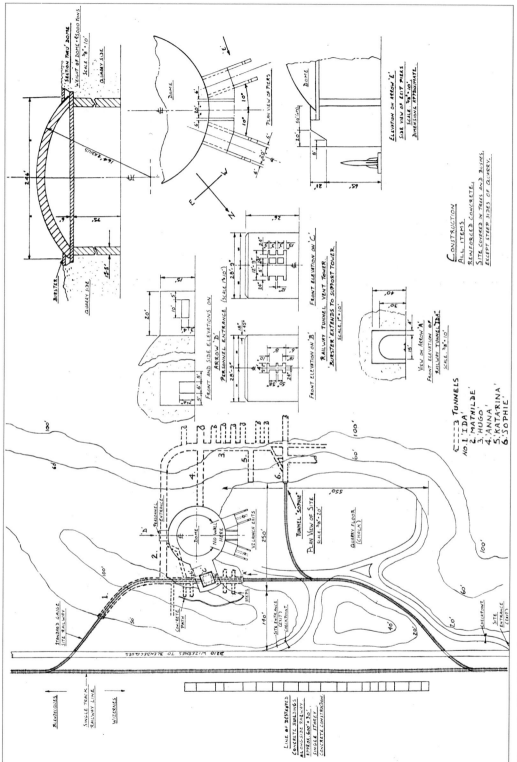

Figure 12. The V2 bunker site at Wizernes.

75 ft (23 m) high, which would have allowed rockets slightly less than this to be launched from the site – considerably larger than the 46 ft V2. The amount of forced labour used at Wizernes is not known accurately, although there is no doubt that for such extensive underground workings, a great deal of manual labour would have been used.

The construction work carried on unhindered at Wizernes until March 1944, a full eight months, although the site had been photographed several times by Allied PRU aircraft. On 11 March 1944 the first bombing raid took place, and these continued on almost a weekly basis until July 1944, by which time bombing had virtually stopped all work at the site due to destruction of access along the quarry floor and construction equipment. Originally a long line of single-storey concrete buildings ran alongside the main single track railway line outside the quarry, covering an area of about 600 ft (182 m) × 30 ft (9 m). These would have provided a similar function to that of the reception station at Watten. They were badly damaged in the bombing and their remains have now completely disappeared. Wizernes had one main operational advantage over Watten: the pre-launch checks and the launch were all carried out at ground level, which meant that no complicated lifting machinery was required to bring the rocket to the surface. There was ample space for liquid oxygen production and storage for alcohol and other essential materials, and there was certainly enough room for a nuclear reactor and the storage of radioactive materials, as there was at Watten.

(vi) Sottevast (Brix) (Reservelager West), Cherbourg Peninsula

There are four large rocket sites in France. We have already looked at two of them, Watten and Wizernes, and all four sites are unique in that the designers, using exactly the same materials, have produced four completely different answers to the same rocket base specification. With Watten and Wizernes the basic structures were more or less complete, and German drawings exist which show how the sites would have looked if they had been completed. Most importantly, though, we have no details of the equipment that was to be installed at these sites, as these are still locked away in the archives somewhere.

Sottevast presents us with another problem. We know it was intended as a rocket base, the contemporary documentation shows this, but construction at Sottevast was not at the pace of Watten and Wizernes. Work started in March 1943, and a year later, in March 1944, when the first bombing raids began to affect building work, the structure was still only perhaps one-quarter finished, virtually in the state it is today. No German drawings have emerged so far which show us what the finished site would have looked like, and so there is some speculation about Sottevast. The main building would have been massive, covering an area of 600 ft (182 m) × 190 ft (58 m), larger than both Watten and Wizernes, with what was most likely an entrance 170 ft (52 m) long × 92 ft (28 m) wide. Alongside the entrance was a concrete air raid shelter for personnel working outside, 100 ft (30 m) long × 31 ft (9.4 m) wide. Sottevast would not have had the imposing presence of Watten; the maximum height today is 20 ft (6 m), and it may have been intended to reduce this, since one of the outer walls is

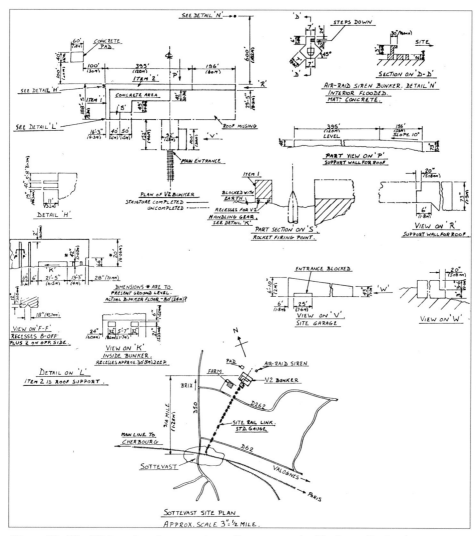

Figure 13. The V2 launch and storage site at Sottevast on the Cherbourg Peninsula.

only 6 ft above existing ground level. Figure 13 shows the site, as drawn by the author, with details of the final layout of the main building as envisaged by British Intelligence shortly after the site's capture in June 1944.

At the present day the site construction resembles a giant 'L' laid on its side, with what appears to be a central open concrete area in the angle, but this concrete area is in fact the roof of the underground section, to which access is now blocked. The only entrances are at either end of the short leg of the 'L', Item 1, and although these are now blocked with soil and covered with concrete beams on the inner side of Item 1, the local farmer said that they were originally very deep, at least 80 ft (24 m). The author believes that this entrance may have been a firing point for rockets, since there is no obvious access from normal ground level. This would explain why this entrance passes right through Item 1, forming a tunnel, which would act as a vent for the rocket exhaust, the width of this tunnel being 21.3 ft (6.5 m), which would have been wide enough for the winged V2, the A9. If the farmer is correct and the depth at this point is at least 80 ft, this means that rockets of this height and more could be launched at this point since they would be in the open, and the top of Item 1 is another 20 ft above ground level. The two legs of the 'L', Items 1 and 2, are in fact two of the outer walls of the main building, and missing are the equivalent on the other side of the open area, which would have eventually been roofed over, with the walls as supports. Underneath the central area, the ground must be excavated to the depth of the entrance at the end of Item 1, the possible launch point, possibly 80 ft, but the interior is hidden underneath the concrete roof of the central inner area. When all four outer walls had been completed, either the whole of the inner area would have been filled with concrete, providing a roof of immense thickness, or two levels would have been provided, the open area now being roofed over and providing the top floor.

The intended normal entrance to the bunker would have been as shown, and would have been positioned in the centre of Item 2, the bunker eventually forming a giant 'T', with the air raid shelter at one side. The author does not agree with the comment on the 1944 Allied inspection that the entrance would have incorporated a rocket-firing point, for reasons described above. The only other concrete on the site is a small shelter on which the air raid siren was located, and a concrete pad, 60 ft (18 m) × 40 ft (12 m), situated about 100 ft north of the bunker. There are no mounting bolts in this pad, nor any other sign that it was for, say, anti-aircraft guns, and hence this may have been a late addition to the site, the intention being to use it as a V2 launch pad. As will be seen from documentation reviewed later, it was intended that Sottevast should play a part in the modified V-weapons offensive.

Sottevast was first bombed on 26 November 1943, followed by a pause until 8 February 1944, and thereafter on more or less a weekly basis until 8 May 1944. During these air raids a total of just over 700 tons of bombs were dropped on the site, and although there are one or two signs of minor bomb damage, the impression is that the air raids did not cause any real problems to the building programme. When the US forces arrived in June 1944 they found none of the devastation as at Watten and Wizernes, but neat rows of recently abandoned and undamaged construction equipment, with all the materials at hand and ready for use.

(vii) Brécourt (Olkeller Cherbourg)

The German technocrats who organized and produced much of the advanced military equipment in the Wehrmacht had a risky policy of giving code names to equipment or projects that could give enemy intelligence a lead as to what the project related to. Typical is the name of 'Freya' given to one of their early and most successful ground-based radars. Freya was a Venus-like figure in Norse mythology who had a magical necklace, Brisingamen, which was guarded by

Heimdall, the watchman of the gods. Heimdall could see a hundred miles by night or day, and hence British Intelligence suspected, correctly, that Freya was connected with some type of radar equipment. The rocket base at Brécourt was given the codename Olkeller Cherbourg, Oil Cellar Cherbourg, and this was too close to the truth for comfort. In the 1920s the French Navy, like those of other modern countries, was converting its coal-fired warships to oil-burning. Cherbourg was then, and still is, a large naval base, as all France's nuclear submarines are built there, and it needed to be able to store a considerable amount of heavy oil for the ships in a secure location convenient for the base. Brécourt is three miles west of Cherbourg and half a mile inland, the site being a small ravine backing on to a hillside. In 1926, tunnels were cut into the hillside and construction started on eight huge underground oil reservoirs, though the last two were never finished. The reservoirs are approximately 240 ft (73 m) × 50 ft (15 m) and 46 ft (14 m) deep, made of concrete with a steel lining. The whole complex was connected by tunnels, with accommodation for personnel and equipment. The site is still under the control of the French Navy, although oil is now stored in above-ground tanks inside the actual base. With permission of Vice-Admiral Canonne, the naval commander at Cherbourg, the author was taken on a guided tour of those areas which are still accessible, including Reservoir No. 3, the adjacent tunnels and part of the German additions to the site.

German forces arrived at Cherbourg shortly after the capitulation in June 1940, and although Brécourt had already been replaced by the newer storage tanks, the possibilities of other uses for the underground complex must have been obvious. It is not surprising, therefore, that when suitable locations were investigated for use as V-weapons sites, Brécourt was chosen on the basis that very little additional constructional work was required. Internally the original oil storage depot was converted as follows. Reservoirs 1–6 (Figure 14) were unchanged, while Reservoirs 7 and 8 were modified to provide offices and workshops for the rocket personnel. The various connecting tunnels and other underground areas were intended for V-weapon storage, plus fuel, warheads and LOX production, and it is possible that some of the other oil reservoirs were intended to be converted into storage, etc., as there is certainly ample room for the production and storage of nuclear material. Supplies were brought to the site by a spur taken off the standard gauge railway that ran along the coast a few hundred yards away, and there are still remains of this track on the site. Each of the original reservoir entrances, together with some of the underground tunnels, were served by a 24-inch narrow gauge railway, most of which is still in place. The entrances into the hillside for Reservoirs 1–3 were given increased security by the addition of bomb-proof doors, similar to Watten. The original French doors were left in place, and 30 ft (9 m) in from each entrance a recess was provided for a concrete and steel sliding door, 12 ft (3.6 m) thick.

The original German plans for the site were based on it being used solely for rockets, but at some time during the alterations it was decided to also use it as a V1 base, and hence the massive blast walls shown in the figure were provided to protect the V1 launch ramp. Item 'H' was intended to have an additional storey, as there are remains of vertical steel reinforcing bars, also evident in earlier photographs, and

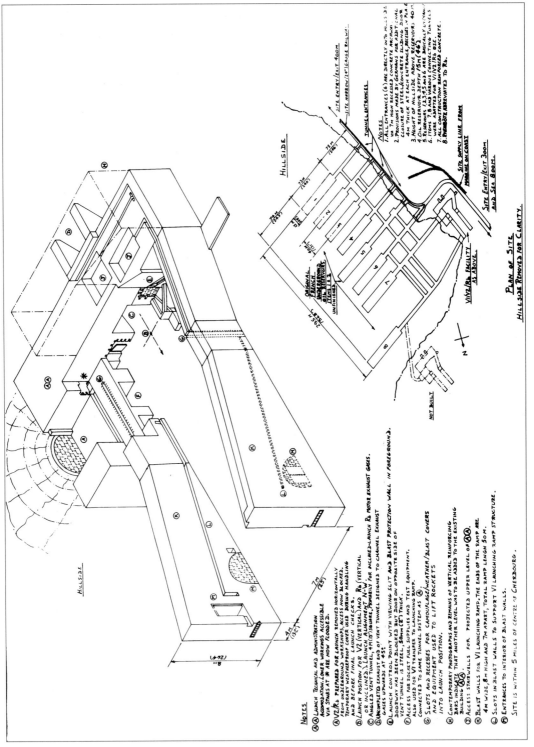

Figure 14. The V1/V2/Rb storage, servicing and launch site at Brécourt on the Cherbourg Peninsula.

there are two rectangular openings obviously intended as stairwells. The additional storey was most likely intended for equipment associated with the launch. The missile exit from the underground storage is at 'A', now blocked-off, but they would have merged horizontally, judging from the headroom available.

Some form of lifting gear would have been required to rotate the rocket into the vertical, or for a V1 it would have been lowered horizontally to the base of the launch ramp. The buildings behind the launch area are accessible above ground. Below ground everything is flooded, but the naval guide said that the workings extend for a considerable distance. The actual V2 launch pad is at 'B' and the exhaust gases would have been directed upwards by the surrounding structures. This is probably why the rocket exit at 'A' is not roofed over, and the reason for the slot between 'A' and 'G'. One of the most interesting features at Brécourt is the 13 ft (4 m) square, angled rocket exhaust vent tunnel, 'D'. The problem of the damage and erosion to the launch pad and associated equipment caused by the red-hot, high-speed exhaust gases was something that became more important as rockets became larger. By the 1960s the larger rockets were placed on an elevated launch pad and the exhaust went vertically downwards before being deflected sideways over a water reservoir. By this means the launch pad and its equipment could be used again within a short period of time. By the 1940s the problem had already appeared with the V2, and at Peenemünde a temporary solution was to build a very large elliptical launch area and use a different location for each launch, the actual rocket sitting on an exhaust deflector known as the 'lemon squeezer', which helped to alleviate the problem. At Brécourt we have a solution to the problem that was years ahead of its time, but in this case it was virtually certain that it was not intended for the V2 or any rocket launched vertically. The V1 can also be ruled out, since it had almost no exhaust until it reached flying speed at the end of the ramp. The tunnel 'D' is angled upwards and then exits at the 45° vent, and there was only one rocket in the German arsenal that could have utilized an angled exhaust vent: this was the Rheinböte, which was launched at an angle, usually of 45°–65°.

A solid-fuel rocket like the Rheinböte reaches maximum thrust many times faster than a liquid-fuel rocket such as the V2, which has a thrust build-up time lasting several seconds as the turbine-driven fuel pumps reach their maximum number of revolutions, so that the thermal shock from a solid-fuel exhaust can be greater than the equivalent liquid motor.

In addition to the four-stage Z-61/9 version of the Rheinböte that did become operational in 1945, a much heavier version was planned, the Rb III, only slightly longer than the Z-61/9 but five times heavier and carrying a warhead equivalent to that of the V2. This version would have had a problem dispersing the exhaust gases, and in a confined launch space, as at Brécourt, the vent tunnel would have been an answer to this problem.

Regarding the use of Brécourt for the V1, the blast protection walls for the ramp are 13 ft (4 m) thick, which is far greater than anything built previously for the V1. These walls contain access passages in places, plus storage areas, and this implies that the V1s intended to be launched from Brécourt were to be given special pre-launch preparation and protection. Once again this implies something other than the standard high-explosive warhead.

The last point worth mentioning about Brécourt deals with the Allied bombing campaign against the V-weapons sites. They were all bombed: both Sottevast and Couville are only a few miles away from Brécourt, and they each received several hundred tons of bombs. But Brécourt was never bombed, not a single missile was ever dropped on the site, and yet aerial photographs were taken of the construction work with the angled V1 blast walls an obvious indication of its intended use. Why Brécourt escaped when other sites nearby were being regularly targeted is a mystery, but as we will see later, this 'escape' meant that Brécourt was to feature in the final stages of the V-weapons offensive organized by SS General Kammler.

THE RHEINBÖTE

The Rheinböte (see Figure 15) was a simple weapon compared to the V1 and V2, as it had no guidance and control system, and its rocket motor had no moving parts; perhaps the most complicated part of the Rheinböte was ensuring that the various stages separated at the right moment. Despite this simplicity, it still required dedicated servicing, assembly and launch teams, together with ground-handling and launch equipment, static and mobile. We know that one type of four-stage Rb did become operational in 1945 from Holland, the Z-61/9. Something like fifty rockets were launched against Antwerp between December 1944 and January 1945 by Kammler's launch group Artillerie Abteilung (Motorized) 709, the actual launch area being close to the V2 launch area, which simplified security and target trajectory calculations. The Z-61/9 version had a warhead weight of 88 lb (40 kg), of which only 55 lb (25 kg) was offensive payload, and a range of between 100 and 150 miles (160–240 km), depending on launch elevation. The rocket had an overall length of 42.7 ft (13 m) and a maximum body diameter of 21.4 in (544 mm); the maximum diameter over the first-stage fins was 57.4 in (1.47 m), and total weight at launch was 3,661 lb (1,664 kg). Because of its long slender shape it was extremely flexible when inclined at an angle of anything from the normal 45° to 65° for launch, and since its target accuracy depended on a precise launch bearing on the target, it was essential to provide a dedicated launch cradle. At the test ranges this was not a problem since the equipment could be purpose-built for the trials, but in operational use, because its own dedicated equipment was not available in time, a Meillerwagen as used to elevate a V2 into the vertical was modified and used for all operational launches. Regarding static launch sites, all the V1 and V2 bunker sites would have been capable of launching the Rheinböte, either vertically or inclined. Brécourt was something special, and it can only be assumed that both the Z-61/9 and the Rb III were intended to be launched from this site. The Rb III weighed eight tons, and with a length of 50 ft (15 m) it would have carried a 1,700 lb (770 kg) warhead a distance of nearly 200 miles (320 km). If fitted with some rudimentary guidance and control system, instead of relying on spin-stabilization, it could have taken over the role of the V2, while the larger and longer-range versions of the V2 were being developed.

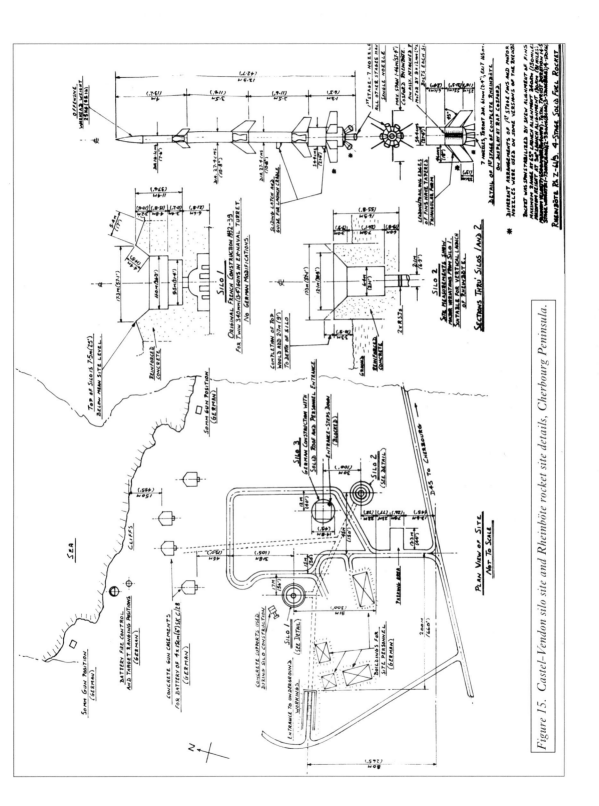

Figure 15. Castel-Vendon silo site and Rheinböte rocket site details, Cherbourg Peninsula.

If Brécourt was the most diverse launching site of the group covered so far, here is one more unusual site that the author believes was intended to play a part in the V-weapons offensive. Four miles further along the coast from Brécourt there is what the author has called the 'silo site'. The location is known as Castel-Vendon. In 1924 the French Navy ordered several 340 mm (13.4 in) guns in turrets from the arms manufacturer, Schneider. These guns were to be added to the coastal defences in Tunisia, Algeria and also further south at Dakar. In addition, two similar twin turrets were to be added to the coastal defences of Cherbourg on the cliffs at Castel-Vendon. The guns arrived in Cherbourg in 1928, and were put into storage at the naval base because of cuts in the defence expenditure programme. In 1935, with the danger of a world conflict looming closer every day, work started at Castel-Vendon to build two massive concrete silos, complete with underground access, for the stored guns at Cherbourg. Work was incomplete when the Germans arrived in 1940, construction having reached the stage (see Figure 15) where Silo 1 was complete, Silo 2 was about two-thirds finished, and the underground tunnels and concealed access to the system were complete. In 1942/3, the Germans started work at the site, and in the first instance they added, as part of the West Wall of 'Festung Europe', a battery of four Skoda 150 mm (6 in) SK C/28 guns in concrete casements, plus two 50 mm guns and separate fire-control and range-finding bunkers on the edge of the cliffs, the main battery being about 150 yards inland. The Schneider turrets and guns stored at Cherbourg disappeared and probably finished up in another section of the West Wall. Since the war, Castel-Vendon has been under the control of the French Navy, but when the author first visited the site in 1974, it appeared to be abandoned, as the wire fencing was down and access was comparatively easy. First impressions, not knowing the pre-war history, led the author to believe that this was a silo site built by the Germans for the V2. Obtaining dimensions of the silos was difficult and dangerous, but initial figures appeared to confirm that the silos would accommodate a V2 vertically. But, because of access problems, only the dimensions of Silo 1 were checked out on this first visit. In addition to Silos 1 and 2, a note was made of a third silo, with the same outer diameter as the first two but roofed over at ground level, with access steps leading downwards, blocked with rubble. In the 1980s the wire fence had been replaced, and therefore no further investigations of the site were made until 1996.

In 1996, accompanied by staff from the Naval Base, a more detailed inspection was made of the site, which was now considerably more overgrown compared to twenty years earlier. The first thing that was noticed was that areas of the site had vanished under a forest of 5 ft high gorse and brambles, including the location of Silo 3. Silos 1 and 2 were still visible, and an inspection of both of them showed that:

1. Silo 1 could not accommodate a V2 vertically because it was not deep enough, being 37.6 ft (11.4 m) compared to a V2 of 45 ft (13.6 m).
2. Silo 2 could not accommodate a V2 because, although it had the required depth, 55.8 ft (16.9 m), the lower section had a diameter of only 7 ft (2.1 m), too narrow for a V2 with fins fitted. The lowest level of this silo was blocked by two steel beams parallel across the diameter, effectively providing a floor.

3. Other differences between the silos are that Silo 2 has a smaller internal diameter than Silo 1. This is a major variation, the main diameter being 21 ft (6.4 m) compared to 36 ft (11 m). This indicates that if Silo 2 was as the French abandoned it in 1940, then the two silos were intended for different guns and turrets. It seems unlikely that Schneider would have supplied two weapons of such different dimensions for installation at the same site.

4. French plans of the site do not show Silo 3, and it must be assumed that it was added by the Germans.

There is no doubt that the site was inspected by the German Army after June 1940 when they arrived in Cherbourg. The site would have been of interest, since work was well advanced and the guns and turrets intended for the site were already in storage in Cherbourg. The OT would have been involved in any discussions on the site's future, and they were well aware of the massive programme under way regarding V-weapons sites large and small since they were responsible for the construction of both the West Wall and the V-weapons sites. In fact, from 1942 onwards, teams composed of Peenemünde staff, the OT and the Army were touring northern France looking for suitable sites, and great interest would have been shown in any existing facility, as happened at Brécourt a few miles away. The author now believes that under cover of building the battery of four 150 mm gun casements, since Allied Intelligence was not particularly interested in additions to coastal defences, modifications were started to convert the site to a V-weapons base using the original French silos as a starting point. Silo 3 was built, and the roof may have been meant only as temporary protection during construction. A relatively easy task was to modify the internal diameter of Silo 2 so that it was more suitable for the vertical launch of a Rheinböte, for even the largest version, with a length of 50 ft (15 m), would have fitted inside Silo 2.

By the 1950s, silo-based ICBMs were the mainstay of the US nuclear deterrent, and even in the 1990s, America, Russia, France and China are still using silos, although they are being superseded by the mobile deterrent in the form of Polaris, Trident and their equivalent. In the 1950s a branch of technology was developed to determine the effectiveness of silo-based weapons. This technology was concerned with determining the protection provided by the silo, the 'hardness value', the spacing and number of silos in a group and how much information was known to the enemy on silo location. The term Circular Error Probability (CEP), which is the radius of the circle into which half the enemy's missiles arriving at the target might be expected to fall, became one of the main criteria for determining the effectiveness of a silo-based missile system. The improvement in accuracy of ICBMs has meant that mobile launch systems are the preferred option. For instance, in 1959 the US silo-based Minuteman I ICBM, with a 1.3 megaton warhead, had a CEP of one mile. In 1977, the submarine-based Trident I had a multiple warhead (yield unknown) with a CEP of 0.1 mile.

The change to mobile launchers has also resulted in a change to solid-fuel motors, safer inside a submarine and able to be stored for longer periods compared to liquid fuels.

Peenemünde was working on the long-term storage of liquid fuels with the development of the Wasserfall (Waterfall) rocket, which was almost a half-scale version of the V2, 25.9 ft (7.8 m) long, and had similar aerodynamics with a different control system. It was intended to keep the Wasserfall ready for launch for up to three months, but development was slow and only four successful test launches were carried out.

THE HOCHDRUCKEPUMPE (HDP), HIGH PRESSURE PUMP

The original site chosen for the use of the HDP against London was a few miles inland from the coast between Boulogne and Calais, a hamlet now famous, with the name of Mimoyecques, German code name 'Wiese'.

Work started, as with many of the V-weapons sites, in April 1943. The HDP barrels, being fixed, had to be aligned precisely on the target, London, and there was no flexibility to be able to vary the target. Also, the barrels had to be inclined at an angle of approximately 45° if the maximum ballistic range was to be achieved, and the shells were unguided, and stabilized by small fins which deployed after the shell left the barrel, spinning the shell in flight. To provide protection for the long barrels, over 450 ft (136 m), the whole operation was based underground, and Mimoyecques provided the ideal location. The Landrethun–Leubringhen main road passing through Mimoyecques is adjacent to some high ground, with a maximum height of 518 ft (157 m), which is aligned directly on London. A loop was taken off the nearby main railway line, and work started in 1943, excavating the hill from both directions. Trains were to enter by the main tunnel, unload supplies and exit at the northern end to rejoin the main line. Originally 25 barrels were planned for the site, in groups of five, but this was later amended, and as built, three groups of five barrels each were provided. Figures 16 and 17, taken from the British mission investigating the effects of the bombing campaign, show details of the underground workings and the shell exit platform on the surface, plus one example of the shell design. From the main railway tunnel, eleven equi-spaced side-tunnels, 160 ft (48 m) long, branched off to the left. These joined a main gallery parallel to the railway tunnel. Almost in the centre of this gallery, three 500 ft (152 m) long shafts, containing five barrels each, inclined upwards at about 45°, to the surface. The exit points of these shafts and the barrels were located in a massive reinforced-concrete platform on the surface, 228 ft (69 m) × 54 ft (16 m) × 17.5 ft (5.3 m) thick at its maximum point. Unfortunately for Mimoyecques, it came within the area in northern France which British Intelligence considered was the most likely location for sites associated with a long-range weapon attack on London and the south-east of England using gigantic mortars. Despite there being very little building activity above ground, it was not long before the PRU aircraft were taking photographs of the site, and the ominous north-west alignment of the openings in the surface slab became apparent. The first bombing raid occurred on 1 November 1943, and these attacks continued on a regular basis until 27 August 1944, by which time the whole area looked like a lunar landscape. On 6 July 1944, the air raid included at least seven 12,000 lb Tall Boy

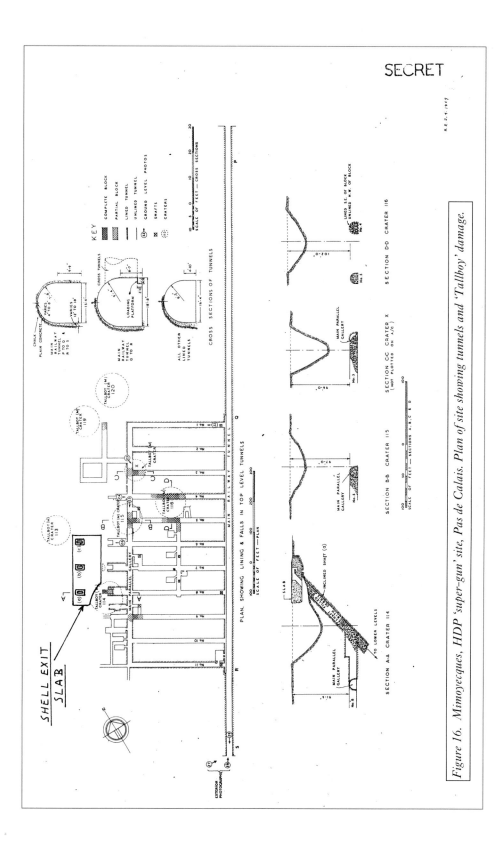

Figure 16. Mimoyecques, HDP 'super-gun' site, Pas de Calais. Plan of site showing tunnels and 'Tallboy' damage.

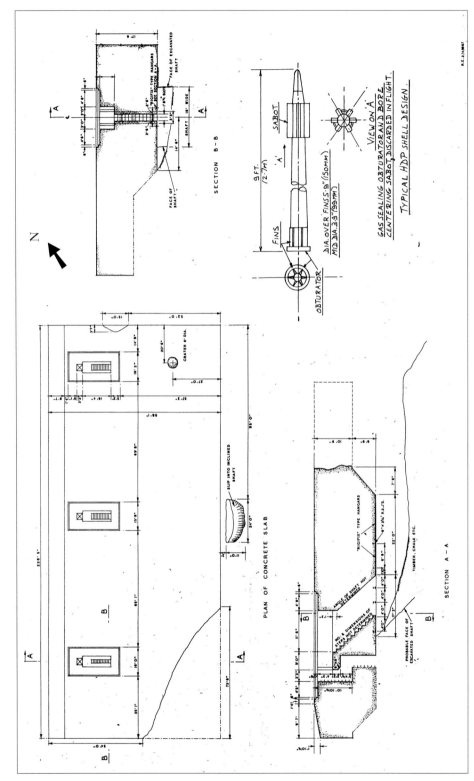

Figure 17. HDP barrel nozzle and shell exit slab, Mimoyecques. There were five barrels per opening, aligned on London.

bombs, four of which caused extensive rock-falls within the tunnel complex. A total of over 4,000 tons of bombs were dropped on Mimoyecques, more than at Watten and Wizernes. Possibly the reason for this was the precise alignment of the barrels on London. At the beginning of the bombing campaign against the weapons sites, Churchill's scientific adviser, Lord Cherwell, had been sceptical of the possibility that the Germans had large rockets, and had advised that they probably had something like giant mortars, which would be buried in the ground, pointing at London.

Unfortunately for the HDP, that is exactly what the site looked like from the air, and hence the massive bombing offensive. By July 1944, problems with producing satisfactory shells for the HDP, coupled with the Allied bombing, produced a reassessment of how the site was to be used. On 12 July 1944 a report was issued from Hitler's HQ following a discussion on the future of the Mimoyecques project. The outcome was that instead of fifteen barrels for the HDP, the number was to be reduced to one group of five in a single shaft. The other two shafts were to be used for two 'Schlanke Berta', Slender Bertha, the Krupp K5 28 cm (11 in) artillery piece. Reamed out to 31 cm (12.2 in) and with a smooth barrel, it was intended to use the shells developed at Peenemünde, in which a rocket motor boosted the range, similar to Iraq's 'super-gun', many years later. In addition, in the open ground in front of the main tunnel entrance, two Rheinböte launchers were to be positioned, which were given the code name 'Meteor'.

The HDP by this time had been given the unofficial code name 'Fleishiges Lieschen', or Busy Lizzie, probably due to the rapid firing rate of the shells. However, by 30 July 1944, another order was issued to the effect that all work at Mimoyecques was to be stopped, as an alternative site near Rinxent was being investigated for all three weapons. This site comprised a railway tunnel for Schlanke Berta and Meteor, and a disused mineshaft for the HDP. The military situation was now changing so rapidly as the Allied forces advanced that these plans were never realized, but for Mimoyecques this was not quite the end. On 27 September 1944, Canadian troops arrived to find the site abandoned, and parts of the HDP barrels and other equipment which had been stored at the site ready for installation had vanished. On 9 and 14 May 1945, explosive charges totalling 36 tons were placed inside the tunnels and under the exit slab by demolition experts of the British Army, and this finally put an end to Hitler's super-gun aimed at London. It was also not quite the end for the HDP. Kammler had not quite given up the possibility of using the weapon, and at the end of November, what remained of the barrels were transported to a site on the banks of the River Ruwer, near Trier, just across the German border north-east of Luxembourg. Eventually two shortened barrels were erected on the river bank, aligned on Luxembourg. On 30 December 1945 the first shells were fired into the city from a range of about 27 miles. Plans to erect a third barrel were abandoned due to the chaotic situation as the Allies advanced into Germany, and eventually both barrels were dismantled after firing about 180 shells in the Luxembourg direction. The barrels were transported back to Rochling in the Saar, and probably melted down as scrap.

All four long-range weapons were further developed after the war, the V2 and Rheinböte technology eventually becoming part of the space-race and the world's armoury. With developments in radar, satellites and mini-computers, the V1 eventually reappeared as the 'cruise missile', but the HDP took longer to reappear. It was in 1991 during the Gulf War against Iraq that the reincarnated HDP appeared as Saddam Hussein's 'super-gun'. Modified and simplified, using the rocket-powered shell idea of Schlanke-Berta, the largest version of the 'super-gun', with a one-metre calibre, was able to carry a conventional, nuclear or chemical/biological warhead over hundreds of miles, and it was aimed at Israel, as described later.

THE NEW ORGANIZATION AND SITES

By October 1943 the mass bomber raids on German cities and industrial centres were becoming a regular feature of the war, and the intensity of these attacks was slowly increasing as the months went by. Peenemünde had been bombed on 17 August 1943, followed by V1 and V2 component and assembly plants. Although the damage at Peenemünde had not been critical, it was purely a stroke of luck that the main weight of bombs had been dropped off the intended target area, destroying workers' accommodation rather than the technical facilities. Of the large weapons sites in northern France, only Watten had been bombed by November 1943, but the 600 tons of bombs dropped there up to that date had seriously disrupted the building programme, and the completion date had to be rescheduled from the original October 1943. No air raids had taken place on the original V1 storage and launch 'ski-sites', but it was now evident to the German planners, from the photo-reconnaissance activity over the sites and the involvement of 'agents', that such attacks were only a question of time. In fact the first sample attack against a ski-site took place on 5 December 1943.

Looking at the overall situation regarding the forthcoming V-weapons offensive against the UK, it was clear that it was extremely unlikely that the original arrangement of sites covering storage, servicing and launching of the weapons would remain intact. Therefore, although work on the original sites would continue as planned, in case the situation changed and as a hoax in some cases, new arrangements would be planned. For the V1, V2 and Rheinböte, these changes amounted to the use of the existing sites if possible, plus a new system of launch sites. The HDP was less flexible, and due to its development problems, no real alternative to Mimoyecques was considered. These new arrangements would be continually monitored in the light of the changing military situation, and, of course, Peenemünde, the Army and the Luftwaffe were no longer in sole command of the programme. The SS were now very much involved, and initially it was the construction aspects which were the beginning of the takeover of the whole V-weapons organization. Construction meant only one person, SS General Hans Kammler, and one of the first recorded meetings when the current V2 situation was discussed was on 1 November 1943, when the Sonderauschuss A4 (Special A4 Committee) met, with Kammler, Dornberger and Degenkolb present.

On 4 November 1943, only three days after this meeting, new orders were issued from Berlin for the special attention of the Army. These orders concerned the deployment of the V2 with reference to storage and launch of the rockets, LOX production and storage, and storage of spare parts and other essential equipment. Four pages of tables were included.

This is an extremely important document for the following reasons:

1. Very little planning documentation for the V-weapons offensive survived the transfer of the Peenemünde and other related files to the USA and Russia in 1945, and almost none of this has reappeared. The Peenemünde files alone weighed around forty tons.
2. The date of this information is highly relevant to the involvement of the SS and the changes to the V2 offensive, and the document probably originated from Kammler's organization.
3. For the first time a reference is made to 'special operations' in the use of the V2.

The document, ref. MI14/865(V), is among a group of assorted V-weapons files in the IWM, London, and Bundesarchiv, Freiburg. It reads as follows.

Der Beauftragte z.b.V. (Heer) Abt.Ia.   Berlin, der 4.11.43.
    Verteiler
    Ob. West
    Ob. West/Aussenstelle
       B.z.b.V.Heer
    nachr:
       OKWW/WFSt/Op.H (West)
       Entwurf
  An
      den Herrn Oberbefehlshaber West (Heeresgruppe D)

Vorg.: Der Fuhrer OKW/WFSt/6624344/43 g.K.Chefs.v.4.10.43
Betr.: Bauten z.b.V.Heer.

Installations of Special Responsibility to the Army.
    A. *Artois Region* (This includes the Pas de Calais to the Somme).
I. *Operations.* *Launch Positions for 2 Companies (Motorized) each with 3 Batteries.*

1. 6 positions one with Leitstrahl. Site location; Field sites: Availability, by 15.12.43.
2. 6 positions, one with Leitstrahl. Site location.: Different field sites to above: Availability, by 15.12.43.
3. 6 positions, one with Leitstrahl. Site location: Different field sites to above: Availability, by 15.1.44.

4. 6 positions, two with Leitstrahl. Site location: Bomb-proof against 500 kg bombs. Availability, by 15.1.44.

Launch Positions for Special Tasks (Sonderaufgaben)

5. 2 positions. Site location: For E-Art between Rinxent and Sangatte. Availability: By 1.2.44.
6. 1 completely protected launch position as a replacement for KNW (Watten). Availability: Planning by OT.
     a)   Main structure complete by 1.5.44.
     b)   Equipment installed from 1.4. to 1.7.44.
Note. The current situation regarding the OT is not known at the present time.

I I. *Logistics and Supply Bases.*   Field Storage. Final capacity 200 V2s. Minus test stand on 15.12.43. With test stand by 31.12.43.

B. *Dieppe Region*
Launch Positions for 1 Company (Motorized).

7. 3 positions, one with Leitstrahl. Site location: Field sites. Availability by 1.2.44.
8. 3 positions, one with Leitstrahl. Site location: Bomb-proof against 500kg bombs. Availability by 1.2.44.

I I. *Logistics and Supply Bases.*   Field Storage. All necessary equipment required for 160 V2: For 40 by 15.1.44. For 120 by 15.2.44.

C. *Cherbourg Region*

Launch Positions for 1 Company (Motorized).

9. 3 positions, one with Leitstrahl. Site location: Field sites. Availability by 15.12.43.
10. 3 positions, one with Leitstrahl. Site location: Different field sites to above, sites being consolidated. Availability by 15.12.43.
11. 3 positions, one with Leitstrahl. Site location: Bomb-proof against 500 kg bombs. Availability by 15.1.44.
12. Position, Brix (Sottevast).

Brix is suitable for use as a temporary bomb-proof storage for Positions 9 to 11. The use of Brix as storage point for 40 V2s is to be investigated.

Current situation, the suitability of Brix is dependent on the OT planning, and availability is not known at the present time.

13. *Olkeller Cherbourg for Special Operations (Motorized).* (Sondereinsatz).

Situation: Bomb-proof accommodation for staff, vehicles, fuel and 30 V2s according to OT plans. The availability is still not known at the present time.

I I. *Logistics and Supply Bases.*   Field Storage. Temporary storage for 80 V2s. 40 V2s, availability by 15.12.43. 40 V2s, availability by 31.12.43.

D. Other Items.

Additional Storage for V2s.

1. Caves, Mery s./Oise, for 500 V2s, availability by 1.3.44.
2. Caves, Bar le Duc, for 500 V2s, availability by 1.5.44.
3. In suitable tunnels or caves, still to be located, for 500 V2s, availability by 1.5.44.

Electrical Batteries.   Large Storage Sites.

4. Caves, Mery s./Oise, for 6,000 batteries, for equipping 1,500 V2s, together with loading facilities. Availability by 15.12.43.
5. Large Storage Sites for spare parts, date still uncertain.
6. Bomb-Proof Sites for overhaul and repair of special vehicles. Caves still to be inspected by Inspector of Defences, West.

Oxygen Production Plant

1. Luttich, 5 sets of production equipment. Availability by 31.12.43.
2. Caves. Caumont, 5 sets of production equipment. One ready for operation by 31.12.43 and four in preparation, available by 31.1.44. Also, foundations for five sets of equipment transferred from Luttich.
3. Caves. Wittringen. Seven sets of production equipment available by 1.3.44. Five sets in preparation, available by 1.5.44.
4. Caves, Rinxent. 1 set of equipment for topping-up supplies. Available 15.12.43.
5. Brix. 1 set of equipment for topping-up supplies. Available 1.3.44.
6. KNW (Watten). Old or new facility, 5 sets of equipment. Date still uncertain.
7. Brix (Sottevast). 4 sets of equipment. Date still uncertain.
8. 5 sets of equipment in reserve.

Oxygen Storage

1. Luttich. 5 storage vessels of 50,000 litres each. Available by 31.12.43.
2. Caves, Caumont. Fast, temporary storage, vessels of 1,000 tons.
   Note. To achieve the maximum day's production for 10 plant items of 360 tons, storage must be in a cool location.
3. Caves, Rinxent. 10 storage vessels for 600 tons. Available 15.12.43.
4. Brix. 12 storage vessels for 600 tons. Date still uncertain.
5. Olkeller. 6 storage vessels for 330 tons. Date still uncertain.
6. Two further oxygen storage sites are being investigated.

The following are notes on the above list.

In the Artois Region, that is from the Pas de Calais to the Somme, there are a total of twenty-four launch sites provided, eighteen of which are field sites and six are protected against 500 kg (1,100 lb) bombs, which implies a concrete thickness of around 6 ft (2 m). It is likely that two of these protected sites were the V1 bunkers at Siracourt and Lottinghen, neither of which had been bombed at the date of the list. Modifications were already under way at Siracourt for the conversion into a V2 bunker. Five of the twenty-four sites were to be equipped with the Leitstrahl radio-beam guidance system which was used before motor cut-off to correct any deviations from the trajectory, overruling the normal control system. Item 5 is significant since it refers to V2s being used for 'special tasks', and the E-Art may refer to a Special Artillery group. Item 6 confirms that KNW, Watten, had been abandoned as a launching site by November 1943, and the alternative bomb-proof location referred to is certain to be Wizernes. The bombing of Wizernes started on 11 March 1944 and continued on a weekly basis until July 1944, by which time the programme quoted, of main structure complete by 1 May 1944, was not achievable. The field storage for Artois was 200 V2s, and interestingly, these sites include test stands after 31 December 1943. Presumably these were for performing detailed pre-launch checks before being transported to the launch sites.

The Dieppe Region, Somme to the Seine, had never been as important as the Pas de Calais and Cherbourg in the original organization, either for the V1 or the V2, and this is reflected in the new arrangements: only six launch sites in total and storage for 160 V2s. The bomb-proof sites are again for 500 kg (1,100 lb) bombs, and this indicates a much more realistic approach to the provision of site protection, as opposed to sites like Watten. It is unlikely that new structures would be provided, but that existing caves and tunnels would be used.

The final region is the Cherbourg Peninsula, and here we have nine launch sites, of which six were field sites and three protected against 500 kg (1,100 lb) bombs. The Sottevast (Brix is the nearest town) bunker was being considered as a temporary storage site for the nine launch sites. Sottevast was bombed for the first time on 26 November 1943, and so this temporary usage would have been feasible on 4 November 1943. What is interesting is that construction work at Sottevast was still at a very early stage in that month, and so only temporary storage was being considered. However, this means that the entrance to the underground workings, now blocked with soil, must extend some distance underground and for some depth, as stated by the local farmer.

Finally, at Olkeller Cherbourg, Brécourt, we have a Launch Group of unspecified size, motorized and whose mission was 'Sondereinsatz', Special Operations. The term 'Einsatz' has always had a sinister connection since the formation of the Einsatzgruppen, special SS formations attached to Amt IV of the RHSA and given the task of supervising the 'final solution' in occupied countries.

The tunnels at Brécourt were to provide shelter for the launch teams, V2s, vehicles and fuel. The site availability was not known, but Brécourt was never bombed, and from the author's own inspection of the site, it could have been used almost immediately for V2 storage, etc., unless special arrangements were required for nuclear material. Is this why the report states that an availability date was still awaited from the OT? Also, only thirty V2s are listed for Brécourt, and yet from the author's own inspection of the underground tunnels there was space for at least 300. So were these thirty V2s 'specials', like the modified V2 in Figure 20? Significantly, there is no mention of using Brécourt for its original purpose, as a V2 launch site. Where was this special motorized group going to launch its V2s, and what were the 'Sondereinsatz'? There is no mention of using Leitstrahl, as at three of the other Cherbourg sites, so was this because it became irrelevant with a nuclear material payload, if the rocket was two or three miles off its target when it was aimed at a large city? Were the special operations from Brécourt a companion to the similar special tasks planned between Rinxent and Sangatte near Calais, and most likely aimed at London? Field storage in the Cherbourg area amounted to only 80 V2s, and this was classed as temporary. From the description of the storage arrangements between the Field Storage, Sottevast and Brécourt, it looks as if the total V2 storage for the area was only about eighty V2s. These were to be distributed between nine field sites, plus perhaps the use of Sottevast as both a firing and storage site. In the site description of Sottevast, the author noted the concrete pad about 100 yd north of Item 1 on the site, and this may have been where V2s were to be launched, pending completion of the site proper.

The total number of V2s available for the ten launch sites gives the impression that there was not going to be a high firing rate on a daily basis. During the final V2 offensive from Holland, the highest daily firing rate achieved by Kammler's launch teams was sixteen in a 24-hour period. The number of launch sites used is not known, but was probably no more than ten. Hence, it appears likely that the Cherbourg sites were going to be used for more specific targets, rather than aiming a large number of rockets at well spread-out areas, such as cities.

The final section of the list, D, covers storage of V2s, LOX, batteries and spare parts, together with LOX production. Points of interest include reference to the Mery s./Oise site or Villiers-Adam, never bombed and scheduled to be used as originally intended for V2, plus battery storage. Bar le Duc is a new site over 150 miles south-east of Villiers-Adam, which gives some idea of the precautions being taken, when all the original V2 storage sites except Villiers-Adam had been abandoned. The LOX production centres were Luttich and Wittringen (Germany), Caumont near Rouen, Rinxent near Calais, Brix (Sottevast) and KNW (Watten). LOX storage was at Luttich, Caumont, Rinxent, Brix (Sottevast) and Olkeller (Brécourt), with two further sites being investigated.

To summarize the V2 organization at the beginning of 1944, we have:

1. Forty-three launch sites, of which twenty-seven are field sites, twelve are protected against 500 kg bombs, one is a bunker site (Wizernes) and one is based at Brécourt. Of these, ten launch sites have Leitstrahl beam guidance equipment. Special V2 launches were to be carried out from two sites in the Pas de Calais, plus Wizernes, and also from the Cherbourg area using Brécourt as a base.

2. V2 field storage sites, four plus two protected for a total of 480 V2s.
3. V2 underground storage sites, three including one to be determined for a total of 1,500 V2s.
4. Equipment storage and workshops, three sites.
5. Oxygen production, seven sites with a reserve of five complete plant items.
6. Oxygen storage, five sites with two more under consideration.

There is no mention of alcohol storage, and this is probably because there were no special requirements for the storage of alcohol, especially with its numerous industrial uses throughout France, for which reason commercial storage could have been utilized.

The field launch sites are of particular interest, and the author has made a detailed study of the Cherbourg Peninsula, as it is a compact area, about thirty miles long and twenty miles wide, and very little new building work has been carried out since 1945 compared with the Pas de Calais, which has obscured some of the V-weapon sites. The ability to isolate the Cherbourg Peninsula from the rest of France was an aid to security as far as the Germans were concerned, and so the area contains a relatively large number of weapons sites, which very often are as they were left in 1944. Despite statements from Dornberger that a V2 could be launched from any piece of flat ground, this was really 'sales talk' to convince the sceptics among the leaders of the Third Reich that rockets were the weapons of the future. In reality, Dornberger's vision of launch teams touring the countryside looking for any piece of flat ground was a vast over-simplification of what was needed to achieve a successful launch.

German documents issued about the same time as the above list, in November 1943, which were probably an addendum, give details of what was required at launch sites, most of which would have been the field sites, from November 1943 to June 1944. The documents give details of what was required for:

1. Official tours of inspection.
2. Launch position, related buildings and supporting arrangements.
3. Road blocks and site traffic checks.
4. Security exercise timetables.
5. Training instructions for launch teams.
6. Building works and their protection.
7. The planning and security of water supplies.
8. Site security troops and their tasks.
9. Instructions for alternative supply points, with maps.

These details show exactly how much planning and organization went into the new generation of mainly field sites.

In addition, PRO file WO 208/3143 contains 1944/5 organization details of several V2 launch companies, including Motorized Battery 902. Battery 902 was intended to launch V2s from field sites, as the above list, and the amount of equipment on the inventory of the 902 is extensive. For instance, it included three motorcycles and sidecars, several staff cars, its own fire-fighting and medical teams, a mobile canteen, its own security detachment with enough firepower in terms of machine-guns and small arms to fight a major battle and a vast amount of communications equipment. All this is in addition to the equipment and transport actually needed to fuel and launch the V2.

There is no doubt that with the SS now controlling site construction, these details originated from Kammler's organization.

It was also essential to have precise details of the launch sites' bearings in terms of latitude and longitude, since for each target an individual trajectory had to be provided, and this required accurate details of both launch and target bearings. What is known about site construction work in northern France is that from late 1943 until early 1944 a new system of field sites was built, and these sites followed a completely new pattern relating to location and facilities. From the previous list it can be seen that the interest in large complicated sites such as Watten had changed, and the roles of some of these sites had been switched from the V1 to the V2. This new generation of sites had to possess several important features:

1. They had to be as inconspicuous as possible, since it was a fact that Allied aircraft now controlled the sky.
2. There had to be as few as possible, since the more sites, the greater the probability of them being discovered.
3. Only the most essential new construction work was to be provided at a site, and this included buildings.

From these basic requirements, it followed that if the site could be provided with near-perfect camouflage and hence remain undetected, it could be used to launch three V-weapons, the V1, V2 and Rheinböte. This would simplify security, the supply organization, trajectory calculations, and importantly, provide launch teams with a familiar environment.

In a relatively small area like the Cherbourg Peninsula, it made a lot of sense to have one site for all three weapons. The problem of site congestion, certainly in the Cherbourg area, was unlikely, as the number of V2s expected to be launched, based on the total storage arrangements of eighty, was not very high.

The problem was the V1, since, unlike the V2 and Rheinböte, it required a long ramp, which took time to build and was conspicuous from the air. The solution was simple and probably came as a result of the SS involvement and the introduction of the new management. The answer was to provide a ramp that could be erected and dismantled in a few hours, say at night, leaving nothing but a few small concrete support blocks in the ground, which could be easily hidden from view. One very conspicuous item missing from the 'new' ramps were the blast-walls, an obvious feature of the original V1 launch ramps.

Concrete pads would be required for all three weapons, plus concrete access roads and one building. For field sites the V2 inventory included an armoured half-track launch control vehicle, which contained sensitive instrumentation,

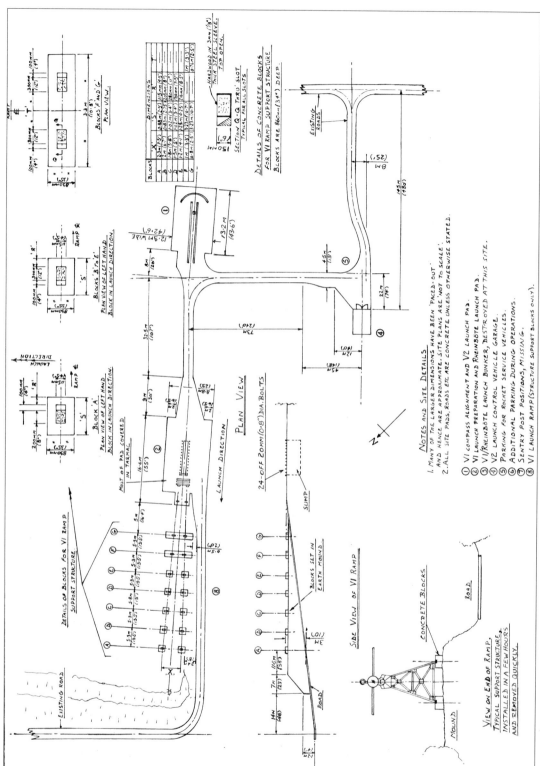

Figure 18. *The simple V1/V2/Rb site at Hameau de Haut on the Cherbourg Peninsula.*

electrical circuits and batteries. It could not, therefore, be expected to travel long distances under its own power, and it was not really practical to transport it from site to site. As every site would have some permanent security, as shown on the above list, a garage would be the ideal solution to provide all-weather protection, and this could also be used for any smaller items of V1 equipment. The only other above-ground constructions would be a small launch bunker for the V1 and Rheinböte, and road-block positions either side of the site area, again as the above list shows. Figure 18 shows one of the thirty combined launch sites built on the peninsula between December 1943 and March 1944; it is one of the two sites where the V1 ramp concrete blocks are still in place.

Out of these thirty sites, fifteen used chateaux or farm buildings and their access roads as camouflage for the sites. The remaining fifteen used existing roads for access between the garage and launch pads, with the occasional garage being built adjacent to existing cottages.

At every site the garage has survived intact, despite it being of block construction, not reinforced concrete, with wooden doors, and it is only the small launch bunker, sentry posts and concrete blocks for the ramps which have been removed at some of the sites. The concrete pads provide a useful hard standing for the farmer, and the garages are a useful store for machinery. The Rheinböte was intended to have its own dedicated mobile launcher, but those fired in 1945 from Holland used a modified V2 Meillerwagen. This was suitable for the 42 ft (12.7 m) length of the Rb and enabled the rocket to be elevated into any firing angle, but it did not provide a rigid base for the launch. This flexibility in the launcher ensured that the Rb achieved a very poor target accuracy during its short operational life. What was really needed was a rigidly mounted launch cradle which supported almost the full length of the rocket, and if a mobile launcher was required, this had to be capable of being raised off its road wheels and bolted rigidly to the concrete of the launch pad. However, the Rb was transported in two sections, reducing the maximum length to just over 20 ft (6 m), which reduced its ground handling problem. The V2 and its Vidalwagen (for general road/site transport) and Meillerwagen (for pre-launch erection to the vertical) had limits to their manoeuvrability and the minimum road radius they could traverse. From the Figure, the site details are as follows:

1. The largest concrete pad on the site contains slots and an arc similar to those found on the floor of the compass-alignment building at the original 'ski' V1 launching sites The pad has a maximum width of nearly 43 ft (13 m), amply wide enough for a V2 Meillerwagen with fuel tankers either side. This 'arc' also appears on the sketch of the V2 field-launch site using the Leitstrahl guidance system (Figure 19).

2. A concrete pad containing a long rectangular sump, covered over with concrete, at the end of which the concrete blocks start for the V1 launch ramp. Either side of the sump is a row of twelve 20 mm (0.8 in) diameter bolts, cast into 150 mm (6 in) deep pockets in the concrete. These bolts were not found at the original V1 launch sites, although there is a wash-down area to hose away traces of HTP and catalyst after each launch, hence the sump.

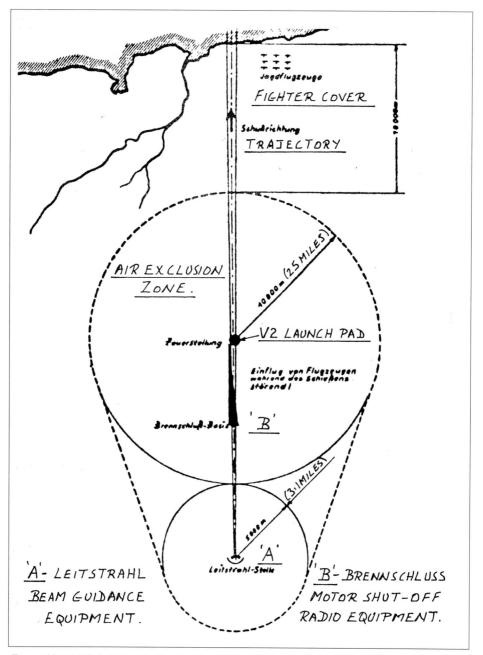

Figure 19. A V2 field launch site, showing the location of the Leitstrahl and Brenschluss equipment.

Each of the twenty-four bolts has a load capacity of 1 ton (1,000 kg), giving a total of 24 tons, but there is nothing associated with the V1 launch ramp that required bolts with this strength. It is most likely that with the V1 ramp dismantled, a Rheinböte launch cradle could have been attached to these bolts and this would have provided the rigid mounting required for an accurate trajectory. Like the V1 ramp, this launch cradle could have been dismantled in a short space of time.

3. A bunker for a small team during a launch of V1 and Rheinböte.
4. A garage for a V2 launch control vehicle and/or V1 site trolleys.
5. Parking for service vehicles, including fuel tankers and rockets awaiting transfer to the launch pad.
6. Additional parking and passing places for site vehicles.
7. Sentry post positions, containing alcoves for ammunition, food, etc. during sentry duty.
8. V1 launch-ramp support blocks, the steel ramp structure being bolted into the hardwood inserts set into each block in steel-lined sleeves. The ramp structure could be erected by this method and dismantled within a few hours. After each use, the wooden blocks and sleeves would be replaced with new items. At some of the sites, these hardwood blocks are still in position.
9. A small, open-topped water tank.

One of the most interesting features of the thirty sites is the variation in the location of Pads 1 and 2 compared to the garage, 4. It is extremely unlikely that the location of any of the site features was on a random basis, with no logic to the arrangement; those who designed the site layouts were professional military weapons experts, and very little was just left to chance. It is noticeable, therefore, that at some sites the location sequence is Garage > Pad 1 > Pad 2, and at others it is Garage > Pad 2 > Pad 1. If the intention was that some sites were to have a preferred V2 launch capability, it would be reasonable to expect that these sites would have easier access from the garage to the larger Pad 1, plus increased parking arrangements. At approximately a third of the sites, the layout is Garage > Pad 1 > Pad 2, plus extra parking, making them more suitable for the V2. These ten sites with a layout more suitable for the 45 ft V2 would tend to support the new V2 operational system given in the previously described list. For the Cherbourg area, nine motorized field-launch teams are mentioned, plus another launch group operating from Brécourt and carrying out 'special missions', but not using one of the 500 kg bomb-proof sites. In fact, although Item 11 on the list is described as using a bomb-proof location, since there are no railway tunnels on the Peninsula, no suitable caves or similar facilities, probably this launch team was expected to use launch sites where existing buildings, such as chateaux, provided the required protection. Hence we have possibly twelve launch teams and a similar number out of the thirty combined sites where the Garage > Pad 1 layout is more suitable for V2 operations.

Because the SS were now in charge of V-weapon site construction, there was a major change to how these new sites were built. In 1943 when the original 'ski' launching sites for the V1 were being built, very often French contractors and labour were used and security was fairly relaxed, but now all this was changed. Firstly the new multi-purpose sites had to be built quickly, and although there was no major construction work involved, concrete surfaces were laid over existing roads, and several concrete pads and parking were needed, together with the ramp blocks, garage, launch bunker and sentry alcove. From the author's conversations with owners of some of the chateaux on which the sites were built, who were living in the houses as children, it is clear that the new regime was extremely harsh. Each construction team was composed of about fifty Russian PoWs with supervisors and guards from the Organisation Todt. It must be remembered that Fritz Todt, the founder of the OT, had originally been a member of Himmler's staff, so the SS influence was not new. It was the winter of 1943/4 but the PoWs were given barely enough food to exist, their clothes and shoes were inadequate and they were regularly beaten if schedules were not maintained. One owner vividly remembered, from all those years ago, the trouble his mother got into with the guards for trying to provide some extra food for the Russians: it was literally a matter of life and death. But this was part of the new urgency to get the V-weapons operational in 1944, and Kammler was now in charge.

At another chateau site, the hot summer of 1998 had reduced the water level in the ornamental lake, so it was decided to drain it and clean out the mud, etc. When it was drained they found dozens of rifles, machine-guns and ammunition dumped by the site troops when news came through of the nearby American landings in June 1944.

CHAPTER 5

Prédefin – the Eyes for Watten and Wizernes

Eighteen miles south of St Omer in the Pas de Calais is the small farming hamlet of Prédefin. In the fields just outside the village is a group of single-storey buildings, some concrete platforms and remains of barbed wire fences. Nothing to attract attention, but it was here that the eyes for Watten and Wizernes were built. Returning to Peenemünde for a moment, one of the essential requirements of such an establishment was the ability to track all test vehicles that were launched, and in addition to send and receive radio and telemetry signals to and from the rockets as they flew down the range. For a ballistic missile like the V2, the trajectory in plan was a straight line, and like modern ICBMs, the ability to maintain this straight line, taking into account the Coriolis effect, was an essential part of their target accuracy. To obtain the most accurate plot of the missile trajectory, the ideal situation was to position the equipment that transmitted and received these signals, immediately behind the launch pad and directly in line with the flight path. As part of this equipment, a Würzburg-Riese radar set was installed on the mainland, five miles behind Test Stand 7 at Peenemünde, and a line of these radars was strung out along the coastline towards the impact point. The Würzburg radar was originally developed by Telefunken as an aid to anti-aircraft gunners, and with its 10 ft diameter dish it could scan through 360° and from –5° to +95° in elevation. Operating on what was for 1939 the very high frequency of 560 megacycles, it could plot the height and range of aircraft to within a few feet at ranges of up to 25 miles. When the need came to improve the range as aircraft performance improved, in 1941 the Telefunken engineers took the most obvious route. The ability to accurately plot aircraft depends on two main variables, the frequency of the transmitted signals and the diameter of the dish. By increasing the Würzburg dish to 25 ft (7.6 m), the range improved to 50 miles in the general scanning mode and 37 miles in the direction-finding mode. The disadvantages of the new Giant-Würzburg were its narrower beam width and therefore reduced general surveillance capability, which produced a poor target acquisition capability; and because of its size, it now required a fixed emplacement, unlike the smaller, mobile version.

When the large sites at Watten and Wizernes were being planned, it was obvious that a radar tracking and signals station would be required. Ideally it should have been positioned behind both sites, but they are located east and west. The next most suitable location was 90° from this position and still in line with both launching sites. The result is that on a map, a straight line can be drawn through Watten, Wizernes and Prédefin in that order, simplifying the three-dimensional trigonometrical problem of radar tracking. Although the Würzburg provided the initial tracking information, an additional long-range instrument was required for the final stages of the flight, and this was provided by a Telefunken 'Mammut' FuMG 52 radar located on the outskirts of the site. The Mammut had a rectangular aerial, 100 ft (30 m) wide × 33 ft (10 m) high, and although the aerial was fixed, it could scan electronically through a 100° arc over ranges up to 186 miles (300 km) and heights up to 82,500 ft (8 km). It operated on a frequency of 120–138 Megahertz on a 6.9–7.9 ft (2.1–2.4 m) wavelength, the operating crew being housed in a bunker beneath the aerial. Compared to the usual German radar station, the site's accommodation and ancillary buildings for signals equipment have been increased considerably. According to a local farmer, the total number of site personnel was around 150, of whom 100 were security.

The additional buildings caused a problem to Allied Intelligence, since it was obviously not a standard radar station, of which there were many in northern France, and the site was put on the target list as a V1 launching site with the ramp identified as one of the long buildings aligned north-west. The site was bombed three times in June 1944, and the launching point is described as being hit with two near-misses. In addition to the radars, a pair of large ear-like sound detectors were located in front of the site, to give early warning of approaching aircraft when the other equipment was in use.

While on the subject of missile tracking and control, apart from Prédefin, another electronic tracking system was intended to be used at Watten. Mention has already been made of the Leitstrahl beam guidance and Radio-Brenschluss motor cut-off systems, and both these were intended to be installed as part of the overall equipment package at Watten. A cable trench in a 100° arc was dug 7.5 miles (12 km) behind Watten, the idea being that the arc would encompass every possible target location in southern England. The signals-transmitting equipment for both Leitstrahl and Brenschluss would be plugged in at the appropriate location in the arc, which aligned the equipment with Watten and the target, in a straight line, hence, like the tracking radars, providing the most accurate and effective use of the equipment. The power for this massive cable and equipment was to be provided by a purpose-built generator installed in a huge bunker in the aptly named village of Rocquetoire, south-west of St Omer. The overall size of the bunker was 105 ft (32 m) long × 64 ft (19 m) wide × 21 ft (7 m) high. Although the cable trench was actually dug, the system was never completed, like Watten, a casualty of the Allied bombing. Figure 19 shows a typical V2 launch pad layout using Leitstrahl and Brenschluss. The larger dotted circle around the launch pad is the flight exclusion and security zone, and the Leitstrahl position includes an arc similar to that found at the new simple sites, Pad 1, on the Cherbourg Peninsula.

A 'composite' V1 at the Imperial War Museum (IWM), Duxford. The fuselage is the long-range F-1 with larger fuel tank and the nose is the 'standard' A-1.

The Duxford type A/ F-1 V1. On either side of the ramp are two of the pistons, one of which was used at each launch. Inserted into the end of the ramp tube, the 'fin' on the piston engaged in a slot under the V1's fuselage and was retrieved after each launch and re-used.

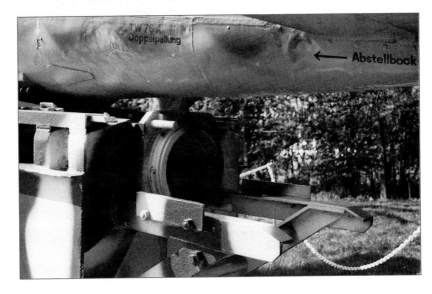

V1 ramp launch tube. After insertion of the piston, the HTP steam generating starter trolley was bolted on to the end-flange prior to launch.

HDP, Mimoyecques. The partially blocked railway tunnel entrance to the main workings, including the gun barrels, firing mechanism and supply storage.

HDP, Mimoyecques. The destroyed barrel nozzle/shell exit slab above the tunnel system. Three openings in the slab each contained nozzles for five 400 ft barrels aligned on London. The background figure gives scale.

A 1 m (3 ft) bore section of the Iraqi version of the Mimoyecques HDP 'super-gun'. IWM, Duxford.

U-534 type IXC/40 at Birkenhead, England. Possibly the last U-boat to leave for Japan, she left Kiel on 1 May 1945 and was sunk by the RAF on 5 May en route for Norway. The bomb damage to the hull is visible above the starboard propeller shaft.

First and second stages of the Rheinböte four-stage solid-fuel rocket, RAF Cosford. The first stage exit nozzles are non-original mock-ups.

A V2 being fuelled for Operation 'Backfire', British controlled launches near Cuxhaven, October 1945. (IWM)

A V2 being transferred from a general-purpose Vidalwagen (left) to the Meillerwagen, using the road-transportable Strabo crane. (IWM)

A V2 being raised into launch position by the Meillerwagen. The 'lemon–squeezer' motor exhaust blast deflector and support for the rocket is already in place. British controlled launches, Cuxhaven, October 1945. (IWM)

The V2 is launched. (IWM)

The V2 launch control vehicle for 'field sites'. A special armoured half-track on the Hanomag 3-ton chassis, it could be parked in the 'simple site' garage when the site was in frequent use. (IWM)

A V1 after ram jet failure, northern France, 1944. The virtually undamaged condition illustrates the stable flying characteristics of the V1. (IWM)

Wizernes V2 bunker. The dome, railway tunnel vent and remains of the rocket launch piers, pictured here before the site was opened to the public on 10 May 1997.

The Wizernes V2 bunker after 10 May 1997. This is the interior of railway tunnel 'Ida' (just beyond branch tunnel 'Mathilde'), showing construction wagons, an air ventilation compressor and the rock-fall caused by British Army demolition charges in 1944.

Wizernes V2 bunker: the railway tunnel vent from the top of the dome, pictured before 10 May 1997.

Sottevast V2 bunker (see Figure 13). The bunker roof was intended to cover the whole foreground area, being supported by the wall pictured and two similar walls (not built) opposite. The rocket launch pad, hidden by the concrete beams, is 60 to 80 ft below ground level.

Watten V2 bunker. The huge south wall of the main building.

Watten V2 bunker: the partially blocked west railway entrance to the main building. The extension provides protection for the 7.5 ft thick bomb-proof sliding door.

Bergueneuse: entrance to the V2 rocket and warhead storage tunnels.

Castel-Vendon, silo no. 2, suitable for vertical launching of Rheinböte.

Simple sites: Chateau de Beaumont. This is the V2 launch control vehicle garage. The usefulness of these buildings for storage has ensured that all thirty on the Cherbourg Peninsula have survived intact.

Simple sites: Hameau de Haut. The photograph shows the left-hand row of concrete blocks for the V1 ramp support structure.

Simple sites: Le Quesnoy. The V1 / Rheinböte launch control bunker. The launch point is 30 ft from the observation slot.

U-234: happier times for crew members during a break in training exercises in the summer of 1944.

I-400, I-401 and I-14 (from left to right) in Tokyo Bay after the surrender. The double inverted U-tube snorkel in its retracted position is visible on all three submarines. (IWM)

I-400: the massive watertight door of the Seiran float-plane hangar.

I-400: the storage hangar for the floats of nos 1 and 2 Seirans, below and to starboard of the main hangar. The floats for the no. 3 Seiran were stored above the aircraft in the main hangar.

Manfred von Ardenne. During the war his 'organization' was engaged on nuclear weapons work for the Reichspost and he employed senior nuclear physicists including Houtermans and Flugge. After the war von Ardenne worked for the Russians on their atomic bomb and although Heisenberg and others belittled von Ardenne's wartime efforts he was awarded the Stalin Prize in 1955 and became East Germany's largest private employer with an internationally recognized scientific reputation.

Brécourt V1/V2/ Rheinböte storage and launch site. Rockets emerged from the hillside underground workings on the left. In the centre is the V2/Rb launch point and the opening for the angled rocket exhaust vent tunnel.

Brécourt V1/V2/ Rheinböte storage and launch site: the end of the V1 ramp protection blast walls. The ramp, never installed, would have been supported in the inclined slots on the inner side of the walls.

Above: An HDP test barrel, pictured in October 1943 at the Hillersleben firing range, 90 miles west of Berlin. The side-branches contained the additional charges which were arranged to fire in sequence and which increased the acceleration of the shell along the barrel. (BA, Freiburg)

The assembled HDP barrel minus breech, as shown above. (BA, Freiburg)

Rheinböte: first and second stages of the rocket en route to the firing range. (BA, Freiburg)

Rheinböte: the assembled rocket on a modified V2 Meillerwagen being elevated to its correct launch angle. Even with extra supports, this makeshift equipment did not provide a suitably rigid launch table for the 45 ft rocket, although dedicated equipment was being designed. (BA, Freiburg)

The only surviving wartime photograph of SS General Hans Kammler, taken in early 1944 on a site visit in northern France.

Wernher von Braun with a group of senior Wehrmacht officers, Peenemünde, 1942. (NASM)

General Walter Dornberger (right) with Heinrich Himmler (centre) inspecting a motor test stand, Peenemünde, spring 1943. On the left is Dr Walter Thiel, in charge of rocket motor development at Peenemünde; he was killed during the RAF bombing raid of 17 August 1943.

Dornberger claimed after the war that the 50 Hz radio beam equipment was never sufficiently developed to provide the target accuracy required, but of course Leitstrahl only operated during the first few seconds of flight, while the rocket aligned itself onto a ballistic trajectory for the target. The Leitstrahl system still provided the least dispersion from the intended flight path, compared to the gyro system, and this is the reason why it was specified in the November 1943 document from Berlin, which gave the V2 organization from 1944 onwards.

CHAPTER 6
Delivering the Ultimate Weapon

A weapon of any sort is useless without an effective means of delivering it, and in the Second World War Germany developed four weapons that fifty years later, with a few modern improvements, have all been used or had the intention to be used with nuclear warheads.

For the Rheinböte and HDP, the only modification required was to replace the high-explosive warhead with a composite one of explosives and radioactive material, to distribute the nuclear material over as large an area as possible. One thing that was missing from these weapons, as for the V1 and V2, was a proximity fuse that would ensure that the warhead was not buried many feet in the ground. Both the Hiroshima and Nagasaki bombs were detonated above ground for precisely that reason. Peenemünde was still experimenting with such a fuse for the V2 when the war ended. The V1 had a comparatively low impact speed at the target, and as it hit the ground at a slight angle, its destruction power was usually greater than the V2: the V2 dissipated some of its warhead in the crater from its Mach 3 impact velocity.

It would be over ten years after 1945 before the nuclear fission process could be incorporated into an artillery shell, but the alternative was nearly as effective, and hence, if the 'super-gun' at Mimoyecques had been completed, it could well have been used with radioactive material in a special shell. In July 1944, when the order was issued from Berlin to modify the site at Mimoyecques, using only one shaft for the HDP and two for Krupp's Schlanke Berta, based on their 28 cm (11 in) K5 (E) long-range barrel, as used on some railway guns, Peenemünde had also been approached to design a rocket shell, similar to the HDP version, but with the muzzle velocity boosted by a small rocket motor instead of the HDP's multiple charges along the barrel. Peenemünde produced two versions of the 'arrow shell', one 6 ft (1.8 m) long for a bored-out version of the K5, 31 cm (12.2 in) with the rifling removed, and the ultimate version, a 52 cm (20 in) smooth-bore barrel, for which a 2-ton 'arrow shell' was designed with a range of at least 120 miles. Stability was provided by small fins which deployed after the shell left the nozzle, imparting a slow rotational movement, as in the Rheinböte, the rocket motor also igniting as the shell emerged from the nozzle.

Both these versions of the HDP idea from Peenemünde could have contained radioactive material in place of the high-explosive filling, as could the original Rheinböte with its offensive warhead of 55 lb.

All this German work during the war to increase the range of conventional artillery, the HDP and Schlanke Berta, was revived in the 1960s by Canadian scientist Dr Gerald Bull. Firstly an example of the HDP was built in Canada, 'Project Harp', using a conventional smooth-bore barrel, without side-charges, but with rocket-assisted shells. Dr Bull's idea was also to use the gun as the first stage of a satellite launcher, but funding was stopped in 1967. In the 1970s Dr Bull also produced a modified artillery shell in which the aerodynamic drag at the base of the shell was reduced by small side-vents, increasing the range of the shell by reducing the overall drag coefficient of the projectile, but unfortunately he exported the idea to South Africa, which was illegal at the time, and he served a prison sentence for his arms dealing, not being released until 1981. Early in the 1980s he sold the rocket-shell HDP idea to Iraq, and in 1988 signed a contract for 'Project Babylon'. The main part of this project was to build a 3 ft (1 m) bore × 580 ft (175 m) long 'super-gun'. The barrel was to be assembled on a 45° hillside near Baiji, 130 miles north of Baghdad, and it was aligned on Israel, 500 miles (800 km) away. A prototype 13.7 in (350 mm) version of the gun was built and assembled before the Gulf War in 1991. Several other long-range weapons were being planned by Dr Bull's Company, Space Research Corporation, SRC, but in March 1990, Dr Bull was 'professionally' assassinated near his Brussels office, shot five times in the head. The affair of the Iraqi super-gun became public knowledge when two British engineering companies, Sheffield Forgemasters and Walter Somers, were given contracts for the 350 mm and 1 m bore barrel sections respectively. They were supposed to be part of an oil pipeline project, but eventually it was realized that they were intended for a long-range weapon. The photograph shows one of the sections of the 3 ft (1 m) bore barrel section on display at the Imperial War Museum, RAF Duxford (see plates). The actual bore of the section shown is 3 ft 5 in (1.041 m), and the overall length is 16 ft 5.5 in (5 m), each section being bolted together by massive 3.25 in (83 mm) diameter bolts. According to Intelligence reports of Project Babylon, all versions of the super-gun were intended for either nuclear or chemical warheads.

The same applies to the Rheinböte, in that if the 1,700 lb (773 kg) warhead version had been completed, this too could have been fitted with an effective nuclear warhead. As it was, the 55 lb (25 kg) warhead of the operational version was too little and too late to have any real impact, even if it had been used with radioactive material.

It was a different matter with the V1 and V2, both with warheads approaching 2,000 lb (900 kg). Of the two weapons, the more effective at delivering a warhead of any sort was the V2. Given the correct launch preparation and check-out, it was more reliable than the V1 by 1945, and most importantly, it was invulnerable to any defensive measures, approaching the target at Mach 3. If the V1 had produced its original specification performance and flown at a cruising speed of 500–550 mph at a height of 1,000 ft or less, it would have probably also been impossible to shoot down. There was certainly little high ground in southern England which would have caused any problems with a pre-arranged flight path that was below 1,000 ft and aimed at London. As a weapon, the V1, with its small-impact crater, was actually more effective than the V2 in its conventional role. The killing over-pressure for the V1 was a 100 ft diameter circle, and the demolition distance for buildings was a diameter of 450 ft from impact, but the V2's destructive power was much less if it produced a large crater.

THE MODIFIED V2

However, the V2 was the most effective weapon at the time, and in Figure 20 there is a comparison between a typical standard V2 and a modified version, German drawing E 2460 B, fitted with a payload compartment between the fuel tanks and rocket motor. The drawings of the standard and modified V2 come from originals in a file of over 2,500 miscellaneous V2 drawings in the archives of the Public Records Office at Kew, London.

From this large number of drawings, the collection only includes two of the modified V2, an assembly drawing numbered E 2460 B and details of the Korsett, E 2450 B, both dated March 1943. This is unfortunate, since on the assembly drawing there are other drawings referenced which would have provided answers to some of the questions and other details concerning the modification. The whole file is a random collection of V2 drawings, many of them original paper copies, and they are now in poor condition, including the copies in question. This caused problems with reproduction, and this is the reason why the author has produced new drawings, to show a comparison between two versions of the V2.

The most obvious changes between the standard and modified V2 are:

1. The addition of a new payload compartment between the fuel tanks and rocket motor.
2. The resulting reduction in size of the fuel tanks.
3. The removal of the normal high-explosive warhead and its replacement with ballast weights.

The new payload compartment had the following features:

1. It formed a very stiff and rigid structure as a result of the longitudinal and lateral 'top-hat' stringer and skin construction. These items were made from mild steel, as was much of the original structure, and hence the whole of the compartment assembly was extremely strong.
2. The method of attaching the new payload compartment to the rest of the V2 was completely different from that used on the original. The standard V2 was divided into four sections for assembly purposes: rocket motor bay; fuel tank bay; control and instrumentation bay; warhead. All four sections were bolted together at bulkheads with as many as thirty-two bolts around the circumference at each joint; the outer skin was attached after the various bays were bolted together. This assembly process would take some time, but it is standard practice with aircraft and missile structures, since normally there is no reason to dismantle the

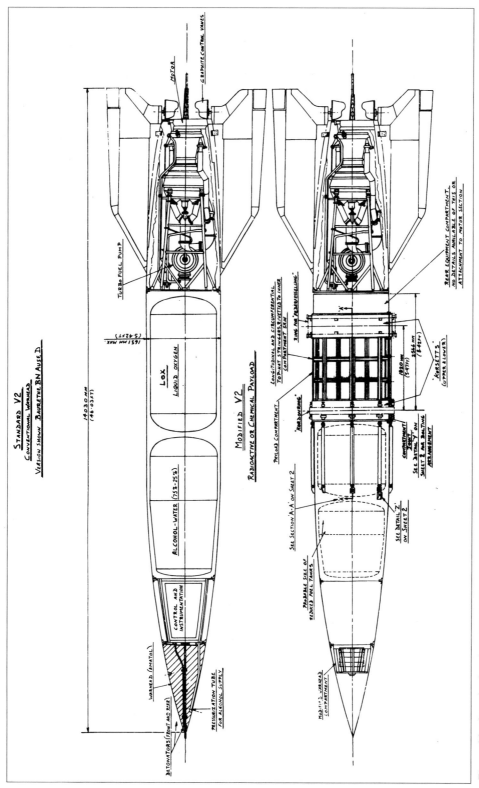

Figure 20. Standard and modified V2s: comparison of assembly arrangements showing the additional payload compartment.

various items after assembly. The new payload section, however, is attached to the body of the rocket using the eight external rods shown. These rods are fitted with screwed connections for adjustment, and also with quick-release couplings. The V2 was assembled vertically, as normal, and the eight rods would have already been inserted into the 'top-hat' sections of the new compartment. The upper body section was then lowered until contact was made with the quick-release couplings. The 'Kordonring' ensured that as the heavy upper body section was lowered, it did not contact the outer skin of the lower fuselage, causing damage. The Kordonring, a solid aluminium alloy ring, was clamped at the top end of the Korsett by a series of screwed clamps welded to the Korsett, which was bolted to the outside of the compartment. Final adjustment to bring the outer skins of the upper and lower sections of the body together, so that they made a neat, flush joint, was made by using the screwed sections of the eight external rods.

3. The new compartment was made in two halves which were bolted together along the longitudinal centreline. The payload was inserted and the two halves were bolted together before being assembled to the rocket.

There are no details available of how the lower end of the compartment was attached to the motor bay, and this would have been included on the missing drawings already mentioned.

The 'Federfesselrung' was intended as the main suspension point for the assembled rocket while it was being transferred into a Meillerwagen or other site-handling equipment.

Apart from ensuring that the new payload compartment could be assembled to the rocket in a matter of minutes, rather than hours, the quick-release couplings also provided another important feature in the event of a launch failure and the rocket falling back onto the concrete pad. The resultant explosion would shear the eight quick-release couplings, and the compartment would separate itself from the rocket, most likely being thrown clear and surviving, dented but intact, complete with contents.

The location of the new compartment at the rear of the V2, rather than utilizing the redundant warhead nose cone, was also an important feature. This would have helped to ensure that on impact at the target, the payload material was likely to be dispersed over a wide area, rather than being buried in a 30 ft deep crater.

The addition of the new compartment would have reduced the total fuel capacity by approximately half. However, the removal of the 1,650 lb warhead, despite the need for ballast weights to correct the aerodynamic trim, and the probability that the contents of the payload container weighed less than half of the fuel, would have helped to compensate for the reduced fuel capacity. The total oxygen/alcohol fuel weight in the standard V2 was 19,750 lb, and the normal launch weight was 28,500 lb.

One of the basic factors affecting the range of a liquid fuel rocket is based on the ratio of

<u>Fuel weight</u>
Total weight

The symbol alpha, α, is used to describe this ratio. Based on the above figures, this gives a value for α of 0.69, which corresponds to the maximum range of 200 miles of the final versions of the standard V2. If these figures are amended for the modified V2, this gives the following approximate results. The weight of fuel becomes 10,000 lb, the total launch weight is now 23,500 lb, based on the original 28,500 lb less the weight of the warhead (1,650 lb), the weight of lost fuel (9,750 lb), plus about two-thirds of the 9,750 lb if it is assumed that the fuel is replaced by a payload material that weighs two-thirds the weight of the fuel (6,400 lb). This results in a total launch weight of:

$$28,500 - (1,650 + 9,750) + 6,400 = 28,500 - 5,000$$
which is 23,500 lb

This gives a new value for α of $\dfrac{10,000}{23,500}$, which $= 0.43$

which may be conservative owing to the ballast weight required.

If the original 200-mile range is now factored by the original α divided by the new α, this gives $\dfrac{0.43}{0.69} \times 200 = 125$ miles.

At this range a modified V2 launched from, say, Watten, could have reached central London, which was less than 120 miles distant.

The 'specific impulse' is another factor which significantly affects the range of a rocket, and this is mainly dependent on the heat released during combustion. The V2 used liquid oxygen (LOX) as an oxidant and a mixture of alcohol (75 per cent) and water (25 per cent) as the fuel, but for simplicity the combined oxidant and alcohol mixture are described as the fuel. The V2's fuel produced a specific impulse of 235, and hence this value contributed to the original range of 200 miles. If this specific impulse was increased by only ten per cent to 259, the range of the standard V2 would increase from 200 to 340 miles; similarly the range of the modified V2 would increase from 125 to 213 miles, regaining the original performance.

There are problems associated with increasing the specific impulse of a rocket fuel, and these include increased combustion chamber temperatures and pressures. The V2's combustion chamber design only just worked with the existing fuel, and any significant increase in temperature resulted in holes appearing in the wall of the combustion chamber.

A considerable amount of work was being carried out on fuels at Peenemünde, both liquid and solid. There were ten in general use by 1942 for the large variety of rockets and motors being developed by BMW, Henschel, Messerschmitt, Rheinmetall–Borsig, Walter and at Peenemünde itself. These were A Stoff (liquid oxygen); B Stoff (petrol); C Stoff (hydrazine hydrate and methyl alcohol); M Stoff (methanol); R Stoff (zyladene tryethalmine, also known as Tonka 250);

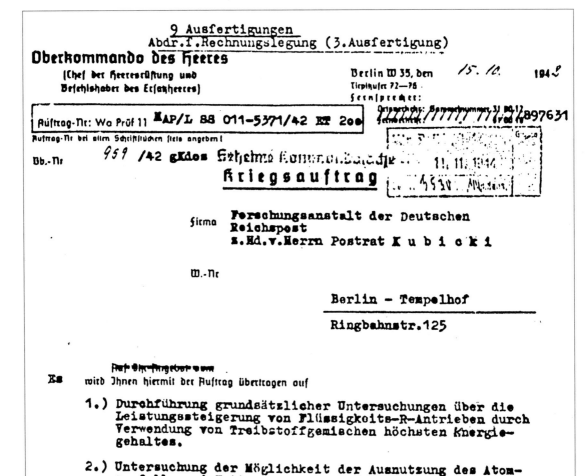

Figure 21. Part of a rocket fuel research contract from Peenemünde to Forschungsanstalt der Deutschen Reichspost.

SZ Stoff (nitric acid); T Stoff (hydrogen peroxide, HTP); Z Stoff (calcium peroxide); Visal (vinylisolbutaether); Vasard 61 (solid fuel).

These chemicals were used in combination of an oxidant (usually LOX, nitric acid or HTP) and a fuel (alcohol, petrol, hydrazine). The concern to provide improved fuels is shown by Figure 21, which is a contract issued by the Army Weapons Testing and Development Section at Peenemünde to the Forschungsansalt der Deutschen Reichspost (Research Institute of the German Post Office). The German Post Office was involved in a variety of research projects which had no connection with the postal service, including nuclear research. The contract is dated 15 October 1942 and is given the second highest priority rating, SS (Sonderstuffe), the same rating as the V2 at the time. The contract is in two parts and states:

1. Initiate fundamental investigations into the power increases obtainable through the mixing of liquid fuels to give their highest possible energy levels for rocket propulsion.
2. Investigate the possibility of the use of the chain-reaction from atomic disintegration, for rocket propulsion.

In other words, the first item was requesting work to improve the specific impulse of the fuel, and the second to investigate the use of atomic energy as a rocket fuel.

At the bottom of the contract is the codicil issued in 1941 on Hitler's orders that no new weapons projects were to be started unless they could be completed within a specified short-term timescale. This was one of the consequences of the early military successes between 1939 and 1941, which resulted in the V2 being removed completely from the priority ratings in 1940/1. It is most likely that similar contracts were issued at about the same time to other organizations, and it illustrates how the interest in nuclear power for rockets was being investigated as early as March 1942. Neither Dornberger nor von Braun made any mention of such a contract or any interest in nuclear power for rockets, when interviewed after the war.

Some confusion has arisen over the modification for the air-burst problem which afflicted the V2 for most of its life, the rocket breaking-up a few seconds before impact, and the modified V2 with the payload compartment. The solution adopted for the air-burst problem also used the term Korsett, but in this case it was used for the reinforcing structure built into the rocket's centre section, unlike the Korsett for the modified V2, which was just forward of the rocket motor bay. Figure 22 is a part-view of a standard V2, showing the reinforcing section in place. This also had a Kordonring, again, for use as the main lifting point of the rocket. As the main structural loads during flight are applied near the centre of the fuselage, it is not surprising that reinforcing the centre section was the main factor in curing the air-burst problem. The fact that it took Peenemünde so long to find a solution to the problem is surprising, but in none of Dornberger's or von Braun's descriptions of the Peenemünde facilities is there a mention of a Structural Test Department where full-size examples of the rocket would have been tested to destruction.

Improved and larger versions of the V2 were also planned, the A7 and A8 having improvements to the structure and motor to increase the range, but these were only marginal improvements. The first major change was the A9, which was a V2 with wings, intended to extend the V2's range to over 300 miles. Two A9s were launched, on 8 and 24 January 1945, but only the second left the pad, reaching a height of 50 miles. The A9/A10 combination was a 112 ft rocket, 30 ft across the fins, with a total weight of 100 tons and main motor thrust of 200 tons, the expected range being over 3,000 miles. But even these 'facts' are open to question. The author has part of an undated US Intelligence report on secret weapons which states, referring to the V2, 'Larger rockets (68 ft in length as

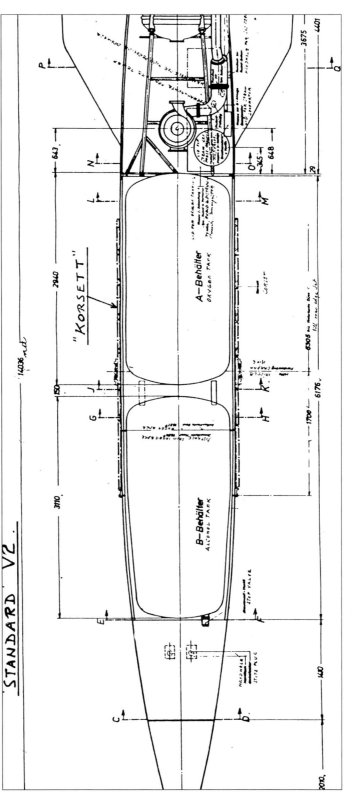

Figure 22. Part of a German DRG 6005B showing the 'air-burst' reinforcement 'Korsett'.

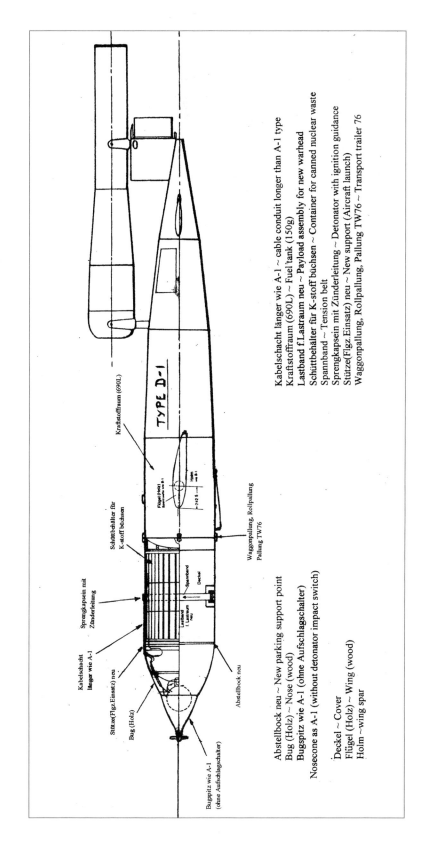

Kabelschacht länger wie A-1 ~ cable conduit longer than A-1 type
Kraftstoffraum (690L) ~ Fuel´tank (150g)
Lastband f.Lastraum neu ~ Payload assembly for new warhead
Schüttbehälter für K-stoff büchsen ~ Container for canned nuclear waste
Spannband ~ Tension belt
Sprengkapsein mit Zünderleitung ~ Detonator with ignition guidance
Stütze(Flgz.Einsatz) neu ~ New support (Aircraft launch)
Waggonpallung, Rollpallung, Pallung TW76 ~ Transport trailer 76

Abstellbock neu ~ New parking support point
Bug (Holz) ~ Nose (wood)
Bugspitz wie A-1 (ohne Aufschlagschalter)
Nosecone as A-1 (without detonator impact switch)

Deckel ~ Cover
Flügel (Holz) ~ Wing (wood)
Holm ~wing spar

Figure 23. A modified V1 with nuclear payload.

against 45 ft) are known to exist, and may appear in small quantities during the year. They would have a considerably larger warhead.'

There was no 'official' version of the V2 which had this length, but both Watten and Wizernes could have handled such a rocket, as could the ex-V1 bunker at Siracourt, which was modified with an exit slot 68 ft long × 18 ft wide at one end.

THE MODIFIED V1

A 'modified' V1 was also designed for the Luftwaffe, the type D-1 (see Figure 23). The new warhead compartment is clearly labelled 'Schüttebehalter für K-Stoffbüschen'. 'Kern' is German for nuclear and K-Stoff is the abbreviation for Kern-Stoff, nuclear material. The full translation is 'Container for canned nuclear waste' and this leaves no doubt as to the purpose of the 'modified' V1.

Significant features of Figure 23 are the use of wood for the wings and nose – steel was used on the 'standard' V1 – and the use of a 150 g fuel tank. The use of the smallest available fuel tank allowed extra space for nuclear material, while to ensure the performance was still acceptable, weight reduction was achieved by the use of wood for the wings and nose. Other important changes compared to a 'standard' V1 are the deletion of the nose-mounted detonator switch, redundant if the V1 were to be detonated above the target; the actual detonator is now positioned above and at the centre of the compartment to achieve the maximum distribution of the nuclear material. Replacing the 1,800 lb HE warhead of the 'standard' V1 with the equivalent amount or more of highly radioactive nuclear waste from either a reactor or particle accelerator (betatron) in the form of crushed granules would result in a deadly nuclear weapon.

The original of the drawing used for Figure 23 came from the Smithsonian Air and Space Museum, Washington DC, and it is part of a folder of drawings showing all the warhead variants of the V1. The drawing, number 824B-Sk 895/a, is dated 19 September 1944 and is related directly with the take-over of all the V-weapons projects by the SS and General Kammler. In the author's opinion such 'sketches' would have appeared in a report produced quickly to illustrate the full offensive capabilities of the V1 to someone who was relatively 'new' to the project, such as General Kammler.

The 'modified' V1 confirms that the V1 bunker sites at Siracourt, Lottinghen, Couville, Tamerville and Brécourt were intended to store, service and launch nuclear weapons, as were the last examples of launch sites built in France, the combined V1/V2/Rb 'simple' sites. It is interesting to note that the first American atomic bomb, the 'Little Boy' uranium weapon dropped on Hiroshima, had a weight less armour and casing of 1,700 lb, almost exactly the same weight as the V1/V2 warhead, and that the gun-type activation mechanism used in 'Little Boy' would have fitted inside the compartment of the 'modified' V2 but was too long for the 'modified' V1 compartment.

CHAPTER 7

Japan – The New Order in the Pacific

If Adolf Hitler and the Third Reich had not looked much further than Europe for its conquests and territorial expansion, avenging old scores with Great Britain and France and the Lebensraum ('living space') of the vast areas of Russia, it was a different story in Japan. From 1900 onwards, Japan had annexed, taken-over and conquered various territories, which allowed Japan to expand her sphere of influence politically and also increased her mineral and food production to supply the rapid industrial expansion that was taking place inside the country. In 1910 Korea was 'annexed', a country rich in mineral deposits and a source of cheap labour. In 1914 Japan joined the war on the Allies' side, but only as a pretext for seizing the German-controlled Pacific islands of Caroline, Mariana, Marshall and Truk, and the Chinese base of Tsingtao. The islands were later ceded to Japan by the League of Nations, efectively extending Japan's perimeter into the Pacific by almost 3,000 miles.

By 1931/2 it was Manchuria's turn. Originally part of China, of considerable strategic value, bordering on Russia and China, it was seized in a rapid campaign, and Japan made the deposed last Emperor of China its puppet ruler. Finally, in 1937, China itself was invaded, following the 'China Incident' in Peking, and by the end of 1938, Peking, Shanghai, Nanking, Hankow, most of the coastline and the most valuable areas of China in terms of material wealth and population were in Japanese hands.

But there were still two major raw materials that Japan lacked if it was to compete on a world scale with the leading countries in the West, oil and steel. The 'screw' then began to turn on European possessions in the Pacific. On 27 September 1940, Japan signed the Tripartite Pact with Germany and Italy, forming what was to become known as the Axis. Article II of the Pact stated that Germany and Italy would recognize and respect the leadership of Japan in the establishment of a 'New Order' in East Asia.

By May 1941, the whole of French Indo-China, including Cambodia, was under the virtual military control of Japan, and France, now soon to be under German domination, could only make token protests. Siam (Thailand) also became an ally of Japan, receiving military and economic aid as Japan fostered national unrest in the area.

Finally, in April 1941, Japan signed a five-year neutrality pact with Russia, protecting her back, as it were, from any possible military threat from beyond Manchuria.

This was a temporary end to the encroachment of Japanese forces, but not an end to the pressures. The first was to stop all supplies to China via British possessions such as Hong Kong, since China was still fighting from inside the vast hinterland; the second was to obtain more oil from the Dutch East Indies, which included Indonesia, Sumatra and parts of New Guinea and Borneo. By June 1941 the Dutch had resisted all efforts by Japan to increase oil supplies in the quantities demanded. Over 80 per cent of Japan's oil at this time came from the USA, relations with whom were gradually becoming more strained as American public opinion hardened against the continuing war in China and the other military conquests in the Pacific. The Dutch attitude effectively sealed the fate of her colonies in the Pacific, as Japanese plans were drawn up to seize by force the precious oil supplies they had been unable to obtain by negotiation. And once again the military plans also included supporting any Nationalistic movements in these possessions, as an added bonus.

But events now took another turn: on 7 December the American Naval Base at Pearl Harbor was attacked, a step from which there was going to be no return. A few days after Pearl Harbor, with the Axis now arranged against America and Great Britain, the Ministry of War in Tokyo produced plans which showed how far the 'New Order' was going to extend into the Pacific and beyond, the 'Hakko ichiu', or 'eight corners of the world under one roof', the one roof being Imperial Japan. These conquests were to be carried out in two stages: firstly the Dutch, British, French, Portuguese and American territory and islands in the Pacific would be taken, including New Zealand, Australia, part of India and the remainder of China, and a 'New Order' would be established in East Asia in which the new nations would have their own governments but overall control would still come from Tokyo. After a pause of ten to twenty years, the final stage would begin. This would result in the occupation of the Central American Republics and the Caribbean Islands, followed by Alaska, the Yukon, Alberta, British Columbia and the State of Washington. This may seem far fetched today, but in just over a year, a large part of the first stage of these plans had been accomplished. By the summer of 1942, Japanese naval forces controlled the whole of the Western Pacific, and on land their armies were at the borders of India and in New Guinea they were less than 400 miles from the tip of Australia. The only American possession left between Japan and mainland USA were the islands of Midway and Hawaii. As in Germany, the summer of 1942 was the high point of the Japanese conquests. The major contributor to this initial success had been Japan's use of naval power, not in the old-fashioned sense of battleship versus battleship, but in the use of combined naval and air-power, using the new floating air-base, the aircraft carrier; in this usage Japan's naval aircraft and its tactics were far superior to anything the Allies had at the time.

But the British and American forces were forced to learn the new lessons quickly, and the industrial might of the USA was soon changing into top gear. The first small but highly significant set-back to Japan's naval confidence came on 4–8 May 1942, in the Battle of the Coral Sea, when two Japanese carriers were badly damaged and one sunk for the loss of one US carrier damaged and one sunk, but it effectively halted the invasion of New Guinea.

Only a month later, at the battle of Midway, the Japanese lost four carriers, one heavy cruiser, 300 naval aircraft and nearly 4,000 navy personnel against the US losses of one carrier, the Yorktown. The invasion of Midway had been intended to shatter US naval power in the Pacific, but instead, apart from the heavy blow to the cream of Japan's naval aviation, it was also a psychological blow which heralded the end of Japanese expansion in the Pacific.

CHAPTER 8

Japan's Long-Range Weapons

If Japan was to achieve the New Order in East Asia and complete the massive territorial expansion into and beyond the Pacific, then it would need weapons capable of being used many thousands of miles from Tokyo. Even with the eventual capture of the US bases of Midway and Hawaii, the distances to the US West Coast were still enormous, making the war in Europe seem almost like a backyard conflict. Here is no doubt, however, that Japan believed that the US Government and the US people were not interested in war, and that they would be prepared to negotiate with Japan, once Japan controlled a large part of the Pacific, including the oil, rubber and mineral wealth of the Dutch colonies. As General Tojo proclaimed after the capture of the Dutch East Indies in 1942, Japan was no longer a 'have-not' nation, but could now negotiate on equal terms with the West, including the USA. The possibility that Japan might negotiate some sort of agreement with the USA, once it had achieved a certain level of territorial gains in the Pacific, had also occurred to Hitler.

In a decoded ULTRA message dated 26 July 1941, from Tokyo to the Japanese Naval Attaché in Berlin, the first part of the message begins:

'Problems of importance at present arising between Japan and Germany are threefold:
(a) Germany's keen desire that Japan should go to war with Soviet Russia forthwith,
(b) Germany's misgivings regarding a Japanese-American settlement,
(c) Japan's declaration regarding the policy which she will pursue.'

As it turned out, Germany need not have worried too much about a settlement between Japan and the USA because less than five months later Japan attacked Pearl Harbor, and despite the early gains in the Pacific, Japan completely misjudged the feelings of the American Government and people in their determination to resist aggression.

However, compared to Germany, the distances involved in reaching its main adversary, the USA, were huge. San Francisco was 5,500 miles from Tokyo and the East Coast cities such as New York over twice that distance. With an invasion now out of the question, the only alternative was to carry out air raids on the East and West Coast cities and the supply route through the Panama Canal. With the islands of Midway and Hawaii still in American hands and their fleet rapidly being replaced, especially with aircraft carriers, after Pearl Harbor, an attack by surface ships was also no longer possible. Even less possible was an attack by land-based bombers. Although Japan had produced aircraft with exceptional endurance, they were sea-based: the Kawanishi Company's Emily and Maisie four-engined flying boats had ranges of over 4,000 miles, but even this was nowhere near sufficient to be able to bomb the US mainland and return. Refuelling an aircraft by submarine was tried on at least one occasion, but it was not really a practical means of producing a long-range bomber.

The only other choice remaining was to build a submersible aircraft carrier which would have the range to reach even the East Coast cities like New York, with aircraft that could carry an effective offensive bomb load. The Commander-in-Chief of the Imperial Japanese Combined Fleet, Admiral Isoroku Yamamoto, had been a supporter of the submersible aircraft carrier concept from the start, and in December 1942, as part of the Fifth Replenishment Programme, a total of eighteen Sensuikan toku, abbreviated to Sen-toku, or Special Submarines, were planned, to belong to Class I-400. Aircraft-carrying submarines were not new, and Japan had built several submarine types capable of carrying a single float-plane. These were classes I-7, I-9, I-13, I-15 and I-54, a total of over 36 submarines, the most modern of which carried the Yokosuka 'Glen', a twin-float catapult-launched reconnaissance aircraft. In 1942 a Glen dropped two small incendiary bombs in Oregon in an unsuccessful attempt to start a major forest fire, but the I-400 class was the first attempt to build a genuine submersible aircraft carrier. As such, they were designed on a massive scale, being the largest submarines built by any nation until the arrival of nuclear-powered boats. Originally based on a two-aircraft concept, the plans were later amended to take three aircraft, with the final design having the following specification:

> Length overall 403 ft (122 m); length at water level 396 ft (120 m); beam 36 ft (12 m); displacement 5,223 tons surfaced, 6,560 tons submerged; draught 28 ft (7 m); four Japanese-built German MAN diesels, total 7,700 s.h.p. via two shafts; electrical power 2,400 s.h.p.; range 37,500 miles at 14 knots; maximum surface speed 18.7 knots; submerged range 60 miles at 3 knots; maximum underwater speed 6.5 knots; eight 21 in (530 mm) bow torpedo tubes with 20 torpedoes; one 5.5 in (140 mm) gun; three 1 in (25 mm) triple-mounted and one single 1 in (25 mm) AA guns; safe diving depth 330 ft (100 m). [See also Figure 24.]

To obtain the required storage space and stability, the hull comprised two cylinders side by side, and the main aircraft hangar, 110 ft (33 m) long and 11.5 ft (3.5 m) in diameter, was on the centre line, with the entrance forward of the conning tower. To starboard was a smaller hangar for the storage of the floats for two of the aircraft and the munitions. The compressed-air-powered aircraft launch ramp was 90 ft (27 m) long, and to its left was a collapsible derrick for recovering the aircraft which fitted into a recess on the deck. The aircraft specified for the submarine was a completely new design by the Aichi Company of Nagoya, the Aichi M6A1 Seiran (Mountain Haze), a two-seater, low-winged, all-metal monoplane with twin floats

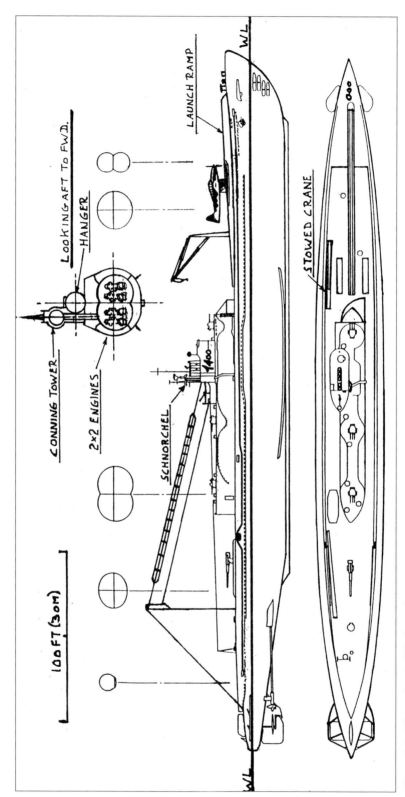

Figure 24. Plans of an I-400 class submarine.

and powered by an Aichi 1,400 hp inverted V-12 liquid-cooled engine. It was the fastest float-plane in the Second World War, with a maximum speed of 300 mph, and it could carry a bomb load of 1,760 lb over a range of 740 miles. The prototype was completed in November 1943, and eventually twenty production versions were built. With pre-heated engine oil, it could be removed from its hangar and got ready for flight within ten minutes by a trained crew.

Both air and sea watch radar were fitted to the submarine, and the hull was coated with the German-developed rubber and cement anti-ASDIC sonar coating. An automatic trimming device was also fitted, which was intended to allow the boat to hover underwater at a depth of between 120 and 160 ft, so as to maintain a set position when the aircraft were returning from a mission.

Although eighteen of the class had been ordered originally, this was amended in 1944, and eventually only three boats were completed, I-400 on 30 December 1944 at Kure; I-401 on 8 January 1945 at Sasebo; and I-402 was converted into a tanker and completed on 24 July 1945 at Sasebo. I-404 was launched at Kure on 7 July 1944, but work was abandoned when almost complete and it was bombed and sunk at Kure on 28 July 1945; I-405 was laid-down at Kawasaki on 27 September 1944, but work was abandoned before the hull was completed.

The decision to amend the order was affected by several factors, including the worsening military situation and the need to use resources on more urgent projects. Also, Admiral Yamamoto had died on 18 April 1943 when his Mitsubishi Betty transport had been shot down off Bougainville by an ambush of US P-38 Lightning fighters, the result of US code breaking. With the death of Yamamoto, his successor, Admiral Toyoda, would have reviewed all the outstanding naval building projects to assess their viability and to see if better use could be made of resources.

In the event a compromise was reached in which five I-400 class vessels were to be built, and in order to provide some replacement for the cancelled I-400s, a conventional submarine design based on the I-9 type was modified as the I-13 class, to take two Aichi Seirans in place of its original one reconnaissance float-plane. The I-13s were large submarines, with a conventional hull layout and a length overall of 373 ft (113 m), beam 38 ft (11.7 m), 4,760 tons submerged and a range of 21,000 miles surfaced at 16 knots. The aircraft hangar was on the starboard side, with the conning tower offset to port. Only two examples were completed by the end of the war: I-13 on 16 December 1944 at Kawasaki, and I-14 on 14 March 1945 at Kawasaki. I-15 was launched on 12 April 1944 at Kawasaki and I-16 on 10 June 1944 at Kawasaki, but neither I-15 nor I-16 was completed before the end of the war. The aircraft launching and recovery equipment was very similar to the I-400s.

If the original building plan for eighteen I-400s had been adhered to, this would have provided quite a powerful bombing force, able to reach either coastline of the USA. Assuming a third of the eighteen would have been unavailable for various reasons, repairs, maintenance, etc., then twelve boats with thirty-six aircraft would have resulted in a total offensive bomb load per mission of 28 tons. In terms of the European scene, this was not large, but if the bombs had been changed to those containing nuclear or chemical/biological material, then it would have become a different story.

Even the amended programme, with five I-400s and four I-13s, would still have provided an effective offensive bomb load if nuclear material had been used.

One of the most significant features of I-400 and I-401 was the type of snorkel fitted. By 1944, Japanese submarines were being fitted with snorkels to allow the use of the diesels for recharging the batteries and increased speed while partially submerged. These snorkels were similar to the later German types, which were permanently erected and could be extended if required, the air intake supplying air to the boat's interior, serving both the crew and the main diesels, and also acting as an exhaust for both uses. On the I-400s, however, the snorkel supplied air only to the auxiliary diesels, twin hydraulically raised pipes acting as both intake and exhaust. This feature on the I-400s had two main implications:

1. As they were built with air-breathing diesel main engines, to provide a snorkel that supplied air only for the auxiliary diesels was almost a pointless exercise, since it would have been just as easy at the time of installation to provide a conventional snorkel.
2. The snorkel design was originally intended for submarines that did not have air-breathing main engines.

Both I-13 and I-14 were fitted with snorkels which appeared to have the same purpose as the I-400s, and these may have been installed as part of the I-400 replacement programme; externally they certainly looked identical to the I-400 version.

The second factor implies that originally the main propulsion system was intended to be by steam power, but this would not be a conventionally fired boiler since this again required an air supply for combustion. The only steam-generated power supply that does not require an air supply is the nuclear reactor, and hence we are left with the only alternative, that originally the I-400 class were intended to be nuclear-powered vessels and that the I-13s were similarly modified.

The I-400s' snorkel was also unusual in that it did not supply air to the interior of the boat for the crew. Even in modern nuclear boats the snorkel provides air to the interior in case a problem develops with the boat's atmosphere-production equipment, and the implication is that perhaps the I-400s had an atmosphere system that they considered ultra-reliable.

The auxiliary diesels in nuclear-powered boats have several functions, and these include providing power for either surface or submerged emergency movement and the ability to charge batteries in the event of problems with the nuclear power plant. Also, the auxiliary diesels allow the boat to operate under its own power while in dock and with the nuclear unit not operating, although this, of course, would not require a snorkel.

However, probably the most important function of the auxiliary diesels in a nuclear boat is to provide power following either a partial or full emergency drop of the shut-down rods to trip the reactor. After a reactor trip and before the auxiliary diesels are fully running, power is supplied by a section of batteries which are dedicated to supplying power to the reactor steam plant auxiliaries, the various pumps, etc., which must be kept running even though the reactor is shut down, to remove residual heat from the core.

The use of two separate engine rooms in the I-400s, one in each of the hull cylinders side by side with each pair of engines driving a single propeller, provided adequate redundancy at the cost of added noise. Virtually all Russian nuclear submarines have two reactors with twin shafts, whereas US, British and French have a single reactor driving a single turbo-generator for the electrical power and a main turbine driving through gears to a single propeller. A single large propeller turning relatively slowly generates far less noise than two smaller propellers turning quickly, and propeller noise underwater is one of the 'killers' of submarines. We have already seen how one of the propellers of U-234 was replaced because it was producing too much noise. We can deduce, therefore, that the I-400s were intended to have two reactors, one in each of the engine rooms, with all the other equipment also duplicated.

From a timing point of view, the fact that the 'nuclear' snorkel was fitted to both I-400s and the I-13s implies to the author that progress with suitable nuclear reactors was well advanced in Japan, and that by 1944, when construction of the boats was under way, it was still a possibility that they would have the nuclear reactors and steam generators, etc. installed during construction. In other words, in late 1943 and early 1944, the nuclear power plant was still a feasible option, but for reasons unknown, but discussed later in the book, it was not possible to install such new and revolutionary equipment and machinery when the military situation did not allow time for the necessary trials and testing programme.

If you only have one or two nuclear weapons, and a replacement time for them of perhaps several months, it is a better option to use the tried and tested diesel main propulsion rather than gain a few knots underwater at the cost of reliability and not being able to actually deliver the weapons.

Japanese submarine design in the Second World War is often considered as inferior to the equivalent European boats, with Germany being regarded as the leaders at the end of the war in boats with high underwater speed, the first true submarines, with their Type XXI 'Electro' boats. The XXIs had an underwater speed of 18 knots due to an advanced hull design with new high-performance lightweight batteries. This was not the full story, however, for Japan was also working on a submarine design with a high underwater speed, similar in specification to the 'Electro' boats. These Sensuikan taka, or Sen-taka, submarines were designed to have an underwater speed of 20 knots, bettering the German boats by two knots, although as built they achieved 19 knots. Five boats were laid-down, but only three completed by the end of the war, I-201, I-202 and I-203, and they did not see operational service.

The Germans imported virtually no finished items from Japan during the war, being more interested in raw materials, but they were very interested in the new S-type submarines.

In 1944 a series of ULTRA messages recorded the German requests for more information on the high-speed boats, and in one reply dated 10 May 1944 it was claimed by Tokyo that four of the boats would be completed by the end of 1944, with a further fifteen in 1945.

If Japan was working on nuclear-powered submarines, an obvious application for nuclear power that was even mentioned by Heisenberg in his lecture to the German Research Institute as early as 26 February 1942, then how did this work originate?

There is little doubt that by 1939 Japan was fully aware of the developments taking place in Europe regarding nuclear fission and its use as a potential weapon. Some of her nuclear physicists had travelled and studied in the USA, and since a state of war did not exist between the two countries until the end of 1941, they were able to extend this knowledge while most of Europe was actually engaged in conflict. It is in the next few years, leading up to 1944/5, that the picture becomes cloudy. Japan, like Germany, had early military successes that most probably produced a similar approach to the use of nuclear power. Any such research and development programme was going to be very demanding on resources, and the final outcome was uncertain, hence such work would continue, but on a low priority. But again by the middle of 1943, there is another similarity to Germany: the military situation was changing to such an extent that it was becoming increasingly doubtful if Japan would emerge victorious. The US, British and Australian forces were beginning to nibble away at the numerous Pacific islands captured by Japan in 1942, and in the air and at sea Japanese forces were usually on the losing side. In the circumstances, interest in unconventional weapons increased, and this included not only nuclear but biological weapons.

In 1940, both the Army and Navy started looking into the possibilities of building a nuclear weapon. For the Army, Lieutenant-General Takeo Yasuda, Director of the Military Technical Air Service, was in charge of the initial studies, and he instructed Lieutenant-Colonel Tatsusaburo Susuki at the Army Aviation Headquarters to investigate the nuclear weapon question and to produce a report of his findings. Among the Japanese physicists still working in America was Ryokichi Sagane, who had worked with Lawrence at Berkeley, winner of the 1939 Nobel Prize in Physics for his invention of the cyclotron. Sagane had also worked at the Cavendish Laboratory in Cambridge, and therefore he had an international reputation. By 1941 Sagane had returned to Japan and was then working on the construction of the largest cyclotron outside the USA, a 60 in diameter version at the Institute for Physical and Chemical Research, know as Rikken, where they already had a smaller 26 in cyclotron which had been working since 1936. Susuki consulted other physicists at Rikken, including Yazaki, who had also spent some time in the USA, and from these discussions it was clear that the experts considered that nuclear power should be proceeded with, including a nuclear weapon. In the meantime, the Navy's investigation into nuclear power was also proceeding under the direction of Captain Yoji Ito from the Electrical Section of the Navy Technical Research

Department. By 1941 these two investigations from the Army and Navy had recruited assistance and advice from several of the leading physicists in the main universities. These included Professors Sagane, Okochi, Nishina, Arakatsu, Yukawa, Kobayashi and Kuroda from Tokyo, Kure and Osaka universities. Yoshio Nishina had also worked abroad before the war; in Copenhagen he had been one of Neils Bohr's research students, and hence was familiar with the leading names in European nuclear physics and knew what problems needed to be solved. If Sagane and Nishina were not full members of the nuclear 'club', like Blackett, at least they were on the fringe and aware of what was happening. Susuki's report to General Yasuda was completed after six months, and with both the Army and Navy now convinced that research on nuclear power should be proceeded with, the work programme was split into four packages, A, B, C and D. The A-Group were to investigate particle accelerators and the effect of high velocity particles on nuclei. The B-Group were to study cosmic rays, since, as already mentioned, there was some concern in Germany and America that if some fissile material, such as U.235 or Pu.239, was assembled, then cosmic ray neutrons might cause premature or predetonation of the material. The C-Group were carrying out general theoretical studies, and the D-Group were looking at the medical aspects.

At this time the approach being taken was very similar to that in Germany, in that packages of work had been handed out to the various experts at the universities. And as we have seen, at this time the actual military need for a nuclear weapon was not obvious, in the light of the success of the conventional armed forces, a situation which did not apply to the USA and Great Britain, where the early military experiences had been in favour of the Axis forces.

By the beginning of 1943, the Japanese studies had confirmed that the manufacture of an atomic bomb was feasible, and a major step forward was the development of a method for producing uranium hexafluoride, a gaseous product of uranium, and essential if the bomb material U.235 was to be separated from U.238. By November 1943 a thermal diffusion plant had been built for the separation of U.235, and this continued operating until 1945, although the 'official' story is that virtually no U.235 was produced from this equipment. On 13 April 1945 most of the plant was destroyed in an air raid.

The picture becomes very cloudy from 1943 onwards, as officially the Army decided there was no longer any possibility of producing a nuclear weapon within the timescale of the present conflict, and this was also echoed by the Navy. However, a new Navy nuclear weapons project had already started, the so-called F-go Kenkyo, or Fission Studies Programme, sometime in 1942. Despite the demise of the original project, therefore, the Navy was apparently determined to continue its nuclear work. Among the scientists involved in the new Navy research was Professor Bunsaku Arakatsu of Kyoto University, a former pupil of Einstein, and he was assisted by Professors Yukawa, Kobayashi, Sasaki and Kuroda. What is 'officially' known about the Navy F-go work is that at least one centrifuge was built for U.235 separation, leading this work were Kimura and Shimizu, and ample uranium oxide was available from Korea. The F-go work is supposed to have ended without any real progress being made, and if both the

Army and Navy work can be summarized briefly, it is that Japan was interested in building a nuclear weapon after the 1939 fission discovery. Scientific opinion was sought and work started on the separation of U.235 using uranium hexafluoride and the thermal diffusion method. The Americans tried the thermal diffusion method and decided that although the process worked, it was not suitable for the mass-production of large amounts of U.235.

Several cyclotrons were built in Japan for isotope separation, and later in the war the centrifuge method of separation was developed, but most importantly at the time of the Japanese surrender, there was neither a bomb design nor the fissile material to use in it.

Most strangely, there is virtually no mention ever made of Japanese work to build a reactor, and yet in any nuclear programme this would have been one of the first objectives, just as it was with the Manhattan Project in America and also in Germany. A working reactor would have confirmed many of the theoretical concepts about fission and the ability to control the fission process.

This is briefly the 'official' history, which varies slightly depending on whose version you are looking at, but the author believes that this is about as close to the truth as the 'Heisenberg version' of Germany's nuclear weapons work: in other words, it is very much a modified version of the truth.

For the official story to be seriously discredited, several factors are required, and one of these is evidence that a massive industrial effort was supporting the scientific work to build a reactor and nuclear weapon. This evidence is most important, since without industrial support, any such work can only be carried out on a laboratory scale, producing, for instance, milligrams of U.235 instead of the kilograms required for a reactor and bomb project.

American author Robert Wilcox has long believed that Japan was building a nuclear weapon, and in his book, *Japan's Secret War*, he has been able to supply some of the pieces of the jigsaw, especially in relation to the industrial support for a nuclear programme.

Wilcox identified a Japanese entrepreneur, Jun Noguchi, as the driving force behind the huge industrial empire in North Korea, based at Konan, now called Kowan, or Hungnam. Since 1910, Korea had been a vassal state of Japan, and any suitably qualified industrialist with the means and the ability was encouraged to exploit Korean resources for the benefit of Japan, and this included labour and minerals, important for the rapidly expanding military industries of Japan. Industry needs power, especially electrical power, and although Korea was not short of coal, it had ample quantities of fast-flowing water in her rivers. One of the first moves Noguchi made, therefore, when he arrived at Konan in 1923 was to start harnessing the three rivers, Yalu, Fusen and Chosen, by building a series of dams and hydroelectric power stations. Wilcox claimed that these stations produced 1,000 MW of electrical power, equivalent to the output of a large modern nuclear power station, a massive amount by 1940s standards. As a matter of comparison, the total power consumption of all the factories and plants associated with the Manhattan Project in America used around 200 kW, a fifth of the Korean output.

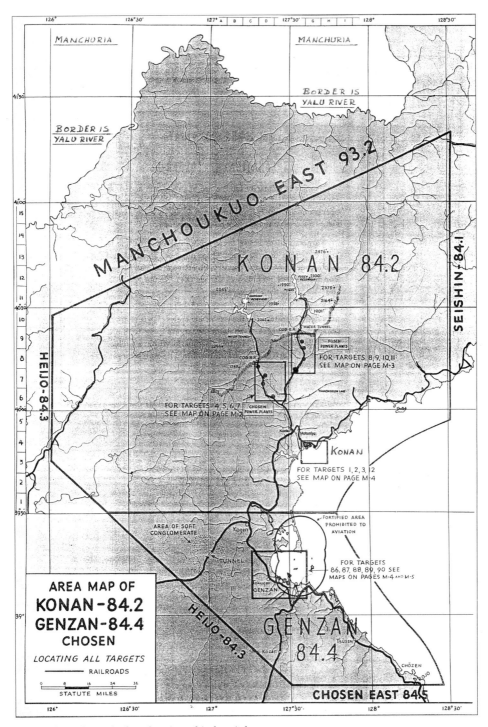

Figure 25. Konan hydro-electric and industrial areas.

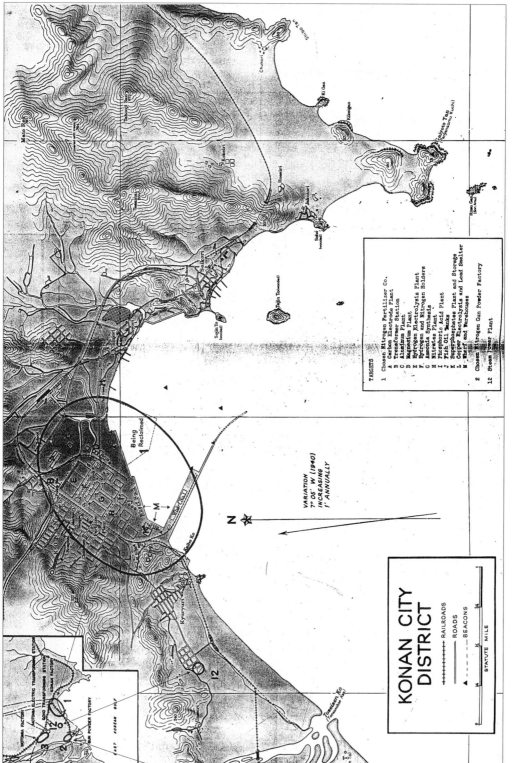

KONAN CITY
DISTRICT

++++++++ RAILROADS
━━━━━ ROADS
▲ ─ ─ ─ ─ BEACONS

STATUTE MILE

VARIATION
7° 05' W (1940)
INCREASING
1' ANNUALLY

N

Figure 26. The Konan industrial area, indicating some of the known materials produced, including the Hydrogen Electrolysis Plant for Heavy Water.

In addition to Wilcox's findings, the author has found the USAF target information for the Konan area, and this provides more details of the industrial output. This information confirms that a vast amount of hydroelectric power was being generated above Konan from the harnessing of the Chosen and Fusen Rivers. Figures 25 and 26 show the locations of the eight hydroelectric power stations behind Konan, and details of the chemical and other plants using this power in Konan. Regarding the electrical power, the effort required to build eight power stations, plus the dams and water tunnels, was enormous, and as the target report states, these power stations generated well over 500,000 kW, plus the additional power which was being supplied from the Yalu River power stations above Antung. One highly significant feature on the large-scale map are the two railway lines heading into the mountains north of Konan. The first rail track has electric transmission lines heading towards the end of the rail track, and this implies a heavy use of power, although the target information supplies no details, which implies that no information was available. If the tracks had served mines or similar, the operations would have been instantly recognizable, but there is nothing.

Wilcox writes in his book that the secret nuclear work was taking place underground in the hills behind Konan, and this is another indication that such work was going on.

The small-scale map identifies the various plant sections, which include the production of carbon; aluminium; magnesium; ammonia; sulphuric, nitric and phosphoric acid; nitrogen, including fertilizer, explosives and rocket propellants; copper; lead; fish oil and glycerine. One interesting section identified is the hydrogen electrolysis plant, which is how the Norsk-Hydro heavy water plant was described, the heavy water being a by-product of hydrogen production and like Norsk-Hydro, it needed huge amounts of electricity. When water is electrolysed, the gas produced is mostly hydrogen, and the residual water is rich in deuterium, which is the main constituent of heavy water, the hydrogen being used in oil refining and the production of ammonia and other chemicals.

Japan never acknowledged that heavy water was produced during the war, but Wilcox refers to it and it is very likely that 'E' is the location of the plant. There are some plant areas that are not identified, and the target report states that 'The present production is unknown'.

South of Konan, in Figure 25, at Genzan, the Japanese had a large oil refinery, which had been owned before the war by the Standard Oil Company of the USA.

The mineral deposits in Korea, especially the north, are well known today, and these have helped North Korea to build nuclear power stations and develop nuclear weapons. The map in Figure 27 shows the known monzanite deposits and mines in North Korea during the war. Monzanite is one of the main sources of thorium and uranium, and other rare minerals can be obtained from it, including gadolinium, which has the highest thermal neutron absorption cross-section of any material, making it the most effective control-rod material available, although commercially it is too costly for normal reactor use. The extent of the monzanite mining operation indicates that thorium was of special interest to the Japanese. The mining of other uranium-bearing ores, including pitchblende, was also

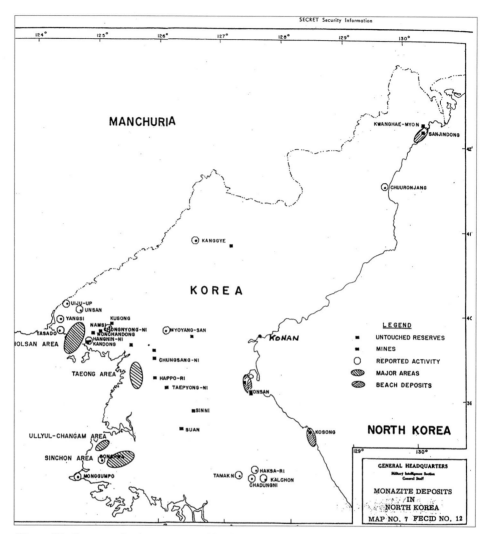

Figure 27. Japanese thorium sources in North Korea.

carried out in Manchuria and Korea by the Japanese, but exact amounts of ore produced can not be quantified. Figure 28 is two extracts from post-war American reports on uranium mining and usage by Japan. Significantly, even by 1948 the USA had still not clarified the situation with regard to certain aspects of nuclear work in Japan, and stated that the amount of uranium ore mined and shipped to Japan from Manchuria and Korea during the war was 'inconclusive'.

Returning to Wilcox's book, further information emerges concerning the nuclear connection with Konan (Hungnam). The *New York Times* published a short article entitled 'North Korean Plant Held Uranium Works' on 26 October 1950. According to the report, during the Korean War, South Korean forces had

'A'

GENERAL HEADQUARTERS
SUPREME COMMANDER FOR THE ALLIED POWERS

OUTGOING MESSAGE   ESS/ST WFM/WJA/am
DATE: 12 April 1948

TOP SECRET

FROM: SCAP

TO : DEPT OF ARMY   PRIORITY   420903

(C-59840) For CSCAD PL.

1. References: Ourad C 58922 to DA for CSCAD PL dtd 28 Feb 48; urad W 96075 dtd 18 Feb 48; ourad C 57734 dtd 3 Jan 48; urad WAR 92991 dtd 25 Dec 47; JCS rad WX 95147 dtd 24 Jul 46; and JCS rad WX 88780 dtd 15 Dec 45.

2. Presence in Japan of 1,898 secret patents, applications and models of Japanese wartime endeavors, presence of radioactive stockpiles in 78 industrial concerns, the necessity for restricting certain areas for military intelligence reasons, and the necessity for compliance with directive contained in para 3e of WX 95147 with respect to the above caused concern over security matters expressed in ourads C 58922 and C 57734. A desire to withhold non-military technical information was not present.

'B'

MINING IN MANCHURIA

10. CONCLUSIONS: The results of the investigation indicate that the Japanese Imperial GHQ, Tokyo, Japan. did, on or about 1 Apr 44, undertake to procure large amounts of uranium minerals from areas occupied by Japanese Military Forces.

a. Mr. Reijiro YAMAMURA, Tokyo-to, Toshima-ku, Senkawa-cho, 1-chome, 6, gave information concerning Japanese military units, civil government agencies, and private companies that engaged in study or exploitation of sources of uranium in Manchuria. His testimony as regards organizational patterns, personalities, and dates, is considered reliable and complete.

11. RECOMMENDATIONS:

a. That further investigation be scheduled by this unit or by ESS to exploit elements of information, as follows:

(1) Information of unreported research or use of uranium in Japan for nuclear fission experiments during World War II

(2) Conclusive information of the amounts, types, and disposition of radioactive materials shipped from Manchuria to Japan during World War II at the order of Japanese Military Forces

b. That this report be forwarded to Targets Branch, Department of the Army (Strategic) Intelligence Division for collation.

FREDERICK G BULL
Major, FA
Commanding

Figure 28. Extracts from US post-war reports on Japanese nuclear activities in the Second World War.

reached the Hungnam-Chosen reservoir, part of Nogichi's original empire, and in the surrounding area they had discovered a huge factory surrounded by an electrified wire fence. One dominant feature was a large 'grain-elevator'-like building and a compound full of high-voltage equipment, apparently powered by two large machines in the centre of the complex. The report went on to say that US atomic energy experts believed that this was a uranium-processing plant and that a second such plant would be found in the area. We do not know how accurate this report was, but the plant was without doubt very large, used a lot of electricity, security was important and it had originally belonged to Noguchi.

Another incident reported by Wilcox during his research in Japan involved an American scientist investigating plans of a Japanese nuclear weapon provided by a Japanese general who had worked in Korea and escaped before the Russians arrived in 1945. Apparently the Japanese had not used the weapon in question because they were waiting for a German submarine to arrive, carrying an improved 'plutonium trigger' for the bomb, as the uranium type they had was not as good. Also, there is a report dated 21 May 1946 from the US Army Chief of Staff's office in Korea which states that there is increasing interest in reports of a research laboratory which was operated by the Japanese at Hungnam, involving atomic energy. Before the Russians arrived at the laboratory, the staff managed to destroy some, but not all, of the equipment. The report also mentioned that nuclear experimental work had been carried out in Japan and that the Hungnam establishment was specifically for developing the military use of nuclear energy. The report by an Intelligence Division G-2 colonel concluded that the evidence that Japan had been developing nuclear weapons could not be ignored. Finally, there is the item that Wilcox started his book with, and which potentially is the most important evidence so far of how the Japanese nuclear work had progressed by 1945. David Snell had been an agent with the 24th Criminal Investigation Detachment in Korea, and later worked for *Life* magazine as a correspondent. In 1946 Snell had interviewed a Japanese Army officer returning to Japan from Korea, where he had been in charge of security for the atomic bomb project at Konan (Hungnam). What Snell took down from the officer and what Wilcox quoted was that on 10 August 1945 (the Hiroshima bomb was on 6 August, Nagasaki on 9 August and Japan surrendered on 14 August), Japan's nuclear weapon was transported from an underground factory near Konan (perhaps at the end of the rail track north of Konan) to the coast, where it was loaded on to a small radio-controlled motor boat. At dawn on 12 August the motor boat, complete with weapon, was guided along the coast and eventually beached on a small island some twenty miles from the observers. A few seconds later the device was exploded in a huge ball of flame, estimated to be 1,000 yards in diameter, complete with the now familiar mushroom-shaped cloud. Japan had successfully tested its first atomic bomb. The scientists and engineers who had organized the test returned quickly to the underground factory and destroyed documents and equipment, plus other completed nuclear weapons, as the Russians were only hours away.

The Japanese weapon was part of the Navy programme, the F-go project which had been largely independent of the earlier Army and Navy nuclear work.

The bombs were to be used in kamikaze aircraft attacks when the Americans invaded the home islands.

This is the gist of the article written by Snell and quoted in Wilcox's book, but there is one further twist to the story. During the Korean war, some US marines were retreating from the Chosen area when they came across an underground factory in a huge cave. It appeared to be a weapons assembly plant, as equipment was still in place and there were radiation warning notices on the walls. A few sketches with dimensions were quickly made of the site, but no detailed examination could be made due to the imminent arrival of enemy forces The opening was sealed with explosives and the marines departed in haste, but eventually a report on their findings was written, and to some extent it is part of the folklore of the US Marine Corps.

This, then, is part of the background to Japanese nuclear weapons in the Second World War. The main theme of the story, that Japan had progressed far enough to actually build and test a nuclear weapon, is not part of the official history of Japan in the Second World War, and virtually all historians take the same line, but we shall assemble all the evidence in the final chapter.

CHAPTER 9

Assembling the Jigsaw

THE GERMAN PIECES

There can be little doubt that in the Second World War, German scientists and engineers were interested, not only in the use of nuclear power for commercial use, but also in its use as a weapon. If a well-known chemistry professor, Paul Harteck, can write from Hamburg to the War Ministry explaining the potential military advantages of nuclear weapons only weeks after the discovery of fission in 1939, then I think we can assume that he was not alone in his thinking; university professors do not usually write to governments without consulting someone at the university in higher authority. Although the reasons why Professor Harteck contacted the military establishment become almost irrelevant, and his cannot have been a major influence, nevertheless from about this time the German military officially became interested in nuclear energy. The next question is, how seriously did the military and the scientists take the prospect of building a nuclear weapon, or indeed using nuclear energy for any other military purpose, such as the motive power for submarines, since the fission process did not require air, or even rockets being designed and built at the new establishment of Peenemünde? For probably two or three years after 1939, any nuclear work proceeded at a low level of priority, as did other new weapons, including the work at Peenemünde, even though it was the most expensive project in the history of the Wehrmacht. The military facts in Germany were that by the summer of 1942, despite not quite achieving the military objectives in Russia, objectives which were staggering for any military organization, and if achieved would have virtually finished Russia, the armed forces of the Third Reich either controlled most of Europe and North Africa directly or could count on assistance if necessary from countries which were either collaborators or neutral. A quick look at a map of Europe at the height of Axis power in 1942 shows the situation better than any words. There was something like euphoria in the air of the German military as they contemplated what had happened, despite the doubters, in such a short period of time. This atmosphere can be illustrated by a report written in May 1942 to outline the Einsatzaufgaben fur Fernstflugzeuge (Special Tasks for the Long Distance Transport Organization) of the Luftwaffe. Proposed routes are shown in four different categories: military routes, supply routes to Japan, US military supply routes, heavy transport routes over hostile territory.

What is surprising is the envisaged world-wide network of transport routes for the Luftwaffe, almost as if there was no likelihood of any opposition to the plans because the enemy would no longer pose any serious threat. The aircraft to be used were the long-range Me264, Ju200, Ju290 and He177 aircraft, with the Blohm and Voss 222 seaplanes being refuelled at sea where necessary. If this somewhat unreal atmosphere was being taken seriously in the Luftwaffe's transport organization, then it is not surprising that the rocket and nuclear work was just being maintained 'ticking over'. It had taken Peenemünde nearly four months to launch the first three V2 test vehicles as they laboured under this lack of urgency, and the nuclear work was struggling under an even greater inertia. Compared to the advances in nuclear physics that had taken place in Germany immediately prior to the war, from 1940 to 1943 very little new information was added to this knowledge. Some indifferent research by Bothe, using impure graphite, resulted in the mistaken conclusion that the thermal neutron absorption cross-section of graphite was too high to make it a suitable moderator for reactor use. Other basic research was being undertaken by others, including Harteck on zero-energy low-temperature reactors and Diebner on heavy-water-moderated natural uranium reactor design, with War Ministry funding. Heisenberg and his group were working on reactor experiments at Leipzig, using the layer concept of uranium and moderator that was the least likely to succeed. However, on 26 February 1942 Heisenberg gave a lecture at the House of German Research in which he outlined the current nuclear situation regarding reactors and weapons. Despite the lecture being low key, with no really important personages in the Third Reich being present, Heisenberg did mention three things which were significant. Firstly he referred to the new element with an atomic number of 94 (plutonium) as being a powerful explosive which could be separated from uranium by chemical means and hence would be relatively easy to obtain; secondly he referred to the use of nuclear power in submarines; and finally he mentioned that beryllium was being investigated as a suitable moderator. Here we have one of the first signs of an apparent contradiction in German nuclear work. Heisenberg's lecture gave no indication of any major advances in reactor design, but at the same time, in an apparently casual 'throw-away' statement, he referred to three items which were to become indispensable elements of nuclear power – plutonium, nuclear submarines and beryllium.

Following the lecture, the Minister of Education, Bernhard Rust, decided that one of his departments, the Reich Research Council, should have some involvement in nuclear research, and Abraham Esau, head of the Physics Office at the Ministry, was put in charge, a move that resulted in increased government interest in nuclear work. Although Heisenberg has led historians to believe that he was the main influencing factor in German nuclear work, we know that, apart from Diebner at the War Ministry, there were also Manfred von Ardenne and physicist Fritz Houtermans who were linked to Dr Ohnesorge and the Reichspost. Houtermans had written a report on plutonium for the War Ministry in August 1941, and the Research Institute (Forschungsansalt) of the Post Office had been asked by Peenemünde in October 1942 to look at the possibilities of using nuclear energy for rocket propulsion. Another new figure appeared on the nuclear scene in 1942. This was Albert Speer, the young, dynamic new Minister for Armaments and Munitions, and the Head of the Organisation Todt, appointed to the posts after Todt's fatal plane crash on 9 February 1942. Speer was not long in trying to get to grips with the nuclear programme. On 4 June 1942, probably at Speer's request, Heisenberg, Hahn, Harteck, Bothe, von Ardenne and others presented the case for nuclear power at the Kaiser Wilhelm Institute in Berlin. Apart from Speer, those present included senior Army, Navy and Air Force officers and their technical advisers. At this meeting Heisenberg was asked by Field Marshal Milch what size of nuclear weapon was required to destroy a city. Heisenberg came out with his much disputed reply, 'as large as a pineapple', or in other words a few kilograms of U.235. Speer evidently came away from this meeting believing that progress was being made towards the building of a working reactor, and eventually a bomb; that the Allies were unlikely to be further advanced than Germany; and that a concentrated industrial effort was not needed, which would have taken the project largely out of Heisenberg's sphere of influence.

This was exactly what was beginning to happen at Peenemünde. Speer must have realized very quickly that Dornberger and von Braun, despite their achievements with the V2, were not the right people the get the V2 organized for mass production. By the end of 1942, Speer was bringing into the rocket project experts from industry to take over key roles in the mass-production programme. It is worthwhile considering for a moment one example of Speer's contribution to the German war effort, since this gives some idea of his abilities in the face of ever-increasing Allied bombing. In 1942 German aircraft and tank production were 60 per cent and 73 per cent respectively of those in the UK. In 1943 the figures were 95 per cent and 160 per cent, and in 1944 they were 149 per cent and 413 per cent, an increase in German production which was quite amazing in the circumstances. Hence, I think we can assume that Speer's ideas worked, and since he was a protégé of Hitler, he could bank on being able to get the Führer's ear when he needed it. In this case Speer was not long in acquainting Hitler of what was required for the rocket programme, especially with regard to the sites in France. On 25 March 1942, Speer outlined to Hitler what was required, and this meeting resulted in an order from Hitler to Peenemünde regarding the construction of the launching site bunkers in northern France.

As we have already seen, 1943 had started badly for the German war machine, and it was getting worse. There was no aspect of the Wehrmacht that was now immune from defeat: the Army in Russia at Stalingrad, Kursk and in North Africa; the Navy and the unacceptable U-boat losses in the Atlantic; and the Luftwaffe and its failure, firstly in the Battle of Britain, and now in its inability to stop the mass-bombing raids on German cities.

All these problems were highlighting the fact that the conventional armed forces of Germany were unable to cope with the combined military resources of the Allies. There is no doubt that one of the crucial psychological, as well as purely military, events was the Army's defeat at Kursk. Of the three branches of the armed forces, the German Army had signified what had been, up till then, the superiority of men, arms and organization. But now, they were suffering from the same problems that they had inflicted on others. As well they might do, since figures found after the war showed that, up to D-Day, 85 per cent of all German military casualties (killed, wounded, missing) occurred in Russia. The end was not a foregone conclusion, but changes were needed and they were needed with some urgency. One of the most obvious candidates for the spotlight was the V2 and Peenemünde. Dornberger and von Braun were ordered to Hitler's headquarters in Rastenburg, East Prussia, for a V2 presentation, complete with films and models, on 6/7 July, one day after the start of Operation Zitadelle at Kursk.

Hitler perhaps had a premonition that Zitadelle was doomed. On the spot, Dornberger was promoted to Major-General and von Braun was awarded the title of Professor. Ideas for a larger rocket were discussed, as Hitler wanted a ten-ton warhead, but instead he agreed, for the time being, that V2 monthly production should be increased to 2,000, adding up to a total of 30,000 by October 1944. Speer and mass-production expert Degenkolb arrived at Rastenburg on 8 July, to be given the new orders for V2 production at Friedrichshafen and Wiener-Neustadt, but noticeably there were no new arrangements made for the V1, HDP or Rheinböte.

Perhaps nerves were jangling in other high places too. Dr Görnnert in Goering's office in Berlin received a report on the nuclear progress from Rudolph Menzel, Head of the Reich Research Council. In the letter, Menzel said that he was enclosing a report from Dr Esau on the situation regarding nuclear research, and that things had progressed well in the last few months, but that the construction of a reactor or nuclear weapon would not be possible in the immediate future, although, he added, it was unlikely that the enemy would have any surprises for them. Although we do not know if Goering actually requested the information at this time, it is a surprising coincidence that the letter is dated 8 July 1943, three days after the start of Zitadelle, and certainly by this time Goering would have been aware of the Army's problems at Kursk. Enclosed with the letter was a sketch of one of Diebner's reactor experiments for the HWA at Gottow; although criticality was not reached, the experiment was technically advanced for 1943, using natural uranium cubes suspended in a moderator of heavy water (about 1.5 tons), the core being enclosed in a graphite reflector to reduce the number of neutrons absorbed into the surrounding structure, which was enclosed in a concrete shield. At the centre of the core was a tube for a neutron source to 'kick-start' the fission process into action, and neutron-absorbing control rods were used. The advantages of using widely spaced lumps of fuel are that some neutrons will slow down to energies less than those at resonance without contacting the fuel, hence they will escape capture and be available for fission; and larger fuel lumps means that resonance neutrons are absorbed at the outer edges of the fuel, leaving the interior protected, which is known as 'self-shielding'.

This reactor design is not that much different in concept and dimensions from the American CP-3 reactor which is claimed to be the world's first heavy-water reactor and dates from May 1944, almost a year later than Diebner's experiment.

The CP-3 reactor used an aluminium tank, 6 ft (1.8 m) in diameter × 8.8 ft (2.7 m) high, and used 3 tons of natural uranium rods, 6.5 tons of heavy water and a reflector of graphite 2 ft (0.6 m) thick. If Diebner's reactor experiment had used more uranium and hence the core had contained more U.235, plus perhaps an extra 2 tons of heavy water, then it is more than likely that it would have become critical, for there was certainly nothing wrong with the reactor technically – it was the quantities being used which were the main problem.

The most important factor in the rocket story now appears on the scene after the bombing of Peenemünde on 17 August 1943 and other factories scheduled for V2 mass production. Before the dust had settled at Peenemünde, Himmler sent Ernst Kaltenbrunner, Head of the SS Security Service, the SD, to carry out an on-the-spot investigation of the suspected security leak that had led the Allies to bomb Peenemünde. Things began to move quickly now, and from 19 to 22 August, Himmler was at Hitler's HQ, persuading him that not only should test-launches of the V2 be carried out under SS control and at an SS site, but that V2 production should be moved to a bomb-proof underground factory. Speer and Saur were informed of the SS involvement on 20 August, and Himmler also informed them that SS-Brigadeführer (Major-General) Dr Hans Kammler would be responsible for implementing the organizational changes. On 26 August, Kammler informed all those involved with the rocket project, including Speer and Dornberger, that:

1. The new underground factory for the V2 was to be at Nordhausen, to be known as Mittelwerk (Central Works). The SS were already responsible for 'administration' in the Nordhausen area with SS-Standartenführer (Colonel) Dr Wagner, and he would be the initial SS representative on the project.
2. The new test site for V2 launches was to be at the SS training ground, Blizna in Poland.
3. A new underground assembly, test and development facility for all future rocket work was to be built at Lake Traunsee in Austria, Projekt Zement.

Pressure was now on Peenemünde to freeze any further changes to the V2 in order to prepare it for mass production, and on 9 September von Braun officially announced that the V2 design was finalized. This, of course, only applied to the standard V2, and variants such as the modified V2 were not affected by his statement; also, the air-burst problem had still not been completely solved, and it would remain unresolved until the centre of the fuselage was strengthened with an additional Korsett.

So what did the huge Peenemünde organization do with its design offices, test laboratories, wind-tunnels, etc., between October 1943 and May 1945, more than eighteen months? Officially, on 8 and 24 January 1945 they launched two V2s with wings, the A9 project, meant to extend the range of the V2 to over 300 miles. Other than that, plus some work on the Wasserfall anti-aircraft rocket, some improvements to the V2 and designing an 'arrow' shell for Schlanke Berta, we are led to believe that this was the sum total of their main activities, which is incredible and another of the Dornberger and von Braun post-war fairytales.

However, not only did the V2 receive an impetus, so did the other three weapons in Hitler's armoury, and their projected operational debuts varied from

December 1943 for the V1 to the summer of 1944 for the HDP, with dates in between for the V2 and Rheinböte. The delay for the HDP was due to the fact that the only way of concealing the 300–400 ft barrel in the relatively bare countryside of northern France was to bury it in one of the few hills in the Pas de Calais. This meant that a substantial firing site was required, and in August 1943 it wasn't even started.

So, what was happening in the search for a nuclear weapon? We know the official story: very little was happening. But what new evidence do we now have that throws a different light on the official story; and what of the original evidence: can we now look at this and say, 'These two together are all part of the jigsaw'?

Heisenberg and Weizsacker had visited von Ardenne in Berlin, at his Lichterfeld house and laboratory in 1940 and 1941, and according to von Ardenne, when the subject was brought up, Heisenberg came out with the statement that a few kilograms of U.235 would be enough for a bomb, a statement later denied by Heisenberg. In February 1942, the Heereswaffenamt, HWA, issued a long report on nuclear progress. The report was put together by Diebner, and towards the end, the report referred to the new element with an atomic number of 94 (now known as plutonium), whose critical mass for an explosive should be 10–100 kg (22–220 lb). Where Diebner obtained his figures from, which are quite accurate, depending on the purity of the Pu.239 (the Fat Man bomb dropped on Nagasaki used 6.2 kg (13.6 lb)), is not known, but it is more than likely that the HWA report was seen and commented on by Heisenberg.

At the end of 1943, Speer must have realized that work on producing a nuclear weapon was going nowhere fast, and Abraham Esau, officially supervising the non-Army aspects of the work through the Reich Research Council, was shuffled off sideways on 1 January 1944, and Walter Gerlach took his place. Gerlach was as different from Esau as it was possible to get: an established physicist and a professor at Munich since 1929, he was not a dedicated Nazi, but was certainly able to ensure that the proper resources were provided for any nuclear work that had any chance of being successful. In other words, Gerlach was not going to be misled by experiments that were going nowhere and requests for money and materials that were inappropriate for the work involved.

The Allied bombing was beginning to seriously intrude on everyone's nuclear experiments. In August 1943 Harteck had been forced to move his reactor and isotope work from Hamburg to Freiburg in southern Germany. Leipzig was badly hit in December, and Heisenberg's laboratory at the university, and his house, were destroyed, although his wife and children had already moved to Bavaria. The KWI at Dalhem was a special target, since Allied Intelligence was aware of its scientific connections, and although the new underground nuclear laboratory was undamaged, other facilities were wrecked, including Hahn's chemistry laboratories, in a particularly heavy raid in February 1944. Hahn and Heisenberg were already beginning to organize their move south, to Tailfingen and Haigerloch respectively. These moves were arranged by Gerlach, whose own university at Munich had been virtually destroyed, as well as his home. For the time being, Diebner's work for the HWA at Gottow went undisturbed, and he was the last to move south from the bombing.

But what about Manfred von Ardenne, and his work for the Reichspost and others? We know that by late 1942 his underground laboratory adjoining his house at Lichterfeld-Ost was operational and contained at least one mass spectrograph for isotope separation, and also, possibly, a cyclotron. Houtermans had been working for von Ardenne since 1941, and in August of that year had produced a report which was re-issued in 1943 and 1944. In this report Houtermans frequently refers to explosives derived from reactors, and he also includes a reference to Element 94, plutonium, which could be separated by chemical means. Once again, the subject of Element 94 surfaces as a weapons material, and as in Weizsacker's and Diebner's reports, one of the main points made is that, unlike U.235, which was difficult to isolate in large enough quantities for a weapon, '94' could be obtained from a reactor and separated by a conventional chemical process.

What was happening between von Ardenne's institute and the Reichspost, since officially it was the Post Office that was sponsoring some, if not all, of his nuclear work? Details of this work are missing, but some information is available for early 1944 which give clues to the importance of this work. Figure 29, dated 24 April 1944, includes three items which had come to the notice of US Intelligence regarding von Ardenne and the Reichspost. Firstly there is a mention of a letter from von Ardenne to Dr Ohnesorge, the Post Office Minister, thanking him for his support in obtaining work in nuclear physics. The last two items indicate that two physicists, D. Lyon and S. Flugge, are now working for von Ardenne. Of D. Lyon we know nothing, but Flugge is different. As long ago as June 1939, Siegfried Flugge had produced a report on the possibility of using U.235 and U.238 as explosives. His 1939 report was updated in 1942, and as a colleague of Hahn and Heisenberg at the Kaiser Wilhelm Institute, he would have known of the latest nuclear developments in Germany. Hence, by early 1944, von Ardenne has at least one senior bomb physicist working on his Reichspost contracts. Von Ardenne's scientific abilities were derided by Heisenberg and others after the war, but in 1945 he went to work on Russia's atomic bomb, and his contribution was such that in 1955 he was awarded the Stalin Prize, and he was not even a member of the Communist Party. Later he established a nuclear research organization in Dresden and became the largest private employer in East Germany, also being appointed a member of the East German Volkskammer, the ruling council of the country. Dr Wilhelm Ohnesorge, the Reichspost Minister, one of the very few of Hitler's ministers to survive the war, also disappeared into East Germany at the end of the war. He certainly had many secrets which would have been valuable to the West, but, like von Ardenne, chose the East.

Nuclear physics and work on reactors and weapons was also being infiltrated, like rockets, by the SS. Initially, at least, the SS were not involved directly in nuclear research; it was more a question of certain administration scientists and engineers who were either members of the SS as a symbolic gesture or actually worked for the SS directly. Himmler awarded 'honorary' SS titles to anyone who he judged was sufficiently important and might be useful in the future, and it was usually unwise to refuse such SS membership. Indeed, von Braun was himself an

THE UNIVERSITY OF CHICAGO

DATE April 24, 1944

TO R. R. Furman DEPARTMENT MUC- PM-35

FROM P. Morrison DEPARTMENT

This document consists of 1 pages and 0 figu
No. 1 of 3 copies, Series A

IN RE: The German Reichspost and Nuclear Research

We now have three independent pieces of evidence that the Reichspost is interested in neutron research or wishes us to think that:

1) Several years ago M. von Ardenne thanked the Reichspost minister, a man named Ohnesorge, for supporting the entrance of von Ardenne's laboratory into work in nuclear physics.

2) In October 1943 (Naturwissenschaften, 31, p. 507) a man, otherwise unknown to us, named D. Lyons, published a mathematical letter on the slowing down of neutrons in homogeneous mixtures. The material of the letter is rather similar to much work done in the early days of this project and also in the published sources. Lyons rather ostentatiously signs his letter as coming from the Office for Special Physical Questions of the Research Division of the German Reichspost (Amt fur physikalische Sonderfragen der Forschungsanstalt der Deutschen Reichspost) located in Berlin-Tempelhof.

3) The information from Swiss sources which you showed us this week mentioned that S. Flugge has left Hahn to go to work for the Reichspost.

It will be clear to you that there is something rather odd in this affair of the Reichspost's becoming interested in a field so very far from the radio and telephone research they have carried out in the past. It is equally strange that we learn about it in such a direct way as from Lyons' note, but confirm it in the rather indirect way of (1) and (3) above. I would suggest that you formulate inquiries about the activity of the Reichspost in the Tempelhof laboratories to whoever will know most about that outfit.

P. Morrison
P. Morrison

PM me
cc: K. Cohen

SECRET

This document contains information affecting the national defense of the United States within the meaning of the Espionage Act, U.S.C. 50; 31 and 32. Its transmission or the revelation of its contents in any manner to an unauthorized person is prohibited by law.

Figure 29. Part of a US report about physicists working for Reichspost, dated 24 April 1944.

SS-Sturmbannführer (Major) by 1945. Incidentally, these honorary titles must not be confused with the SS rank held by Kammler and others. Kammler's final rank was SS-Obergruppenführer (General) und General der Waffen SS, the significant item being his Waffen SS title, which was his actual 'working' rank, and the distinguishing factor between his and many of the other honorary SS titles.

Typical of this inter-relationship in the SS was Wilhelm Osenberg, who became Head of the Reich Research Council in March 1943. Osenberg was an SS officer, and he also did some work in the RHSA's Security Office, in its cultural section, IIIC.

One of the most capable of the SS scientists, and typical of how many highly intelligent and qualified young men became working members of the SS, is Helmut Fischer.

Fischer had a PhD in mathematics from the prestigious Heidelberg University, and he became head of the RHSA's Scientific Office, a job which entailed frequent contact with both the Army's HWA and the Reich Research Council, especially on nuclear matters. This also meant he had contact with Heisenberg, Diebner, Gerlach and Ohnesorge of the Reichspost. The bizarre relationship in the SS of those involved in mass-extermination programmes and science is shown by the fact that Fischer's chief in the RHSA was Otto Ohlendorf, who had been in charge of Einsatzgruppen D in 1941/2. Ohlendorf was an intellectual and economist, and another example of the recruitment policy of Himmler. The other three Einsatzgruppen in the East were Group A, Walter Stahlecker (Dr Law); Group B, Arthur Nebe, Head of Criminal Police; Group C, Otto Rasch (Drs Law and Political Science).

Ohlendorf had returned to his 'desk job' later in 1942 as Head of Amt III of the RSHA, and SS-Brigadeführer (Major-General). He was executed for war crimes in 1951. Strangely enough, in January 1945, it was Ohlendorf who persuaded Speer to expedite the completion of Paul Harteck's new heavy water pilot plant, code name SH200, a co-design with Austrian chemist Hans Suess, which was being built by I.G. Farben at their huge Leuna plant. This association between Harteck, heavy water and the SS continued until the end of the war.

The Harteck-Suess heavy-water plant used the fractional distillation system, and even after the war, claims were made by I.G. Farben against the USA for infringing patents on the new heavy-water manufacturing method.

The Ohlendorf-Fischer connection with nuclear reactors and weapons becomes more involved from 1944 onwards. Fischer is believed to have been partly responsible for a document that appeared in October 1944, coming officially via Führer Order No. 219 of 1944, which was concerned with implementing the urgent construction of a nuclear weapon. After the war, a copy of this report eventually found its way to the Wiesenthal Archive in Jerusalem, from where it was brought to the attention of Professor Rose while he was writing his book, *Heisenberg and the Nazi Atomic Bomb Project*. Some details of the report appear in his book. Professor Rose thinks that the report may have originated in the Reichspost, since the word 'Forschungsansalt', Research Institute, appears in the title, and this description was used by the Reichspost for its nuclear organization. It is a lengthy report and it contains many sections where details, including figures relating to calculations, quantities and references, have been omitted by the author. Professor Rose believes that this was either because of lack of time or because the information was just not available to the original author. Some of the topics included in the report are as follows:

1. Reference is made to a reactor experiment where neutron multiplication had been controlled, resulting in a power increase from 0.5 W to 200 W. This implies that the reactor multiplication factor, 'k', had gone slightly beyond 1.0, allowing a controlled power increase. Hence criticality had been achieved, although the additional neutrons could have come from an external neutron source.
2. Comments are made that for both U.235 and Element 94 (plutonium) only fast neutrons would produce an explosion, rather than thermal (slow) neutrons, and that the bomb material would have to be concentrated very quickly in order to avoid incomplete fission in the form of pre-detonation or 'fizzle'.
3. Details of achieving the fast assembly of the fissile material are referred to, and a 'gun-type mechanism' is described. Two bomb types are mentioned, together with details of the casing, timer and detonator, the second bomb design being dropped by a parachute, type AS12/44.
4. The preferable method of delivering the weapon would be by V1 or V2.
5. Four different methods of U.235 separation are quoted: centrifuge, Clauss-Dickl tube, Hertz's membrane diffusion, mass spectrograph.

On a pessimistic note, the author of the report concluded that it would take 100,000 individual items of separation equipment to produce one kilogram of U.235 in 24 hours. Alternatively, a 200 W reactor would take 11,400 years, if it was operating continuously, to produce one kilogram of plutonium. This is not very far out, as a 1,000 MW reactor designed to produce plutonium could produce one kilogram in 24 hours.

The report also refers to Gustav Hertz, who had originally been excluded from the government nuclear work because of his non–Aryan ancestry, but had worked for von Ardenne from 1944, and joined him in working for the Russians from 1945 onwards. Hertz specialized in isotope separation, which was also one of von Ardenne's interests.

Professor Rose is sceptical about exactly how much nuclear reactor and weapons knowledge the author of the report actually had, especially since there are many gaps in the text, where numerical quantities and other technical details are missing. In the author's experience, this omission of certain sections of an unfinished technical report is commonplace where the report's author is awaiting in-puts from other technical sources. The fact that the report discusses the gun-method (as used in the Little Boy Hiroshima bomb) for assembling the fissile material as fast as possible is hardly commented on by Rose, other than to say that the report's author did not realize that this would be too slow for a plutonium weapon. The Little Boy weapon used a modified 3 in bore gun barrel, 6 ft long with the rifling removed, and about 55 lb of U.235 was fired at about 77 lb of U.235 acting as the target, the total of 132 lb being the critical mass of that particular package of U.235, the fission process being kick-started by a burst of neutrons from a polonium/beryllium neutron source at the centre of the U.235 'target.'

What does not seem to have been considered is the obvious situation where two sub-critical masses are fired at each other, colliding in the centre of the gun-barrel with a resultant velocity of 6,000 ft/sec if they are each travelling at 3,000 ft/sec, a simple question of dynamics. Certainly if the Little Boy fissile material had collided at 6,000 ft/sec instead of 3,000 ft/sec, one would expect it to have fissioned more than the reported 25 oz out of the total Little Boy U.235 material of 132 lb, an efficiency of 1.2 per cent. Regardless of how much more efficient such a modified gun-type of weapon would have been, using two sub-critical masses fired towards each other, it would have taken much longer to modify a standard 3 in gun barrel for this type of operation than it did for the actual Hiroshima bomb.

If there was one thing the Manhattan Project did not have by April 1945, it was an abundance of time. No time to test the Hiroshima type of bomb and only one test of the Nagasaki plutonium-type of bomb, and this was a static test compared to the parachute drop and detonation above ground of the Nagasaki bomb.

At Farm Hall on 14 August 1945, Heisenberg also mentioned a gun-type mechanism, but these comments, just as when, on the same date, Heisenberg suddenly produced an accurate figure for the critical mass of U.235 and Pu.239, are dismissed by the US nuclear historians as being guesswork, with no real technical foundation.

However, returning to 1944, two events occurred beyond the control of those working on weapons. On 6 June the Allied forces landed in Normandy, and on 20 July there was an attempt on Hitler's life at his Rastenburg headquarters. The D-Day landings immediately disrupted operational plans for the V1, V2 and Rheinböte in Normandy. Although there were very few weapons sites between the Seine and Cherbourg Peninsula, the Peninsula itself had two large V2 bunker sites, (Sottevast and Brécourt), the silo site, thirty of the new combined simple sites and a number of the original V1 ski sites which were still in operational condition. The Couville site and Tamerville had already been officially written out of the operational plans. The July bomb plot did not cause severe injury to Hitler, though his right arm and leg caught some of the blast and his eardrums were damaged. Of the four who were killed, the most senior was General Gunther Korton, Chief of the Air Staff, a name that reappears later in the story. On the same day as the bomb attempt, Hitler appointed Himmler as successor to General Fromm, one of those implicated in the plot, as Commander of the Reserve Army and Chief of Army Armaments, which included the Heereswaffenamt (HWA). Himmler was now effectively in charge of all the Army rocket projects, including the V2, Rheinböte and HDP, as well as having a direct involvement with Diebner and his nuclear work for the Army. On 6 August, Himmler appointed the newly promoted SS-Gruppenführer (Lieutenant-General) Dr Hans Kammler as his Commissioner, with responsibilities for all the weapons projects. In a somewhat futile attempt to stave off the inevitable, on 1 August Speer and Dornberger planned to turn Peenemünde into a Limited Company, the Elektromechanische Werke GmBH. Siemens Director Paul Storch was appointed General Manager and von Braun Technical Manager, but all to no avail. Despite protests from Speer, the SS and Kammler continued to increase their influence in the rocket programme, so that by the end of September, Kammler was in control of development, production and testing. Nordhausen (Mittelwerk) was now fully operational, producing 600 V2s in September 1944, 650 in October, 650 in November, 618 in December and a further 1,806 from January to March 1945. Of those produced in September and October, 400 were allocated for training and testing. Due to the Allied bombing, scientific work could no longer be carried out in Berlin, and by the middle of 1944, Heisenberg and his team were building a new reactor experiment at Haigerloch, not far from Hahn at Tailfingen. Diebner and his Army team were moving to Stadtilm in the autumn of 1944, where in a requisitioned school building they were working on a nuclear weapon. The choice of Stadtilm for Diebner's final weapons work is highly significant, since within a northerly arc of about 60° and 60 miles in radius from Stadtilm, all the major rocket work was being concentrated by the SS. The V2 and other weapons work was transferred to Bad Sachsa, north of Nordhausen, in late 1944. Satellite rocket factories were set up at the nearby Bleicherode, Sondershausen and Sommerda, with the main assembly work at Klein Bodungen. There were motor test-beds at Lehesten, and liquid oxygen was produced in a nearby railway tunnel. Moving in towards the pivot of the arc near Stadtilm, using forced labour the SS had constructed a huge complex of underground bunkers, to where the political and military organization of the Third Reich was finally going to be moved when Berlin became untenable. Most of the underground facilities were located in Thuringia.

The resources used to construct these underground complexes were enormous, despite the fact that the labour was supplied from special camps set up in the area, satellites of the main concentration camps. The policy of moving the 'heart' of the Third Reich underground must have been based on the assumption that the enemy forces on the ground had been brought to a standstill many miles away. Otherwise there is little point in being underground when the enemy occupies all the territory above you, destroying your freedom of action.

At Bad Salzungen the gold reserves and other objects of value were stored. In the Jonas Valley (Jonastal) and at Ohrdruf were the Führer's HQ and Communications Centre respectively, and the remaining administration was to be carried out from Schmucke. Another underground complex was built at Crawinkel, and this was linked to Ohrdruf and Jonastal. The area was captured by part of General Patton's Third Army, the 4th Armoured Division, and after the war Colonel Robert S. Allen described the Ohrdruf bunker as extending like the spokes of a wheel, 50 ft underground and many miles in length. It was fully equipped with living quarters, recreational facilities, air-conditioning and sewage systems, giant fridges and all the amenities for a small town.

The whole area, including Nordhausen, became part of East Germany after the war, but although Germany is now unified, there have been no official efforts to investigate these underground workings. The fact that these facilities do exist, and considering their intended purpose, has led to speculation as to what actually exists underground. Among the rumours and claims of strange occurrences in the Ohrdruf-Jonastal area in particular are stories of strong magnetic fields, strange lighting effects and the most bizarre claim, that a thick electric power cable was discovered, with one section above ground. The cable was 'live', and when it was cut, no power losses were reported in the surrounding areas, leading to further speculation that there is a generator still functioning underground after sixty years.

We are now into 1945. Diebner and the Army weapons team were established in the school at Stadtilm, Heisenberg and his group were preparing a reactor experiment at Haigerloch and Hahn was nearby at Tailfingen. At Stadtilm and Haigerloch they had between them several tons of heavy water, graphite and uranium oxide, the exact quantities of which are unknown, but certainly the amount of heavy water must have been at least five tons and perhaps as much as twenty. In 1939 the only commercial producer of heavy water in Europe was Norsk-Hydro at Rjukan, information that was well known to all those interested in nuclear research. The output of heavy water in 1939 was about 250 lb per year, but after the Germans arrived in April 1940 the plant was taken over by I.G. Farben, and with the assistance of Paul Harteck, additional equipment was installed which increased production to five tons per year.

Not until February 1943 was part of the heavy-water production plant destroyed by Allied commandos. Then, in November 1943 an Allied bombing raid further damaged the plant, although causing little disruption to the heavy-water section. Nevertheless, these Allied raids convinced the Germans that further attacks were likely, and they decided to transfer the remaining stock of heavy water, about twelve tons, to Germany. The journey involved crossing Lake Tinnsjo, and on 19 February 1944 the railway wagons were shunted aboard a ferry at Tinnoset. However, despite the security guard, during the night Norwegian agents placed explosive charges on board which destroyed the ferry and its cargo while it was crossing the lake the following day.

The vulnerability of the Norsk-Hydro operation had been obvious to the Germans, and Paul Harteck had arranged with I.G. Farben to build a heavy-water plant at their Leuna site, and this was operational by January 1945. Summarizing this information to get a realistic figure of the amount of heavy water available to Diebner and Heisenberg in 1945 is difficult, but the fact that twelve tons was being shipped to Germany in February 1944 indicates that production had been stepped up between 1941 and 1943, from five tons a year to possibly twice that amount. It was unlikely that the twelve tons had been stockpiled for very long because of the urgent need for it in Germany. In addition, Paul Harteck had developed a new method of producing heavy water, and I.G. Farben had built a pilot plant which started production in January 1945. Hence it can be assumed from these various sources that Diebner and Heisenberg had at least five to ten tons. Natural uranium metal or oxide, that is without the U.235 amount increased, was not in short supply because US forces found nearly 1,000 tons of uranium ore near Stassfurt, north of Nordhausen, awaiting processing at the nearby Auer plant.

Germany had produced other nuclear materials, in particular beryllium and zirconium, and the amounts of beryllium quoted in the ULTRA messages are far greater than anything that even the Americans appear to have had available for their nuclear programme, according to Hansen's book. Boron, lithium, neon and thallium were also among the nuclear materials being shipped by submarine to Japan. The cargo-submarine traffic between Germany and Japan from 1944 to 1945 had become well established, and we know from a German report that for 1944 nineteen boats were dispatched to the Far East, of which at least eight reached their destination, six were missing and five were *en route*. For the return trip, twelve boats were dispatched, of which four were missing, five had to return to port and three had arrived at the time the report was written, 5 January 1945. Of these three, two were German and one Japanese (I-29, which was sunk on the return trip). Some boats had reached Penang before 1944, and U-532 arrived on 30 October 1943 and surrendered in Liverpool on 10 May 1945 on the return leg of the trip.

What cargo items were sent to Japan by submarine in 1943/4 which could be classified as nuclear is unknown at the present time. For 1945 the situation is different, and mention has already been made of U-864, U-873, U-234 and U-534, of which both U-873 and U-234 had nuclear cargoes, U-864 may have had nuclear material on board, and U-534 was sunk on 5 May 1945, later to be raised and put on display at Birkenhead. It is certain that it did not contain a nuclear cargo, although the Danish owner is being very secretive about the U-boat's contents.

None of these last boats to leave for Japan reached their destination, all being sunk except U-873 and U-234, which surrendered to the US Navy.

The Allies were now faced with a deadly dilemma: they knew that certain submarines *en route* to Japan in 1945 contained nuclear cargoes, and some of the actual details were known from the loading lists. At least one, U-864, of these submarines leaving Kiel and Bergen for the Far East had been sunk, but here again, the information on which boats had been sunk could not be guaranteed to be 100 per cent accurate.

In addition, the Allies could never be absolutely certain that their code-breakers had received all the relevant messages between Berlin and Tokyo, since the amount of message traffic was enormous and something could have been missed that was crucial. And now there was U-873 and U-234.

U-873 left Norway for Japan on 1 April 1945, and U-234 on 16 April 1945, possibly a day or two before each loading list was transmitted to Tokyo. Before very long it would be clear to the Allies that both U-boats had slipped through the anti-submarine patrols and were on their own in the vastness of the Atlantic, almost impossible to track down. The loading list had most likely revealed some, if not all, of the details of their nuclear cargo, and there was now something else for Washington to think about.

In fact there had been something for Washington to think about, apart from nuclear weapons, since November. PRO file W0 219/298 may not give the

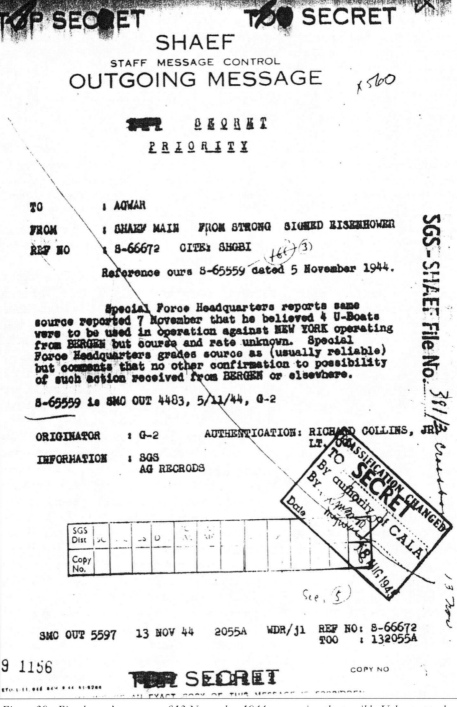

Figure 30. Eisenhower's message of 13 November 1944 concerning the possible U-boat attack on New York using V1s.

complete story, but at least it gives us some idea of the problem. The first Top Secret message is from SHAEF HQ (Supreme HQ Allied Expeditionary Force) in Europe, signed by Eisenhower and dated 1 November 1944. The message reads:

'To: AGWAR CITE WDGBI
Following passed for what it is worth.
Special Force report quoting Danish source states U-boat will be leaving European waters shortly to launch V-1s against NEW YORK.
Date of report 30 October.'

Seven more messages followed between SHAEF and AGWAR as an attempt was made to verify the information and Allied Naval sources confirmed that it was technically possible to launch a V1 from a U-boat.

One of the messages, dated 13 November, is shown in Figure 30 and shows that the number of U-boats had grown to four and that the departure point was Bergen, although no details of course and date were available.

This information must have set the alarm bells ringing again in Washington. One can imagine the sort of discussion that was taking place. A V1 could be launched from a U-boat, as it was little different from launching a float-plane from the foredeck, and many nations had submarines capable of this, but the submarine would also need a watertight hangar to store the missiles. The V1 could be dismantled and stowed inside the U-boat, but it would take some time to reassemble it for flight, a dangerous occupation in the seas around New York. As far as the US knew, no U-boats had been fitted with a hangar on the deck, but any form of attack on New York, from conventional explosives to warheads filled with gas, chemicals or nuclear material, had to be taken seriously and now we know there was a V1 designed to carry a nuclear payload (Figure 23). Allied sea and air patrols around the Norwegian U-boat bases were increased. The U-boats were safe underneath eighteen feet of concrete in the submarine pens, but once they were in the North Sea it was a different matter. Since the date of the first warning message about the V1 attack was 1 November, and the comment was that 'U-boat will be leaving European waters shortly', it is reasonable to assume that the Allies believed that December or early 1945 was the proposed date for the attack, and this was the period when Allied anti-U-boat forces could be expected to be assembled in the general New York area. If the submarine hunters were in the North Atlantic, this would give any submarine heading south a better chance of getting past the Azores, which was becoming something of a 'black spot' for submarines travelling between Germany and Japan. The only known submarine leaving for Japan in December was U-864, a Type IXD2, under Raif-Reimar Wolfram, which left Kiel in December 1944 for Bergen. It was damaged in an air raid on the submarine pens at Bergen, and did not leave for Penang until 9 February 1945. The loading list for U-864, German codename 'Caesar', was transmitted from Berlin to Tokyo on 28 February (ULTRA 1623 refers), and the list is unusually explicit about the cargo, which included technical drawings for the Me163 and 262, Junkers, BMW, Walter and Zeiss, but the only items not identified were 'Reference material for engineers travelling on board'. These were described as 'CASPAR 63: total 69 packages'. Now, Caspar was one of the 'three wise men', travelling to Bethlehem with gifts of incredible value, and so these unidentified packages must have been something special. U–864 was unlucky, because the day it left Bergen it was torpedoed while submerged by HM Submarine *Venturer*, but the news was not transmitted from Berlin to Tokyo until 4 April 1945 (ULTRA 1777 refers). This message confirmed that U–864 was missing, presumed lost, and that the German engineers on board were Klingensberg and Schmers, together with Japanese engineer Yamato and 'temporary official' Nakai of Mitsubishi. Nakai had apparently been studying 'the chemicals used in rocket aircraft', and his father, a DSc, was a teacher at the Imperial University.

In general, though, December and January U-boat activity from Norway had gone quiet, which might have given the impression that the V1 attack on New York had been abandoned. And then suddenly, from the middle of February, it all changed. In the space of a few days at least nine boats left, heading north: U–518, 530, 546, 548, 879, 880, 995,1001 and 1230. By April, all these boats were clear of the Allied U-boat patrols in the North Sea, and in addition both the 'nuclear' boats, U–873 and U–234, left Norway for Japan, and they also escaped the patrols.

The story now takes another twist. Paul Just, commander of U–546, writing after the war, says he received a message on 18 April from U-boat Command, in which he and five other boats were ordered to form a search line on 20 April only 100 miles wide in the vicinity of the New York–England convoy route. To Paul Just this was madness, but there was radio silence and it could not be queried. Six boats in such a small area was suicide, and so it turned out. Four boats, U–518, 546, 880 and 1235, were sunk between 15 and 24 April in an area north-west of the Azores, although Just and 32 crew members survived. The identity of the other two boats is not certain, but one was probably U–530, which was in the New York area at the time, and ignoring surrender orders, sailed to South America, reaching the River Plate on 11 July 1945.

What is certain is that in the latter half of April, both U–873 and U–234 were in the North Atlantic heading south towards the Azores, and if the US U-boat hunters were diverted north towards the New York area, both U–873 and U–234 would stand a better chance of getting through to Japan.

This decoy plan has all the hallmarks of Kammler: if six U-boats and their crews had been lost but U–864, U–873 and U–234 had got through, the end would have justified the means.

But what of the original New York warning messages in November, the first referring to one U-boat leaving shortly? The only U-boat leaving in December of any real military significance had been U–864, with its unidentified 69 'CASPAR 63' packages. Because these items were apparently stowed inside the U-boat, we can assume that they were not radioactive. If so, were they parts for a nuclear reactor, was 'CASPAR 63' the '2,000 or more core clamps, Kernehaspe' referred to in the order sent from Tokyo to Berlin on 16 January 1945 (ULTRA 1443 refers)? It was still three weeks before U-864 left Bergen, and the parts could have been easily flown from Germany to be loaded before 9 February, complete with the engineers who were familiar with them.

The last message in PRO file WO 219/298 is dated 18 November 1944, but it is likely that more warnings followed early in 1945 to keep Allied Intelligence alert to a later attack on New York, for by 18 November the number of U-boats involved had increased to four. If there were later warnings, this would explain the six U-boats used as decoys in April 1945.

Certainly, there has never been any information that indicated that a U-boat had been modified to launch a V1.

If General Groves and Washington were now living on a diet of crises, as is very often the case, things could only get worse. Part of the ALSOS mission, oblivious to what was happening at sea, arrived at Stadtilm on 12 April, and Dr Fred Wardenburg, an ALSOS physicist, sent a message to the senior nuclear physicist on the mission, Samuel Goudsmit, in Paris: 'Sam, ALSOS has found another goldmine, Pash' (Boris Pash was the mission's chief).

What ALSOS had found at Stadtilm was actually very little in terms of hardware, as all the equipment and materials had gone, including several tons of heavy water and uranium, spirited away by the SS. What they did find was some documentation, obviously not the most important, plus a very talkative Dr Berkei, who, in the words of Fred Wardenburg, 'knew everything about Stadtilm and Haigerloch'.

We now come to what must have been shattering news to Groves and Washington, especially since only a few months earlier, after ALSOS had captured the first German nuclear physicists and some of their papers at Strasbourg University, Boris Pash had informed General Groves that the USA had nothing to fear from a German nuclear weapon. General Groves now learned from Pash that at Stadtilm, the Army weapons people had a betatron and details of the 'target' material, that is the material being bombarded by the high-energy particles in the betatron. What General Groves in Washington did not know was for how long the betatron had been operating and how many others there might be in secret locations. The other worrying factor was that no nuclear equipment or material had been found at either Stadtilm or Haigerloch. Why had it been removed, the war being almost over, or were there still some surprises hidden underground in the mountains? General Patton's forces, which had reached the Ohrdruf area on 11 April, had no time to examine all the underground workings, but there was no doubt that they were something special.

One of the scientists captured near Stadtilm was Dr Ernst Stuhlinger, one of Peenemünde's senior engineers, an expert on rocket propulsion and fuels, and one of those who eventually accompanied von Braun to America. What was Dr Stuhlinger doing in Stadtilm?

Not only had a senior Peenemünde engineer been found at a nuclear weapons site, but a senior nuclear physicist, Pascal Jordan, had been traced to Peenemünde. Jordan was an old student colleague of Heisenberg's and had studied under Max

Born at Heidelberg, helping him to unravel some of the secrets of the atom. Both Stuhlinger and Jordan had the sort of status that guaranteed that they must have been involved with some important work connected with rockets and nuclear physics, and they would have not been alone; at least they would have had a team working for them. Washington needed answers to these questions fast, but at least there was one possible factor in their favour: both U-boats would take about three months to reach Japan, and Germany should have surrendered long before then. Here again, nothing was clear-cut. Suppose they refused to heed the surrender messages and decided to press on regardless to Japan? The USA could not send an individual message to them demanding their surrender, since this would obviously imply that the USA knew the importance of the cargo, and especially of U-234, and give the game away immediately. In the background was always the recurring question, 'What if another U-boat has already reached Japan with a similar nuclear cargo to that in U-234?' They had no absolute guarantee that another nuclear cargo had not already arrived or was on its way to Japan ahead of U-234. The others included not only surface ships and submarines, but air transport, and there is no doubt that air transport was used, though what is not certain is how many flights took place, as the evidence is conflicting. The main advantage of using submarines was the fact that they could carry large amounts of cargo, 200 tons was not unusual, but the disadvantage was the length of time, at least three months, it took to reach Japan or vice versa. Air transport was much faster, as it could take as little as 35 hours non-stop, but the amount of cargo was limited, and a Ju290 with additional fuel tanks and armament removed might be able to carry between one and two tons of cargo.

From the middle of 1942, Japanese conquests in the Pacific and their occupation of Manchuria and parts of China provided three main air routes from Europe. PRO file WO 208/120 gives the intended routes based on Allied Intelligence as at May 1942. The routes were:

1. Northern Route.
   Landplanes: Scandinavia–Tsitsihar(China)–Tokyo.
   Seaplanes: Finland(Lake Oulu Jarvi?)–Dairen–Tokyo.
2. Central Route.
   Land/seaplanes: Rome–Odessa–Nanking/Peking or,
   Rhodes–Van, Turkey (avoiding the Mosul oilfields)–Kabul–Paoto– Peking.
3. Southern Route.
   Rhodes–Arabian Desert–India–Rangoon–Tokyo.
   Alternative landing at Van if Turkey allows it.
   Emergency landing at Akayab.

The keen interest shown by Japan in starting an air-link between Germany and Japan was demonstrated by an ULTRA message, no. 1846, dated 4 September 1942, from Tokyo to the Japanese Naval Attaché in Berlin, which lists the landing points for the southern route and ends with the statement, 'Since we are anxious to put this air-link into operation as soon as possible . . .'. Despite this interest from Japan in starting an air-link by the southern route, there were concerns to avoid territory still

```
AM WHI

STN X


1                              1014 GMT                    TP

TO:-   AI.4.E FOR AI.3.B

        FOR F.O. FRANK

FROM:-   RAF SCTN   GC AND CS

11TH APRIL 1942

ZIP/ASI   NO 9467    --.87.
```

ITALIAN AIR ATTACHE TOKIO, NOW RETURNED TO DUTY, SENT TO
ROME ON 9/4/42 A LONG REPLY TO THE SIGNAL SUMMARIZED IN OUR
A.S.I. NO.OEIY   CONCERNING COMMUNICATION BY AIR BETWEEN ITALY
AND JAPAN.   THE FOLLOWING POINTS CAN BE MADE OUT.

THE SENDER HAD MADE CONTACT WITH THE JAPANESE GENERAL

STAFF AND AIR INTELLIGENCE SERVICE.   THESE WERE IN FAVOUR
OF THE SCHEME AND HAD ASSURED HIM OF THEIR FULLEST CO- OPERATION.
THE GENERAL STAFF APPROVED THE SUGGESTION OF THE AIR
INTELLIGENCE SERVICE THAT ALL DETAILS CONCERNING THE FLIGHT
SHOULD BE DISCUSSED BETWEEN THE AIR INTELLIGENCE SERVICE
AND THE SENDER AND BY HIM COMMUNICATED TO THE AIR MINISTRY IN
ROME (FOR DISCUSSION WITH THE JAPANESE (?AIR ATTACHE) THERE).
THE JAPANESE AUTHORITIES HOWEVER DID NOT AVPEAR TO FAVOUR THE
PROPOSED ROUTE AND (SUGGESTED) A MORE NORTHERLY ROUTE:
ROME - PAUPING - (TOKIO). THE FIRST (QUESTION TO BE DECIDED)
WAS THAT OF THE ROUTE, AND THE NEXT THAT OF THE TYPE OF
PLANE TO BE EMPLOYED.

THE NAME OF COLONEL SHIMYS/ SHIMITSU IS MENTIONED BUT IS
NOT CLEAR WHAT PART HE IS PLAYING IN THE NEGOTIATIONS.

CTNS WORD AFTER 9467 TO READ AA. 87
WORD AFTER SHOULD BE TO READ DISCUSSED
WORD AFTER DID NOT TO READ APPEAR
IN LAST PARAGRAPH PLEASE INSERT THE WORD IT AFTER

MENTIONED BUT
PASSED TO H.Q. R.A.F.   M.E. IN SUMM NO 204
TIME SENT 1020 GMT FMW +++

Figure 31. RAF decode of a message from Tokyo to Rome, dated 11 April 1942.

```
                       J
     M5
     MOST SECRET : OFFICER ONLY
     TO: D.M.I.
         D.N.I.
       D.D.I.3 AIR MINISTRY
      FROM: DUTY OFFICER HUT 3
     MOST SECRET.
     =============
                 THE FOLLOWING SUMMARY OF B.J. 110022 AND 110015 HAS BEEN
     PASSED AS ULTRA 26 TO DELHI FOR A.HQ INDIA AT REQUEST OF D.D.I.3
               TOKYO INFORMED ROME ON 2ND OCTOBER THAT SECOND ROME-TOKYO
     FLIGHT COULD NOT TAKE PLACE OVER NORTHERN ROUTE AS PREPATAIONS
     ON THE SOUTHERN ROUTE WERE ADVANCED.   JAPANESE INSISTED
     SECRECY AS TO FLIGHT SHOULD BE OBSERVED.   ON OCTOBER 11TH. ROME
     INFORMED TOKYO THAT BOSE WOULD LEAVE ITALY BY AIR FOR JAPAN ON
     OR AFTER 15TH. OCTOBER. INFERENCE THAT FLIGHT WILL BE MADE IN
     MID-OCTOBER BY SOUTHERN ROUTE.
      B/A/W                      HSM/MS                 2115/15/10/42 GMT
      CCN 4TH LINE LAST GP TO READ ...PREPARATIONS
      SENT BY BB/DC+
       RD TKS VBC
```

Figure 32. RAF decode of a message from Tokyo to Rome, dated 15 October 1942.

in Russian hands. Japan had signed a Five-Year Non-Aggression Pact with Russia on 13 April 1941; and with Germany, Japan's ally, now locked in mortal combat with Russia, Japan did not want to risk an 'incident' that might threaten her Manchurian border with Russia, if a German plane on its way to Japan landed in Russia. For Germany, the problem with an air-link in September 1942 was that they did not have suitable military aircraft for such extended flights. The Luftwaffe had only two aircraft types suitable as long-distance transports, the FW200 Condor and the Blohm und Voss BV222 Wiking flying boat. The FW200 was originally a civilian transport, and by the time it had been modified to suite Luftwaffe requirements with defensive armament, protection for the crew and general strengthening of the airframe, it was on the limits of its range for such flights. The BV222 was never available in large numbers, and by the end of 1942 only three examples were flying, and these were required for more urgent duties, including supplying the Afrika Korps in Tripoli. In addition to the lack of suitable aircraft, the supply situation in Germany regarding materials from Japan, such as tungsten, rubber, tin and opium, was not critical, and so this removed any urgency from the planning. It was different in Japan, where the value and superiority of German developments in electronics, alloy steels, chemicals and military hardware was recognized.

From the available ULTRA messages, it appears that the first flight to Japan was by Italy, and this flight and the Italy–Japan link in general was discussed in three messages dated 8 and 11 April and 15 October 1942, of which two are shown in Figures 31 and 32. The message of 8 April 1942 between Rome and Tokyo is brief, mentioning only that the proposed air-link was being discussed, and that the route was Rome–Oman–Bangkok. The relevant points of the three messages are:

1. BJ is the abbreviation for Britain–Japan, given the code name 'Black Jumbos' by British Intelligence for all Japanese Diplomatic messages using the 'Purple' machine.
2. Bose refers to the Indian Nationalist leader Subhas Chandra Bose, who eventually left Europe in U-180 and transferred to Japanese submarine I-29 on 27 April 1943, south of Madagascar.
3. The route favoured by Italy, Rhodes–Oman–Bangkok, could be undertaken by a flying boat, since all these locations were sea-based. The more northerly route preferred by Japan, Rome–Pauping–Tokyo, also had reasonable access to the sea. Pauping is probably a misspelling for Peiping, now known as Beijing, China, and under Japanese control in 1942.
4. From the message of 11 April 1942, it is clear that the Japanese were fully in favour of the air-link, and as it says, 'had assured him of their fullest cooperation'.
5. Using Rhodes rather than Rome would reduce the distance to Japan by at least 500 miles in each direction.

The Italians had a history of long-distance flights in the 1930s, and in 1930 and 1933, using the Savoia-Marchetti S55 twin-engined flying boat, flights were made from Italy to Brazil non-stop, and from Italy to Chicago via Iceland, Greenland and Labrador, in stages. The S66 was a three-engined development of the S55, and both types were still operational in 1942.

The ULTRA messages do not mention cargo, and there is no confirmation that a second flight took place. Certainly Bose did not go by air to Japan.

By 1943, the supply situation regarding strategic materials was beginning to change, and some items were now becoming scarce, including tungsten (Wolfram) and natural rubber. Several ULTRA decoded messages between Berlin and Tokyo dealt with discussions on the proposed flights. ULTRA 78, dated 15 February 1944, states that an air-link was established in 1943, and although no details are given, it implies it was a German-organized operation. The route question was now becoming one of the major problems from 1944 onwards. The loss of some territory in the Pacific was reducing the number of options for a southern route. The northern routes were safer, but the flight path included passing over parts of Russia, and Japan did want to give that country any pretext to cancel the 1941 Non-Aggression Pact and threaten the Manchurian border.

Subsequent ULTRA messages, including no. 169 dated 6 May 1944, from Berlin to Tokyo, refer to the transfer of the new German Air Attaché to Tokyo, General Kessler, who eventually became one of the passengers on U-234. Other topics raised in ULTRA 169 were the use of Junkers Ju290 or Ju390 aircraft and the necessity to use a northern route which avoided Russian territory, since the southern routes were now impossible due to the rapidly deteriorating Japanese military situation in the Pacific. The availability of the four-engined Ju290 and the possibility of using one of the pre-production six-engined Ju390s had changed the long-distance transport situation in that with extra fuel, both the Ju290 and Ju390 could fly non-stop to Japan via the Polar route. In January 1944, the second prototype Ju390 had flown from the Mont de Marsan Luftwaffe base south of

Bordeaux to a point north of the US coastline near New York and returned safely, confirming its long-distance performance.

ULTRA message 283, dated 7 June 1944, from Berlin to Tokyo, also deals with Kessler's flight, and states, 'also as to the aircraft to be used, they could assign the one that was got ready last time for the Asia–Europe service', implying that the previous flight did not take place. By 20 August 1944 there was an air of urgency in the transfer of Kessler to Tokyo, and ULTRA 698, Berlin to Tokyo, spells out some of the concerns related to the military situation. ULTRA 957, dated 25 September 1944, refers to Kessler and his party either using the several German submarines that were due to leave for Japan towards the end of October, or two Ju290 aircraft. The whole Kessler affair now took another turn, his appointment in Tokyo being cancelled and then reinstated (ULTRA 1506, of December 1944, refers). The final message in the Kessler affair was ULTRA message 1792, Berlin to Tokyo, dated 12 April 1945, only days before the end of Hitler and the Third Reich.

This four-page ULTRA message refers to Kessler flying to Japan in a specially modified Ju290 using a great circle route to avoid Russia, over the North Pole from Bardufoss in Norway to the Bering Strait, across the sea to the east of Kamchatka to Paramushiro Island, Japan. Passengers would be Luftwaffe Major-General Wild, the new senior adviser, 'and one other man already mentioned who would be a passenger', presumably General Kessler. Due to compass problems over the North Pole, astro-navigation would be used and the most suitable dates for this were three days around either 28 April, 20 May or 15 June.

This message raises several questions, including the following:

1. Major-General Wild's Luftwaffe career shows that he was captured in Norway on 8 May 1945 by British troops and detained as a PoW until 1 July 1947, an unusually long time for an ordinary serving officer. If the flight did take place, he was certainly not one of the passengers.
2. Reference to 'one other man already mentioned' appears to be a strange way of referring to General Kessler, if indeed this was the intention.
3. What happened to the Ju290 prepared for the flight to Japan? The date of ULTRA 1792 is five days before Kammler's message to Himmler at SS HQ (see Figure 33), that the Junkers 'truck' was not available.

A Ju290 did leave Germany on 25 April 1945, bound for Barcelona with a group of high-ranking Nazi leaders, this plane, the only Ju290A-6 produced, had originally been intended as Hitler's personal aircraft, but was transferred to KG-200, which was engaged on special missions. However, this particular aircraft was not a long-range version. The aircraft arrived safely in Barcelona and later served with the Spanish Air Force, although the passenger list was never divulged.

There is one further mystery concerning Junkers, and this relates to the Ju390. Only two prototypes were built, Versuch numbers 1 and 2, and although V-1 was found after the war, V-2 was never found.

The mystery of flights to Japan now becomes even more involved, as Washington now realised that they had to worry, not only about submarines, but aircraft as

Funkspruch	+	marconigramma	—	nauiogramma	—	nauiogram
Fernschreiben	±	Telescritto	—	Telegrama	~	Dialkopieny telegram	—	Távirat
Fernspruch	—	Fonogramma	—	Fonograma	—	Telefonný telegram	—	Távmondat
Blinkspruch	±	Fototelegramma	—	Telegrama optica	—	Signalizačný telegram	—	Fénytávirat

Nachr.-Stelle — Posto di collegamento — Unitatea de transm. — Ústredňa (stanica) — Hiradó állomás	Nr. Čis. Szám	Befördert — Trasmesso — Transmis — Odoslaný — Továbbitva				
		an a câtre do hová	Tag Giorno Ziua Dňa Nap	Zeit Ora Ora Hodin Idő	durch da (nome) de câtre telegrafista távirász neve	Rolle Ruolo Rola Svazok (kotúč) Tekercs

Vermerke — Annotazioni — Observațiuni — Záznamy — Megjegyzések

Angenommen oder aufgenommen — Accettato o ricevuto — Primit sau recepționat — Prijal — Átvette vagy felvette			
von — da — de la — odosielateľ — honnan	Tag — Giorno — Ziua — Dňa — Nap	Zeit — Ora — Ora — Hodin — Idő	durch da (nome) — de câtre — telegrafista — távirász neve

++-   GEHEIM -- SVMS . 258 17.4 1190 = =

Dňa — Nap | Hodin — Idő | Důležitost — Sürgősség

AN SS- FHA. AMT ROEM 2 I ORG. ABT. ROEM 1 B/ROEM 5 ==

An — Al — Câtre —
Adresa — Cim:

BETR.: LKW. JUNKERS.-

GEMAESZ FUEHRERBEFEHL GEHEN MASSNAHMEN STRAHLFLUGZEUG(

MILITAERISCHEN VORAUS.-

BIN DESHALB NICHT IN DER LAGE GEWESEN, GEWUENSCHTEN

LKW. FREIZUSTELLEN.==

BAUINSP.D.W.- SS REICH-SUED ,

GEZ. DR.ING. KAMMLER SS-OGRUF. U. GEN. D.WAFFEN-SS +

Figure 33. Kammler's Junkers 'truck' reply to Himmler, dated 17 April 1945. LKW is the abbreviation for 'Lastkraftwagen' – heavy truck.

well. Appendix 3 is the Interrogation Report of General Kessler after his capture on board U-234 by the US Navy. The date of the report is 31 May 1945. U-873 had been unloaded with its two tons of beryllium, and its commander, Friedrich Steinhoff, was dead, but the nuclear cargo on U-234 was still intact; what it contained was no secret, if perhaps all the details were not known.

A few days earlier, U-234 crew member Leutnant Pfaff had told his interrogators that the nuclear containers were 'gold-lined', a fact that will be discussed later, but this definitely confirmed that the USA had a nuclear problem on its hands.

Washington already knew about the betatron at Stadtilm, and all they were waiting for now was for the actual Stadtilm documents to arrive from Germany.

The whole interrogation of Kessler is taken up with questions regarding transport flights between Germany and Japan. The concern is obvious, but Kessler was not a transport officer, although perhaps Allied Intelligence suspected he was connected with the nuclear cargo, or at the very least might know something. Kessler's statements regarding the Italian flight in 1942, that the Japanese Government objected strongly to the flight, treating the pilots very discourteously, is not supported by the ULTRA message which shows how much the Japanese were in favour of the air-link with Italy. Why was Kessler so positive about the Japanese objections, which were clearly not true? It is unlikely that Kessler had incorrect information, hence it must be assumed he was lying, but why?

What was special about the first Italian flight? It is a fact that new long-distance flights on what is expected to be a regular route very often have at least one proving flight to confirm that the route and facilities are satisfactory. Was the Italian flight via Odessa the proving flight for later German flights? The Luftwaffe did not have suitable aircraft to spare in 1942. Odessa is on the Black Sea, and the original central route was Rome–Odessa–Nanking/Peking, all these locations suitable for the Savoia-Marchetti S55/66. The problems with believing Kessler's answers are increased in Question 7, when he is told about a former Luftwaffe pilot who claimed to have made two return flights between Poland and Manchuria in early 1944, and that two other pilots made similar flights. Kessler denied emphatically that such flights could have taken place, but there is significant corroboration of the flights by historian and author William Green. His history of the Ju290 states that three Ju290s were recalled to Germany in the spring of 1944, and within 48 hours all their unnecessary weight, including armour and weapons, had been removed and extra fuel tanks fitted. The aircraft were flown from Mielec in Poland via Odessa to Manchuria with special cargoes, returning to Mielec with urgently needed raw materials. Green would not have known about the Kessler interrogation and the Question 7 statement from a German pilot, so these two statements are completely independent. What is definite about the Mielec–Odessa–Manchuria flights is that they could not have taken place after the beginning of April 1944, since on 10 April, Odessa was recaptured by Russian forces after a rapid advance along the Black Sea coast by the Third and Fourth Ukrainian Armies under Marshall Malinovski.

What was on these flights from Mielec to Manchuria and back: were these cargoes also nuclear material on the outward or both flights? Was the use of Mielec significant? Here again there is another strange coincidence. V2 launches and other weapons testing was transferred from Peenemünde to the SS range at Blizna (Heidelager) late in 1943. Mielec is approximately fifteen miles north of Blizna and the nearest airfield, but there were dozens of other airfields in Poland, including Luftwaffe airbases at nearby Krakow and Lvov, which would have had better facilities for long-range flights, but Mielec was the Blizna airfield!

Why did Kessler deny that such flights took place when it appears virtually certain, with independent corroboration, that they did?

Other points of interest in the interrogation report are that in Question 1, Kessler referred to scarce material such as antimony and tungsten. The reference to antimony is unusual, since it never appears in the ULTRA messages dealing with the movement of material between Germany and Japan. Antimony has some military uses, since as an alloy it is used in ammunition cases, with lead in the plates for batteries and in engine bearings. It also has some nuclear uses, with beryllium as a neutron source, and the isotope of antimony, Sb.125, which can be obtained with neutron bombardment, is highly radioactive as both a beta and gamma emitter, and it has a very useful half-life of two years.

Kessler's statements that the preparations for flights to Japan were made 'without advance consultation with the Japanese' was clearly untrue, since there are several ULTRA messages describing the Japanese interest in starting an air-link and the Luftwaffe Chief of Staff's discussions, firstly with General Korten, and after the Hitler July bomb plot, with General Koller, Korten's successor, about such flights with the Japanese diplomats in Berlin. Kessler was obviously lying, and the impression is that he was trying to distance himself from any connection with flights to Japan. If this interpretation is correct, then there had to be a good reason for his action. The only valid reason why Kessler should want to give the impression that no flights took place is that he knew that the cargo being transported was not just normal military stores, in which case there would have been little reason for keeping it a secret, but something very special.

But suppose General Kessler was not lying about the 'without advance consultations with the Japanese'. Perhaps he really didn't know that his name was being used as the main passenger on a flight to Japan, and this also has implications, as explained later. Perhaps it was always intended that he should go by U-boat to Japan.

There is one other item concerning flights between Germany and Japan. There is an unconfirmed report that Japan did try to make one flight on 7 July 1943. Using a Kawanishi Type 97 H6K5 Mavis flying boat, an attempt was made to fly from Singapore to Germany, but the plane disappeared over the Indian Ocean.

What conclusion can we make about transport flights between Germany and Japan? From the ULTRA evidence there is no doubt that in 1942 Japan was very interested in starting an air-link from either Italy or Germany, the objective being to obtain high-technology military hardware from Germany. From the German point of view, in 1942, there were no obvious military advantages in an air-link, and certainly they did not have suitable aircraft available; hence the first flight used an Italian aircraft and crew, as a route-proving flight for future possible use. From the middle of 1943 onwards, things had changed for both Germany and Japan.

Germany was now beginning to experience shortages in strategic war materials, and some of these could be supplied by Japan. From the Japanese side, there was an even more urgent need to obtain German high-technology materials and equipment, as the war was developing into a war of technology, especially in the air and in electronics, as well as with the important nuclear developments. But by the end of 1943, the question of routes was of major importance to Japan. Territorial losses and Allied air-power in the Pacific meant that southern routes were no longer possible. Northern routes were still available, but this meant flying over Russian territory, and Japan did not want to endanger the Non-Aggression Pact with Russia. However, up to early 1944, it looks virtually certain that a number of flights took place using German aircraft, Ju290s, and crews, from Mielec in Poland, via Odessa to Manchuria. Both the outward and inward flights carried cargo that was most likely connected with rocket and nuclear technology, as the relatively small cargo capacity of the Ju290 meant that only critical and urgent items used this route. How many flights took place is unknown, but it was probably at least four, and may possibly have been ten or twelve, as improved versions of the Ju290 were available from late 1943 and Odessa was in German hands until April 1944.

It is clear that General Kessler was lying, certainly during some of his interrogation in May 1945, and he was probably trying to protect himself from a lengthy spell in a PoW camp or worse if he gave the Allies any hint that he might know something about nuclear weapons. Fortunately for Kessler, the Allies were unlikely to divulge to him exactly how important the nuclear cargo was on U-234, and so, most conspicuously, the topic was not raised in the questioning.

However, returning to U-boats, the Allies, but especially the Americans, were by the end of April 1945 in a crisis situation about the two boats U-873 and U-234, and were checking every message sent between Europe and Tokyo. Both boats had now slipped through the Allied anti-submarine defences around Norway and were into the Atlantic, which was like looking for a needle in a haystack. Unless they broke radio silence there was almost no chance of them being found and sunk.

In Washington, General Groves, head of all nuclear work in the USA, and instigator of ALSOS, was in a massive predicament. From the information passed back to him from ALSOS in Europe, which had included the interrogation of those German physicists at the renamed 'Strassburg' University in November 1944, he had told his military and political chiefs that it was virtually certain that the Germans did not have an atomic bomb. Now, however, everything was going 'pear-shaped', and not only might the USA be in danger from a nuclear attack, but his head was on the block. U-195 had arrived in the Far East on 28 December 1944, and as in previous cargo-loading lists, although the Allies had an ULTRA-decoded version (not in the PRO files), not every item was described, some just having a reference number. But now there was a gleam of light: the news was that, with the Russians in Berlin, Hitler had committed suicide on 30 April and Grand Admiral Doenitz was his successor. Peace would not be long now, and on the night of 8/9 May 1945, the guns finally fell silent. The Third Reich had survived the death of its leader by seven days. In the meantime, U–873 and U–234 were ploughing relentlessly on through the Atlantic rollers, and it is assumed but not confirmed that both boats were following a similar course for Japan, separated as they were by about fourteen days.

From the radio messages now filling the air waves, they knew that Germany had surrendered and what was expected of any U-boats still at sea, and they also knew that Japan had severed all relations with Germany and German citizens were now considered as aliens.

Other radio broadcasts from America had been picked up, and these stated that Japan declared itself free from all treaties and contracts with the Third Reich and would continue to fight on alone.

The instructions from the US East Coast naval radio stations were that all U-boats were to disarm torpedoes and jettison the detonators, but all torpedoes were to be retained. All ammunition was also to be jettisoned and the guns secured facing astern, a black flag was to be flown from the extended periscope and navigation lights were to be illuminated. The exact navigational position was to be given and all further movements were to be on the surface. For all Atlantic areas a port of surrender was given, and for both boats this was Halifax, Nova Scotia, Canada. Discussions were held among the crew and passengers on U–234, and presumably also on U–873, as to what action was to be taken. The majority on U–234 were for surrendering to the USA, although some wanted to proceed to Japan, and others to South America. The two Japanese officers had taken an overdose of sleeping pills and were now in a coma, their requests being to be buried at sea. On 13 May, U–234's captain, Fehler, instructed the chief signals officer, Hirschfeld, to contact Halifax with their identification and position. Once U–234's position had been established, it is clear that the USA had no intention of allowing the boat, with its nuclear cargo, to land anywhere but a US naval port. Hirschfeld reported to Fehler that it appeared that all transmissions from U–234 were being jammed, and shortly afterwards a warship appeared on the port quarter, the American destroyer USS *Sutton*. When it was within range, U–234 was ordered to head for the Gulf of Maine and ignore all further radio communications from Halifax. It was now clear that the USS *Sutton* had been the source of the jamming, and with the destroyer astern they now headed for Maine on the surface and with a black flag attached to the periscope.

Captain Fehler was now concerned about the Japanese. He knew that if they were still alive when they landed, the Americans would try to revive them. He instructed the medical officer to ensure they died peacefully, and a few hours later he reported that they were dead. The bodies were sewn into weighted hammocks, and despite *Sutton*'s signals asking why they had stopped, they were slipped into the sea after a short ceremony. The position was 47° 07' N 42° 25' W, approximately 1,000 miles from land. Soon afterwards a prize crew from the *Sutton* came on board, and on Saturday 19 May, U–234 entered Portsmouth harbour, New Hampshire.

What exactly was going on inside U-873 before the surrender is not known, but presumably there were similar discussions with the crew as on U-234, and a similar realization that although Halifax was supposed to be the port of surrender, efforts were being made to ensure that it was a US port they entered. At all events, Commander Friedrich Steinhoff decided to surrender to the Americans, and here another mystery starts. U-873 surrendered to the US Navy on 11 May, three days before U-234, and entered Portsmouth on 17 May, two days before U-234 arrived. Obviously the US authorities, especially Washington and General Groves, were waiting for both boats, but Steinhoff was the first to arrive, and it can be imagined he walked into a hornets' nest of questions, with the USA in no mood for niceties. U-873 was carrying nuclear materials, 100 kg (220 lb) of thallium and 1,402 bars of beryllium, but what had happened to the remainder of the zirconium shipment mentioned in Figure 4, and the '2,000 or more Kernehaspe', the core clamps? If they had been on U-864, they were now at the bottom of the North Sea.

A couple of days behind Steinhoff was U-234 with the big prize, and it was not unreasonable for the US interrogators to assume that Steinhoff knew everything; after all, he had connections with V-weapons. His brother was one of Peenemünde's top scientists and had been one of the Peenemünde team who had masterminded production of the V2 at the underground factory of Mittelwerk, Nordhausen, where human life meant very little indeed.

But there was a possible V-weapons connection between Peenemünde's Dr Steinhoff and his U-boat commander brother, Friedrich Steinhoff. From May to June 1942, U-511 was seconded to Peenemünde for 'Operation Ursel', where it underwent rocket-launching trials while submerged, the rockets being 8.3 in (210 mm), short-range solid-fuel missiles mounted on the U-boat's casing. The commander of U-511 at the time was Friedrich Steinhoff, but U-511, now under Fritz Schneewind, had finished up in Japan. Leaving Lorient in May 1943, it had arrived at the Kure Naval Base in August 1943, returning Admiral Nomura to Japan.

But in Portsmouth, USA, with U-873 safely in port, it was now Friedrich's turn, and let the reader be in no doubt that Allied Intelligence knew how to extract information from the enemy when needs must, and now time was of the very essence.

There were many questions that needed quick answers, and these included the obvious, such as whether the rocket tests with U-511 were intended as a trial before a full-scale attack on New York using other U-boats, and whether U-511 had gone to Japan complete with its rocket-launching equipment. Closer to home were the questions about U-873 and U-234 and their respective cargoes.

Whatever happened to Friedrich Steinhoff, one thing is sure, U-234 entered port on 19 May, and on 20 May Steinhoff 'committed suicide', as the official story goes. Was Steinhoff 'pushed' or did he go voluntarily, had he already divulged so much that he knew what fate awaited him from fellow U-boat crew-members, since the USA certainly wouldn't want him after this was all over? Or were the US personnel just a little too over-enthusiastic in their interrogation techniques? We will never know the details, only the end results.

After U-234 arrived at Portsmouth, its nuclear cargo remained undisturbed for several weeks; the exact date of the unloading is not known but it was early in July. The local press had given full coverage to U-234's arrival because the passengers included several high-ranking Nazis, two Japanese officers had committed suicide, and there was talk of secret weapons on board and other newsworthy items, which made good reading at the end of the war in Europe. An unloading list for U-234's cargo was released, and this is reproduced in Appendix 2. This list includes the thallium, fuses and 'uranium oxide (10 cases, 56 kg, marked for Japanese Army)'. What is not mentioned is the Me262 jet aircraft that was supposed to have been transported as a kit of parts; however, we are not particularly interested in the Me262.

The nuclear cargo was stored in tubes in what had been the mine shafts on U-234, and according to the signals officer, Wolfgang Hirschfeld, American scientists arrived with radiation monitors to check exactly how much radioactivity was leaking from the containers.

Crew member Leutnant Pfaff had been in charge of the loading of the containers in Kiel, and he now volunteered to supervise the unloading of the containers, and also supplied other information which allowed the American physicists to predict more accurately what exactly was in the containers. Figure 34 is a brief report of Leutnant Pfaff's statement to the US Navy at Portsmouth, and it contains some highly significant information. Firstly, it must be assumed that Pfaff was not a nuclear physicist, but because he was the loading officer, he had been given just enough information for him to do his job properly. There is one important fact to recognize about uranium oxide from the very start. It emits so little radioactivity that it can be carried in a paper bag, and the normal method of transporting it for Union Minière was in strong wooden barrels, mainly because of its weight: uranium metal weighs 1.7 times more than lead, so even in its unrefined state it is a very heavy substance. Not only does the oxide emit little radioactivity, but in this state it is material easy to handle. Hence, if it was uranium oxide, the instructions related by Pfaff concerning how it should be unloaded do not make a lot of sense. But Pfaff also volunteered another vital piece of information, and one which he probably imagined would also buy him more considerate treatment by his captors. The uranium oxide, he said, was 'loaded in gold-lined cylinders'. Unfortunately, he did not mention how thick the gold was, knowing this would have enabled the investigators to have estimated much more accurately the energy levels inside the containers.

It is very unlikely that Leutnant Pfaff knew why the cylinders were gold lined, but everyone knew the value of gold, and this must be worth something. Pfaff was right, gold is valuable, and if it was less so, it would be used a lot more in the nuclear industry than it is, but on U-234, the gold was not there for its intrinsic value but for its unique nuclear properties.

Gold has not one, but three, important nuclear properties which make it a unique metal. Perhaps the most obvious of these properties relates to gamma radiation. This is very penetrating, and the ability of a material to stop, or 'attentuate', this radiation is directly dependent on the material's density, and it is also dependent on the atomic number of the material, because the higher the

```
SECRET                              27 MAY
262151 (P)


FROM:        CNO

TO:          NYPORT

INFO:        COMONE

SUBJECT:     MINE TUBES, UNLOADING OF
        INTERROGATION LT PFAFF SECOND WATCH OFFICER U-234 DISCLOSES
HE  WAS IN CHARGE OF CARGO AND PERSONALLY SUPERVISED LOADING
ALL MINE TUBES.
        PFAFF PREPARED MANIFEST LIST AND KNOWS KIND DOCUMENTS AND
CARGO IN EACH TUBE.
        PFAFF STATES LONG CONTAINERS SHOULD BE UNPACKED IN HORIZONTAL
POSITION AND SHORT CONTAINERS IN VERTICAL POSITION.
        URANIUM OXIDE LOADED IN GOLD LINED CYLINDERS AND AS LONG AS
CYLINDERS NOT OPENED CAN BE HANDLED LIKE CRUDE TNT.
        THESE CONTAINERS SHOULD NOT BE OPENED AS SUBSTANCE WILL BECOME
SENSITIVE AND DANGEROUS.
        PFAFF IS AVAILABLE AND WILLING TO AID UNLOADING IF RNEDT DESIRES.
        ADVISE.


DISTRIBUTION
COMDT                                        CTM
C/S
DUTY OFF
ACO (A)
DIO
D ORD OFF
```

Figure 34. Message concerning the unloading of mine tubes, and giving details of Leutnant Pfaff's statement about the gold lining of nuclear containers on U-234.

atomic number, the better the stopping power, especially for gamma rays at higher energies. Lead, which is the material most associated with radiation shielding, and gold have almost identical atomic numbers, 82 and 79 respectively, but gold is 1.7 times more dense than lead, and hence you can say that gold is nearly twice as good as lead at stopping gamma radiation of all energies. If space was at a premium, as in the mine shafts of U-234, you could achieve the same level of gamma shielding with a gold thickness almost half that of lead.

If the first nuclear property of gold is fairly straightforward, the next start to get more involved. Neutrons do not occur naturally (apart from some in cosmic radiation), but are produced in the fission process, in the disintegration process following high-energy photon (gamma) bombardment or when certain elements are bombarded with particles to form neutron sources. For example, when beryllium is bombarded by alpha particles (rays) from radium or polonium, it will emit neutrons at a very high rate, and this neutron emission can be used to initiate (kick-start) fission reactions. They are also produced from certain heavy nuclides, such as californium 252, which fission spontaneously.

All these neutrons have different energies and speeds, and as they gradually slow down and lose energy due to collisions with nuclei of the material they are travelling in (moderators slow neutrons down without absorbing them, since in U.235 slow neutrons fission more readily than fast ones), they go through resonance periods. These resonance periods produce a sudden increase in neutron absorption cross-section by factors several thousand times the normal, a property which can be of great value in some circumstances. Reactor control rods have to absorb neutrons of all energies if the fission process is to be controlled or snuffed-out as soon as possible, and since neutrons are produced during the fission process, reactors have to have shielding capable of absorbing neutrons because neutron radiation is extremely hazardous.

Gold is one of the few materials that has several of these resonance periods, and it has very high neutron-absorption rates at the lower (thermal) neutron energies.

The third nuclear property of gold involves alpha particles (rays), which are produced following fission and during the decay (disintegration) process following bombardment by protons, deuterons, photons (betatron) and neutrons. Alpha particles are highly charged, heavy particles with short ranges and little penetrating power: a sheet of paper will stop alpha radiation, but they are capable of producing ionizing radiation in material through which they travel – in other words the material becomes radioactive. Because alpha radiation occurs over a short range, its energy is deposited over a short distance, and hence is concentrated in a small area, making alpha radiation dangerous, especially if it enters the human body.

Gold is the most efficient absorber of alpha particles available, and it is used as a standard by which the alpha absorption of other materials is calculated.

I think we can assume that the highly professional German scientists who assembled and prepared the nuclear containers on U-234 did not use a gold lining for some purpose other than its nuclear properties, and certainly not for its intrinsic value. Also, I think we can assume that Leutnant Pfaff was correct when he said the containers were gold lined. So, what do the three nuclear properties of gold mean as far as the material inside the containers is concerned?

There are several possibilities, perhaps the most obvious being that the material in the containers was irradiated material from a reactor and it was still very active. The voyage to Japan was scheduled to take about three months, and if the material was then intended to be used as a radioactive package, to be dropped on US West or East Coast cities, the radioactive half-lives of the material would have to be at least four to six months. Many radioactive isotopes have half-lives of more than four months, including cobalt 60, iron 55, zinc 65, manganese 54, zirconium 93, caesium 134, strontium 90, etc.

Alternatively, the betatron particle accelerator could produce radioactive isotopes similar to those from a reactor, and it could also produce a neutron source from beryllium. The threshold for disintegration of beryllium is 1.6 MeV, and if the betatron used at Stadtilm could produce electrons with energies greater than this, then using beryllium as the target material would result in the beryllium becoming a neutron emitter. Finally there is the alpha particle aspect, for many radioactive isotopes emit alpha at the same time as gamma and beta particles, and it depends on the individual isotope. There is also polonium which is a powerful emitter of alpha particles, and the normal industrial practice is to contain the alpha radiation by gold foils.

If Leutnant Pfaff knew some details about the nuclear containers on U-234, what happened to passenger Captain Gerhard Falck, who was supposed to be the expert on the nuclear containers? His name is never mentioned after the surrender of U-234 and his post-war fate is a mystery – he just vanishes from the scene.

Another U-234 passenger was also of interest to US Intelligence. A secret ALSOS report dated 23 July describes the search for information on Dr Ing. Heinz Schlicke. On 23 June and 14 July 1945, two ex-associates of Dr Schlicke, Dr Kupfmüller and Dr Barth, were finally located and interrogated in Germany, the objective being to discover why Dr Schlicke was going to Japan on U-234. The interrogators are described as 'Agent Madeira and Expert Consultant W.F. Colby', and they had some difficulty in locating the two ex-associates, but persevered. What they learned was that Dr Schlicke was carrying 20,000 microfilms, he was an expert on radar and other electronic equipment, and the U-boat he was on left Germany between 15 March and 1 April 1945 for Japan via the Cape of Good Hope, a voyage expected to take about three months.

But the real reasons behind the interrogation appear part-way through the report. We do not know the question, but the reply was: 'Kupfmüller cannot believe that Schlicke had any knowledge of proximity fuses or took any with him.'

Why were the US interrogators so interested in proximity fuses, and why did they go to so much trouble to try and find out if Dr Schlicke had any connection with these devices? At the time of the interrogations, Dr Schlicke was in US custody following the surrender of U-234, and he would already have been questioned in Portsmouth, New Hampshire. But evidently his answers were not considered sufficient, and corroboration was required that he knew nothing about proximity fuses. So what was the fuss about? In normal circumstances there would have been no fuss about proximity fuses, but these were not ordinary circumstances and 'fuse' was another name for detonator. In June/July 1945, the nuclear alarm bells were still ringing in Washington, as we shall see in the final chapter.

Professor Blackett believed that the USA was considering using radioactive material as a nuclear weapon, and Appendix 4 is a letter dated 25 May 1943 from Robert Oppenheimer, scientific head of the Manhattan Project, to Enrico Fermi, on the subject of using strontium as a radioactive poison. Strontium 90 has a half-life of 28 years and is absorbed via the food chain into bones, which can be fatal.

In the UK a secret investigation was carried out and the results published in February 1952 under the title 'Radioactive Isotopes for Radiological Warfare', in which various materials were irradiated in a reactor and their radioactivity and half-lives listed. This PRO report, ADM 204/1173, concluded that as a tactical weapon, the ideal was to use materials with half-lives of between one week and one month so that the enemy would be forced to abandon territory but that it would not remain unusable for more than a few weeks.

THE JAPANESE PIECES

When U-873 and U-234 left Kiel in March 1945, the group of four submersible aircraft carriers, I-400, I-401, I-13 and I-14, joined the 1st Submarine Division under Captain Tatsunosuke as part of the Sixth Fleet operating from the Kure Naval Base, and commenced training in the Inland Sea for their next mission, although I-14 did not join the group until 15 March. On 12 April, I-401 was slightly damaged by an air-laid mine and had to return to Kure for repairs, remaining there until 1 June. From April to July the movements of the four submarines became critical in relation to the voyages of U-873 and U-234. Both left Kiel at the end of March, and by the end of April they were through the Iceland–Faroes Gap and into the Atlantic. From previous similar voyages, both U-boats could expect to reach Penang, Singapore, by early June. They would unload their cargo for transportation by air over the remaining 3,500 miles to Japan, which would take two or three days, or proceed directly by sea to Japan, which would take an extra two weeks. There is some evidence that the U-boats were going direct to Japan via South America and Cape Horn, for safety reasons, in which case they should have reached Japan by the end of June.

On 14 April, I-400 left Kure for Luta (Dairen), on the tip of the Kwantung Peninsula, the major port for men and supplies being transported by rail to Manchuria. Dairen had another more sinister connection, with bacteriological warfare. Unit 731, the Japanese germ warfare organization attached to the Kwantung Army in Manchuria, had its HQ at Harbin in Manchuria, from where experiments were carried out with various types of plague viruses, sometimes on live human subjects. Dairen was the HQ of the South Manchurian Railway Sanitary Institute, which acted as a 'front' for scientists and technicians joining Unit 731. The Institute produced bacterial specimens used by Unit 731, and their laboratories were also used for Unit 731 experiments. Was this unusual voyage of I-400 connected with germ warfare and its use as an alternative to a nuclear weapon? The story of Japan's wartime germ warfare work is told in the book by Peter Williams and David Wallace, *Unit 731*, and it is clear from their account of the work and experiments on live subjects that there would have been no moral scruples about using any germ agents which Unit 731 produced, if the opportunity had arisen. The return journey of I-400 to Dairen was 2,000 miles, and the submarine arrived back at Kure on 27 April. Officially, the reason for the visit to Dairen was to get diesel fuel, but the seas around Japan at this time were extremely hazardous for any sort of naval craft. I-401 was still being repaired after mine damage, and it appears very strange to send the sole survivor of the class on a 2,000-mile trip for fuel, especially when Dairen was not the only source available. On 27 May, I-13 and I-14 left Kure for the Nanao Naval Base on Japan's west coast, stopping *en route* to refuel at the Korean port of Chinkai, next to Pusan. This means that there was a much closer alternative to Dairen, and the proximity of the large port of Pusan virtually guaranteed a supply of fuel. There is no doubt the fuel situation was critical in the Navy, and how the last stocks were used provides a highly significant part of the story. On 6 April the pride of the Imperial Navy, the 73,000 ton battleship *Yamato*, was dispatched from Kure on a suicide mission in a vain attempt to stop the US landings at Okinawa, only 700 miles away, and eventually beach the ship as a static battery with its 18 in (460 mm) guns. This was a suicide mission because *Yamato* was sent out with only enough fuel for a one-way trip and with no air-cover. Only a day out from Kure, *Yamato* was intercepted by US carrier-borne aircraft and quickly overwhelmed by a massive onslaught of torpedoes and bombs, sinking in a huge explosion at 14.17 p.m. on 7 April.

The now repaired I-401 was refuelled at Kure, taking on over 1,300 tons of diesel oil, arriving at Nanao Bay on 4 June, followed by I-400 on 5 June, to join I-13 and I-14. On 3 June the Seiran float-planes of the 631st Flying Corps arrived at Nanao Bay, and all four submarines started their operational training, each with a full complement of aircraft. The training was officially described as a prelude to an attack on the lock-gates of the Panama Canal, as originally planned in 1942, but the 1942 planning also included attacks on US East and West Coast cities. However, the military situation in 1942 was completely different from that in 1945, and what in 1942 would have been a useful objective for Japan, to disrupt the flow of Allied supplies when they were trying to recoup their losses, in 1945 would have been only a very brief setback to the Allies. It is possible, though, that a combined attack was still envisaged in that if perhaps two or three months' breathing space could be obtained by blocking the canal, this would be enough to transport a nuclear weapon to either the East or West Coast of the USA.

The exercises at Nanao Bay lasted until 12 June, and on or around this date there was a sudden and significant change to the plans. The Panama Canal mission was abandoned, and instead the target was changed to the US Naval Base at Ulithi Atoll, 1,000 miles west of Truk Island, which was still in Japanese hands. ULTRA message 1909, dated 17 May 1945, from the Japanese Embassy in Berne, Switzerland, to Tokyo, provided the first evidence that U-234 had surrendered to the US Navy, because the message also mentioned that two Japanese officers were on board, although the U-boat was not identified. Final confirmation that the submarine was U-234 was provided on 4 June 1945, when ULTRA message 1949, from Stockholm to Tokyo, quoted an article in *Time* magazine that U-234 had surrendered and two Japanese officers had committed suicide. Strangely enough, none of the ULTRA messages of this period mention U-873, although there are at least three relating to U-234, and the sinking of U-864 and U-843 are mentioned in messages to Tokyo.

The cancellation of the Panama Canal mission resulted in the following changes to the Seiran-carrying submarines. On 20 June, I-13 and I-14 unloaded their Seirans at Nanao Bay and proceeded directly to the Maizuru Naval Base.

They arrived on 22 June, and work started immediately to modify their hangars to accommodate two dismantled Nakajima C6N1 Saiun (Painted Cloud) reconnaissance aircraft. The Saiun was the fastest carrier-launched reconnaissance aircraft of the Second World War, with a maximum speed of 390 mph and a range of 2,800 miles. Some versions could carry a single torpedo, offset to starboard under the fuselage. The plan was that I-13 and I-14 would each transport two of these aircraft to Truk, from where they would carry out reconnaissance flights to Ulithi, 1,000 miles to the west, in preparation for a attack by the Seirans of I-400 and I-401. The chances of this amended plan being successful were remote. Although Truk was still in Japanese hands, it had been devastated by attacks from US carrier-borne aircraft, and had been virtually unusable as a base since February 1944, being left to 'wither on the vine', like many other isolated Japanese bases. On 2 July, with the modifications completed, I-13 and I-14 left Maizuru for the Ominato Naval Base at the northernmost tip of Honshu. They arrived on 4 July and on the same day they each loaded two dismantled Saiuns. On 11 July I-13 left Ominato for Truk, but five days later it was sunk some 400 miles to the west of Tokyo by a US hunter-killer group led by the escort carrier CVE *Anzio*. On 13 July I-400 and I-401 left Nanao Bay for Maizuru, where they spent seven days taking on supplies and topping-up with fuel. They left on 20 July for Ominato, arriving on 23 July. In the meantime, I-14 had left Ominato on 14 July, arriving at Truk on 4 August without incident, and the two Saiuns were unloaded. On 23 and 24 July respectively, I-400 and I-401 left Ominato for the Ulithi area, the date for the first part of the operation being 17 August. However, on 15 August Japan surrendered and the attack was cancelled. The three submarines were ordered back to Japan, and surrendered to US naval forces between 27 and 29 August after dumping their Seirans overboard. After a period of evaluation later in 1945, the I-400s, which were the largest submarines built by any country up to the advent of nuclear power, were sunk in the Pacific.

THE FINAL PIECES

The contents of the nuclear containers on U-234 were eventually examined early in July 1945. What they contained we do not precisely know, but what we do know is that it was not un-processed uranium oxide. The US atomic bomb project now took on a note of urgency, and as we have seen from Figure 3, all information relating to Stadtilm was to be sent direct to Washington, which meant General Groves, head of the Manhattan project. Although the Allies had broken the Japanese codes, there was no absolute guarantee that every message between Germany and Tokyo had been intercepted, and hence there was the possibility that other submarines had already made the journey to Japan carrying a similar cargo to that on U-873 and U-234. The messages that had been intercepted showed that the nuclear material that Japan was ordering from Germany was meant for an advanced reactor and weapons programme, and that the amounts of some of these materials, such as beryllium, were greater than those available to the Manhattan Project. At Los Alamos, HQ of the scientific side of the Manhattan Project, Robert Oppenheimer and his senior physicists must have been very worried about the revelations which had come from the ULTRA messages and culminated in the reality of the cargo of U-873 and U-234. General Groves would have had to consult Oppenheimer and others to get a real understanding of what the transfer of the nuclear material to Japan really meant, as there was always the chance that it might have been some sort of elaborate hoax by Germany and Japan, but the cargoes in the U-boats told the truth, that this was no hoax.

Just when General Groves and ALSOS were congratulating themselves that Germany no longer posed a nuclear threat, their whole world had been thrown upside down, and no longer was it only Germany, but Japan as well. Some revelations were more worrying than others. 'Ordinary' U.235 and Pu.239 bombs were one thing, but the Germans had also been supplying lithium to Japan, and lithium can be used to produce tritium, and tritium was one of the ingredients of a 'super-bomb' using the 'boosted fission' process. In addition to that, lithium was also an essential part of the hydrogen bomb. Details or even mention of boosted fission, fusion and the hydrogen bomb were so secret that no more than a handful of people knew about it, but the Japanese had been ordering lithium at the same time as zirconium, neon and 'core clamps', and for the same department.

It was now early July, and there was no time to be lost at Los Alamos. A plutonium bomb using the implosion technique to compress the fissile Pu.239 was assembled in some haste, and on 16 July, on the top of a 100 ft tower in the New Mexico desert, it was successfully detonated. Only three weeks later, the Little Boy uranium bomb was dropped on Hiroshima, and two days later it was Nagasaki's turn, with the plutonium Fat Man bomb.

Time had been running out for everyone in the last few months, and now it was Japan where the seconds were ticking away. Russia declared war on Japan on 8 August, the day before Nagasaki, and invaded across the Manchurian border, quickly overcoming the Japanese resistance. But the vast Konan empire of Noguchi was untouched, and the hydroelectric power stations were still churning out millions of watts, with a mad scramble under way to complete something before it had to be destroyed or fell into Russian hands. Snell's description, as reported by Robert Wilcox, of a Japanese nuclear test on 12 August now looks more than just a good story thought up by another of the defeated Japanese.

On 13 August, the US code-breakers intercepted a message from Tokyo, and the relevant part of it is reproduced in Figure 35. The message was in several parts, and Item (3) reads:

'At 1005I the Yokosuka Naval District ordered:
   Today, alert Operation Homeland #3 and #4 and F Operations.
At 1033I Sasebo reported that 'Operation Homeland #3, #4, #5, #6 and #7 has been alerted.'

Note: The Navy (F-22) comments that Operation Homeland #3 and #4 are believed to involve the Tokyo area and that 'F Operations' have not previously appeared in the traffic.

'MAGIC' SUMMARY

they were scheduled to return to the Tokyo area.

(2) At 0759I on the 13th, Air Flotilla 71 (Tokyo area) was ordered to "engage in interception operations immediately", apparently against attacking Allied carrier planes. (According to another message, the Allied attack began at 0530I.) At 1211I "about 12" Jill dive bombers in the Tokyo area were ordered to "activate [word missing] offensive search".

(3) At 1005I the Yokosuka Naval District ordered:

"Today, alert Operation Homeland #3 and #4, and F Operations."

At 1033I Sasebo reported that "Operation Homeland #3, #4, #5, #6 and #7" had been alerted.

Note: The Navy (F-22) comments that Operation Homeland #3 and #4 are believed to involve the Tokyo area, and that "F Operations" have not previously appeared in the traffic.

(4) On the morning of the 13th, 44 Zeke single-engine fighters were ordered to move from the Nagoya area to the Tokyo area (20 on the afternoon of the 13th and 24 on the 14th). Later the movement apparently was postponed until the 14th.

b. Okinawa area:

(1) An order issued at 2301I on 13 Aug

-4-

Figure 35. F Operations, 13 August 1945. Part of a US decode of a Japanese message.

The significant item in this message is the reference to 'F Operations', because 'F-go' was the code name for the final Japanese nuclear weapons programme, under the control of the Navy.

The Yokosuka Naval Base near Tokyo was probably the largest in Japan, with a large part of the facilities underground in the adjacent hillside. PRO File WO 208/886 is the American target description of the Yokosuka base, and this describes how the hillsides had been excavated to provide what they believed were an underground oil storage depot, perhaps like Brécourt, near Cherbourg. But, also like Brécourt, the final purpose of the underground workings were probably nothing to do with oil storage. It is also a fact that some of the nuclear-related materials ordered by Tokyo, in particular boron, were described on the ULTRA messages as being destined for the Yokosuka Naval Base. Boron is a very powerful absorber of thermal neutrons and an essential ingredient of some reactor control rods, and boric acid is used in water-moderated reactors to shut down the reactor in an emergency if the control rods fail to operate correctly. The important word regarding boron is thermal, or slow, neutrons, because the property of boron here relates to neutrons that have been slowed down as used in a reactor. This implies that the boron was to be used in a nuclear reactor, and the tunnels of Yokosuka could well have been where some of the Navy 'F-go' work was being carried out.

If Japan did test a nuclear weapon on 12 August 1945, what sort of device might it have been? We have three, and only three, fissionable choices for the primary weapon fuel, and there is nothing else. Firstly there is U.235, which can only be obtained by separating it from uranium, of which 99.3 per cent is U.238 (fissionable only by fast neutrons, and hence useless for our purpose) and only 0.7 per cent is U.235. Then there is plutonium Pu.239, which is obtained when U.238 captures neutrons, and instead of fissioning, eventually decays to Pu.239, which can then be separated from U.238 by chemical means. Finally there is U.233, obtained in a similar way to Pu.239, except that the starting point is thorium Th.232 instead of U.238. The Little Boy U.235 bomb dropped on Hiroshima used about 130 lb of fissile material, of which only 1.5 lb actually fissioned before the remainder evaporated in the fireball, because the gun-method used to compress the U.235 was so slow compared to the speed of the fast neutrons producing the fission. The actual amount of U.235 in the 132 lb is not known, but it was probably about 90 per cent, i.e. enriched to 90 per cent. Quite low values of enrichment, as low as 40 per cent U.235, will form a critical mass, especially if a very efficient reflector of neutrons, like beryllium, is used.

Taking the U.235 option first, suppose an amount of fissile material with about 50 per cent enrichment had been produced in Noguchi's vast Konan empire, and it had been decided to explode the device as a gesture: although time had run out, given a few more months several much more efficient bombs would have been produced. Because it was only 50 per cent U.235 and the gun-method was used, the device exploded in a 'fizzle' of incomplete fission, but was still an effective weapon.

Alternatively, did Japan have sufficent Pu.239 or U.233, which behave very similarly when used in a bomb, the advantage of U.233 being that it does not have any elements that produce spontaneous fission? Plutonium isotope Pu.240

fissions spontaneously, and although most of it can be removed from the Pu.239, traces remain and these produce neutrons, accelerating the explosion process, and hence the need for something faster than the gun-method. The implosion method in the Pu.239 Nagasaki bomb used a number of explosive charges, or 'lenses', focused on the Pu.239, and these were exploded simultaneously to quickly compress the Pu.239 into a critical mass. One essential feature of the implosion method was the need for very efficient and fast-operating detonators. Among the various requests for material sent from Tokyo to Berlin, one particular item keeps on recurring in the ULTRA messages and was included in the cargo of both U-873 and U-234. The item is fuses, and fuses are just another name for detonators.

As we have already seen, US Intelligence and ALSOS thought that U-234 passenger Dr Schlicke might know something about 'proximity fuses', and they went to some trouble to check this out with his previous associates in Germany.

The concern about fuses (detonators) was based on two main applications. First, the use of a proximity detonator for nuclear weapons such as the 'modified' V1 and V2, to distribute the nuclear material above the target, or even for a weapon dropped by parachute, like the US bombs. Secondly, special detonators were required for a plutonium bomb. The Nagasaki 'Fat Man' weapon used thirty-two fast-acting detonators, fired simultaneously, to initiate explosive charges (or 'lenses'), which compressed the fissile material into a 'super-critical' mass very quickly. Japan may have wanted fuses for either or both of these reasons.

If Pu.239 was not used, was it U.233, which originates from thorium, and like Pu.239, needs a uranium reactor in the first instance to start the conversion process from Th.232 to U.233? Korea had vast deposits of monzanite from which thorium (and uranium) can be extracted, and this was being extensively mined by the Japanese. Once more we come back to Konan, where everything was possible. The implosion method could be used with any of the three fissile materials, and if it had been used in the Hiroshima bomb it would have ensured that more than 1.5 lb of U.235 fissioned. The Nagasaki bomb was nearly twenty times more efficient at using its fissile material than 'Little Boy', which gives some idea of the improvement in the two methods.

There was also the lithium, which can be converted to tritium either in a reactor by bombardment with neutrons or in a particle accelerator like a betatron. Tritium together with deuterium provides the fusion fuel for a 'boosted-fission' weapon. Fusion occurs momentarily at the centre of a fission explosion, and fusion-bred neutrons possess energies a lot higher than those resulting from fission. Hence, if the numbers of these high-energy neutrons could be increased in the fission bomb, it would result in a more effective weapon, by a factor of at least ten over the 'ordinary' fission device. If beryllium was also close to the fusion process as a 'tamper', the extra fusion neutrons generated by the beryllium would also add to the explosive effect. The two fusion fuels can be used either in their gaseous or their liquid forms, the deuterium being obtained at the same time as heavy water, and Konan had an electrolysis plant. The actual fusion fuel is placed at the centre of the weapon, which is provided with a hollow core. The use of the hollow core at the centre of a boosted-fission weapon for the fusion fuel would mean that this hollow could no longer be used for the neutron source, a mixture of polonium and beryllium, whose neutrons 'kick-started' the fission reaction. Hence a boosted-fission weapon would have to be provided with an external neutron source.

Whatever type of weapon Japan was working on, based on the materials ordered from Germany, the reactor technology and associated work must have been very advanced. There was zirconium for the fuel tubes and adjacent structure, and note, in Figure 4, that the order from Japan specified a purity of at least 99.5 per cent. Hafnium is also a constituent of zirconium and is a powerful absorber of thermal, slow neutrons, and so it must be removed, otherwise the fuel tubes will act as a neutron poison; ideally the hafnium content should be not more than 0.01 per cent. Beryllium is a neutron reflector, moderator and neutron source for both fission and fusion, in fact in any nuclear application where neutron absorption has to be a minimum and the expense and toxicity of beryllium is not a problem. Boron is for control rods and a general reactor poison for removing neutrons. Thallium is used for scintillation counters for radiation measurement. Lithium is a producer of tritium and a fission booster, and neon can be used to detect the passage of nuclear particles. Diamond dies are used for core instrumentation wire and high-frequency insulation.

All these are very high-technology nuclear-related materials, and just the quantity alone of beryllium ordered by Japan would have made Robert Oppenheimer extremely envious.

Finally we have the nuclear components, 'Haspekerne', which was translated by Allied Intelligence the wrong way round, and should have been 'Kernehaspe', core clamps, most likely referring to fuel rod, control rod or insulation attachments in the core, in which case, if 1,000 were to be used, with the remainder as spares, they could be for a single reactor of several hundred thousand watts, or a number of reactors of less power. Significantly, as a general rule, reactors very rarely have components which are interchangeable with other reactors. So, was Japan engaged on a reactor-building programme that was based on a German design? The ULTRA messages show that Japan had bought plans for military hardware from Germany which included everything from radar to jet aircraft, so it would be logical that if Germany had developed a superior reactor, Japan would be interested in using some, if not all, of the design.

Also, it must be remembered, the ULTRA messages in the PRO files are only a fraction of the total message traffic between the two countries.

If Japan was using these materials for a high-technology reactor and weapons programme, where does that leave Germany, where the material originated? It leaves us with many unanswered questions about German nuclear technology in the Second World War, and makes those who appear on the Farm Hall tape recordings very good candidates for 'Oscars'. Why was no mention made by the famous ten at Farm Hall of the transport of these nuclear materials to Japan, and why was the nuclear cooperation between the two countries also never mentioned? But it goes further than Farm Hall: in all the dozens of the post-war interviews given by Heisenberg and his colleagues, again there is no mention of Japan.

However, we can pick up the trail of the man who knew all the answers, SS General Dr Hans Kammler. 'Operation Pinguin', Kammler's V2 offensive from Holland, ended at the end of March 1945, but the V1 was not quite finished. Kammler's last recorded message was sent from Prague on 23 April 1945, when he ordered the destruction of the V1 equipment in Berlin. It is more than likely that these V1s were nuclear versions – otherwise why would Kammler take the trouble to order their destruction? Trainloads of 'standard' V1s were lying abandoned on the rail network across Germany at this time. By now Kammler was almost at the very top, for on 27 March, on the personal orders of Hitler, he had been placed in complete charge of all jet aircraft production and development, over the heads of Speer and Goering. According to Goebbels's diary, Kammler had a long meeting with Hitler in the bunker on 3 April, and among the items discussed were changes to the Luftwaffe. By this time the main group of Peenemünde staff, including von Braun and Dornberger, plus all the important Peenemünde documents, had been moved by Kammler from Bad Sachsa to the safety of Oberammergau, on the edge of the Austrian Tyrol, a distance of over 300 miles, bypassing Nuremberg and Munich – quite an achievement by rail when the Allies were bombing everything that moved, and illustrating the influence that Kammler still had. This large group stayed in the area until they surrendered to the US Army on 2 May.

After his last meeting with Hitler in Berlin, Kammler moved to Munich, from where he sent another of his last messages, which has already been referred to briefly (Figure 33). This message, dated 17 April and addressed to Himmler's HQ, contained some very strange wording. It starts:

'Reference: Junkers truck.
 Work on expediting jet aircraft production is proceeding in accordance with the Führer's orders. The truck could not be handed over because it was needed by Kammler's organization.' End of message.

The letters GEZ before Kammler's name are short for Gezeichnet (signed by), and mean that the message was signed in person by the sender.

From this reply which is headed 'Junkers truck', it appears that the fate of the truck had been Himmler's main reason for contacting Kammler in the first place. The Junkers truck that so concerned Himmler was either a Ju290 or the missing Ju390 transport plane, and was very possibly the aircraft prepared for the Japan flight taking General Wild and 'one other passenger', which was scheduled to leave from Norway on its trans-Polar flight on one of 'three days around the 28th' (April). Was Kammler's reply to the Head of the SS a message that sealed Himmler's fate? Himmler, most of all Nazi leaders, would have had few illusions about what fate awaited him with the Allies, since the British and American newspapers had explicit stories of the concentration camps, with pictures of their victims. After the German surrender, Himmler wandered about northern Germany, between Flensburg and the Danish border, with his moustache shaved off and the papers of a discharged Gestapo agent, until he was arrested by British troops at Bremervode, north of Bremen. While being examined by a British doctor at Luneburg on 23 May, he swallowed a cyanide capsule concealed in a tooth. Himmler's behaviour has all the appearance of someone who had an escape route neatly planned in case his secret peace feelers with the Swedish diplomat Count Bernadotte failed, but it had all gone wrong, leaving him with no escape route. The news of Himmler's 'treachery' was one of the last straws for Hitler, and on 29 April, unable to reach Himmler, he ordered the SS liaison officer, SS General Hermann Fegelin, who had attempted to escape from the bunker, so raising Hitler's suspicions of Himmler, to be taken outside and shot in the bunker grounds, despite the fact that he was married to Eva Braun's sister, Gretl. It is extremely likely that Kammler knew of Himmler's secret peace negotiations, which had been going on for some weeks, and hence the message of 17 April, when Himmler was told by Kammler that *he* was still obeying the Führer's orders and that the Junkers truck was no longer available – especially not to traitors.

Was the Junkers truck also intended as a possible escape route for Hitler and his secretary Martin Bormann? Bormann's body was never positively identified, and the circumstances of Hitler's death still leave some unanswered questions, especially the lack of any scientific DNA evidence that the burned remains found in the bunker grounds were those of Hitler. Certainly, there is no doubt that Kammler had Hitler's trust in the last few days of the Third Reich, and he had the ability and organization to arrange such a flight if it was required by Hitler; and from Himmler's message, it is clear that Kammler still had control of the escape equipment. From the ULTRA message, it is a fact that the Polar flight was being arranged: the capture of General Wild in Norway, and General Kessler's boarding of U-234 at Kristiansand, confirms the plan was going ahead, but for some reason the aircraft to be used vanished. Was the aircraft the Junkers truck? General Wild, an ordinary Luftwaffe transport officer with no connections with the SS, secret weapons or war crimes, was kept in prison for two years by the Allies. Why?

Was this unusually long detention because Allied Intelligence suspected that there was still a mystery about the whole business. There were very few 'fools' left in the Third Reich in 1945, and a wise man would arrange more than one escape route, just in case. It is certain that Berlin had no illusions about the security of messages sent to Tokyo. The Germans had broken British naval codes as early as 1940, and the Enigma machines were just routine: every ship in the German Navy had one, and the Army had thousands, so there was little security there. If several escape plans were being made for Hitler, and perhaps Bormann, or other leaders of the Third Reich, the last thing one would expect is for their names to appear on the escape plan details that were bound to be intercepted by the enemy.

Was General Wild and the messages about the flight to Japan with Kessler just a convenient 'red herring', and was Kessler's interrogation denial about discussions having taken place with the Japanese about the flight because he genuinely did not know about them, because the flight was never intended for him in the first place?

But of course, flights were not the only method of leaving the 'sinking ship'. The 'Birkenhead U-Boat', U-534, was probably the last submarine to leave Germany *en route* for Japan, on 1 May 1945. U-534 was sunk before it reached the safety of Kristiansand, Norway, where it would have taken on supplies and passengers before leaving for Japan.

By this time Hitler and Bormann were perhaps already dead, but there were others, such as Himmler, who were very much alive. What was the U-534's mission? So far, nothing has been found on U-534 which gives any indication of why it was going to Japan, but they are still looking: the U-boat's log was only found late in 1998, and there is a lot of hidden storage space on a U-boat. One thing is sure, it had ample supplies of wine, beer and spirits on board to make the passengers comfortable on a long voyage, and these can be seen at Birkenhead.

Kammler's last recorded message was from Prague on 23 April, and after this date there was nothing. Kammler author Tom Agoston, in his book, *Blunder*, and the recently revised German version, *Teufel oder Technokrat? Hitlers graue Eminence*, has examined in detail all four accounts of Kammler's death and found all four unsubstantiated. The most credible report was supplied by Kammler's last driver, who is still alive, and this was investigated in 1999 by a journalist associate of Agoston's who actually returned to the Pilsen area where Kammler was supposed to have killed himself, with the driver who claimed he buried the body. They actually found the wooded location where it was supposed to have occurred, but the driver then admitted to the journalist that it had all been lies with the purpose of providing a cover for Kammler's disappearance, but he could provide no further information about Kammler. So there is a strong possibility that Kammler, together with his secrets, survived the end of the Third Reich.

The information he had put him right at the very top of the wanted list for the East and West. Kammler's information was in three main areas: the V-weapons, which included the V1, V2, Rheinböte and HDP 'super-gun'; secondly the nuclear work; and thirdly the secret work being carried out inside the Skoda works near Pilsen. In the closing stages of the war all V-weapons work, including the Peenemünde team, was concentrated in a triangle south-west of Berlin, stretching from Bad Sachsa and Nordhausen in the north to Stadtilm in the south.

At Stadtilm, and also possibly in the nearby underground complexes of Ohrdruf and Crawinkel, the final nuclear weapons work was undertaken, again supervised by the SS, who were responsible for removing all the nuclear material and equipment from Stadtilm and Haigerloch before the Americans arrived. A total of between five and ten tons of heavy water vanished, and this alone had a market value in 1945 of between $2 million and $4 million. Finally there is the Skoda works at Pilsen, sixty miles from Prague. We know that the SS had a weapons research establishment attached to the Skoda works, the largest industrial complex in Czechoslovakia. Tom Agoston interviewed the German wartime Skoda chief, Dr Wilhelm Voss, on several occasions after the war, and he was able to confirm some aspects of the SS involvement at Skoda. Dr Voss was never charged with any war crimes after the war, although he was also involved in the arms industry in Germany, Austria and Italy, and had the honorary SS rank of Sturmbannführer (Major). Dr Voss was able to tell US interrogators investigating his wartime work that the Russians had captured the vast majority of the SS's secret weapons work when they occupied the remains of the Skoda works in 1945. Dr Voss's wartime work proved valuable in the 1950s when he went to Egypt to reorganize their armaments industry, a job in which he was able to utilize many German ex-wartime specialists from the military and industry, including Focke-Wulf and Messerschmitt. With the arrival of the Russian technical specialists in Egypt in 1955, Voss returned to Germany and died in 1974. The information he gave to the USA regarding his work at Skoda during the war is still classified in the US archives. The subject of exactly what work was being undertaken by the SS at Skoda is very much a question of speculation. What is known is that in the Prague area, at the Rusin airbase and the Letov aircraft works, development work was being carried out on special versions of the Heinkel He177 heavy bomber and the Ju290 transport. There is evidence that He177s were being modified with a lengthened bomb bay and pressurized cabin, for them to be used, it is claimed, as atomic bomb carriers. At any rate, it is apparent that the facilities and personnel of the right quality were available in the area.

Professor Blackett is also involved in the Skoda story. On page 20 of his 1948 book, in the section dealing with air power in Europe during the Second World War, he refers to the bombing of the Skoda works by the Allies on 25 April 1945. As he points out, about one-third of the until-then undamaged Skoda works was destroyed in the air raid. By 9 May the whole area was in Allied hands, and Professor Blackett is puzzled by this apparent 'wanton destruction', as he describes it. His puzzlement bears an uncanny resemblance to his words on the urgency with which the atomic bombs were dropped on Japan, and again the reason he puts forward is the rapidly advancing Russian forces. According to Blackett, the most common opinion in Prague at the time was that the raid took place to destroy an industrial competitor or to prevent Skoda falling into the hands of the Russians. In both cases, Blackett was perhaps unaware of German and Japanese nuclear developments, and certainly of the possibility that the SS were using Skoda for secret weapons work, which would have given the Allies a more plausible reason for the bombing raid, rather than claiming, as they did, that it was a legitimate military target.

Perhaps the most bizarre aspect of the Skoda story involves flying saucers. The story as repeated in several books is that two flying saucer designs were actually constructed, one in the Pilsen area, the German designer being Miethe, and one in Breslau by Rudolph Schriever. The Miethe disc had vectorable jets around the circumference, and is supposed to have made its first flight from the Prague area on 14 February 1945, reaching a height of 37,000 ft and a speed of 1,200 mph, approximately Mach 2. The Schriever disc had fixed jets around its edges, but no flights were made before the Breslau factory was captured by the Russians. There are three points to make about the flying saucer stories. Breslau was surrounded by Russian forces by late January 1945, and despite eventually being a hundred miles behind the Russian front line, did not surrender until 6 May, four days after Berlin. Was secret weapons work being carried out in Breslau, and was this the reason for the fanatical defence, specifically ordered by Hitler? Secondly, work on flying saucers continued after the war in the USA and Canada, and in particular A.V. Roe in Canada produced some flying designs, of which only the unsuccessful were made public. Finally there is the question of UFOs, a question that will not go away, despite repeated attempts by governments to provide explanations, such as meteorological balloons, ice formations, fakes and delusions of one sort or another. In 1998–9, the BBC made a series of programs on UFOs, and although a large percentage of so-called sightings could be explained away for the reasons above, a small number remain which defy explanation.

It is a fact that by the end of the war, Germany was the leader in high-speed flight, and companies such as Arado, Junkers and Messerschmitt had considerable experience in jet propulsion. Apart from the research carried out by the individual aircraft companies, only a few miles north of Nordhausen and Bad Sachsa, near the village of Volkerode, the Luftfahrtforschungsansalt Herman Goering (Herman Goering Aerodynamics Institute), was involved in research on weapons and aircraft. The 'father' of modern aerodynamics, Theodor von Karman, visited the site in 1945 with a group from America, and he said the whole thing was incredible, over a thousand people worked there and the Allies knew nothing about it. The facilities included four wind-tunnels, low-speed, high-speed and two supersonic tunnels, and more than sixty buildings, with laboratories, workshops and accommodation, all camouflaged with trees planted on the roofs and an airfield with hidden runways.

Kammler disappeared in 1945, but the search goes on. Tom Agoston's book on Kammler has been reprinted and revised several times in German, and members of the German and Dutch media are still probing the story, looking for that elusive new evidence. One of these people who is in contact with the author has a map which has been authenticated as originally belonging to Kammler. The map includes the Thuringia area of Germany where Nordhausen and Stadtilm are located, and Ohrdruf is circled in pencil. Further south in the mountains, another area is marked in blue, although there is no lake there: is this the location of the missing heavy water?

With regard to some of the nuclear questions, the author believes that Kurt Diebner could also have provided some of the answers. Diebner died in 1964, but from 1948 until his death he worked in Hamburg as a private consultant on nuclear power, especially with regard to ships. After his death, his personal papers relating to much of his wartime work vanished, including a secret patent for a reactor first issued from the Heereswaffenamt in 1941/2 and numbered T-45. Professor Rose relates the story of this particular patent and how, while the Americans seized 144,000 patent files, at least 37,000 secret patent files were destroyed by the Germans before the fall of Berlin, although some secret patent documents are in the Washington archives and still classified.

We have other clues to Diebner's involvement in nuclear weapons. When the Germans occupied France in June 1940, the HWA lost no time in visiting Frederic Joliot-Curie and his nuclear laboratories at the Collège de France in Paris. One of the first visitors was Kurt Diebner in early August 1940, only days after the Germans entered Paris. When Samuel Goudsmit of ALSOS interviewed Joliot-Curie in 1944 about his wartime involvement with the Germans and their visits, Joliot-Curie was specific about Diebner. Goudsmit's ALSOS report on his interview with 'J' (Joliot-Curie) states:

'J was interviewed at length by a German Army man named Diebner, physicist once co-worker of Pose. He had evidently studied in great detail all of J's official government contacts which might have had a bearing on TA [code for Tube Alloy, US name for nuclear programme]. This information he got from captured files from French Intelligence. Diebner acted very authoritatively and seemed to have a thorough knowledge of the TA problem. If the Germans do any work on TA, J expects Diebner to be a key man in the administrative set-up.'

What is remarkable is the speed with which German Scientific Intelligence obtained and translated the captured French nuclear information and transmitted it within days to the HWA and Diebner.

Diebner knew about the betatron particle accelerator at Stadtilm, but not a single mention was made of it during the Farm Hall recordings, evidence that deserved an Academy Award for acting. Other evidence that there may have been other betatrons operating comes from ALSOS after their arrival at the renamed Strasbourg University. Heisenberg's colleague Weizsacker had been made a professor at the university in 1942, and he and other German nuclear physicists did research there from 1942 to 1944. During this time there were reports of bright blue flashes coming from some of the laboratories where they were doing this work. Such blue flashes are produced by visible radiation as it passes through air or water, so-called 'Cerenkov radiation', and are typical of what could be produced by a betatron during its operation.

In late 1944, US Intelligence was very active searching for evidence of German secret weapons. Two reports refer to atomic bomb test sites in Germany, and state that 68 ft rockets existed. Figure 36 indicates that an apparatus was used at Strasbourg which produced an electric arc of enormous power for research into the disintegration of matter. Disintegration of matter is the original method of describing the nuclear decay process, following neutron capture, fission or nuclear bombardment, by which new isotopes are produced, and the equipment described sounds very like a particle accelerator, perhaps another betatron.

Figure 37 is a page from another US Intelligence report dated 24 January 1946, and it concerns the interrogation of a flak expert named Zinsser who was flying in an He111 south of Lübeck in northern Germany in October 1944. Zissner's statement includes references to an atomic bomb test site, a cloud shaped like a mushroom, strong electrical disturbances and a description of the cloud as being dotted, after a short period of darkness, with all sorts of light spots, which were in contrast to normal explosions, of a pale blue in colour. Mushroom-shaped clouds can be formed by any large explosion, conventional or nuclear, but the electrical disturbances and the colours indicate that this was not a conventional explosion.

Before the US first atomic test bomb on 16 July 1945 at Alamogordo, New Mexico, it was estimated that the explosive yield would be less than 13,000 tons of

SECRET

AMERICAN EMBASSY
OFFICE OF THE MILITARY ATTACHÉ
1, GROSVENOR SQUARE, W. 1
LONDON, ENGLAND

17 April 1945

Subject: Secret Weapon Experiments In "German Redoubt".

To   : Major F. J. Smith, Room 5119, New War Dept.
           Bldg., Washington, D. C.

          On 14 April 1945, at 1034 hours, the French
Telegraph Service broadcasted the following which is
thought to be of interest to your office:

    "German border: Somewhere in the "German redoubt",
there are reported to exist great underground laboratories
where scientists and technicians have been ordered by Hitler
personally to go on with experiments with new secret weapons.
The Fuehrer feverishly follows their work. The weapons are
said to include 'V6', the famous atomic bomb. They had already vainly tried to work on this in the thick-walled,
windowless casemates discovered in Strasbourg. They contained a special apparatus for producing an electric arc of
enormous power, which was used for researches in the dis-
intergration of matter. In addition to reserves already
accumulated, the laboratories in the 'redoubt' are still
producing gas. One of these gases is harmless in the open
air, but becomes toxic by contact and chemical combination
with the substances in the intake tube (cartouche) of gas-
masks, meant to neutralise the action of other gases."

          For the Military Attache:

                              H. K. CALVERT
                              Major, F.A.
                    Assistant to the Military Attache.

SECRET

Figure 36. A US report, dated 17 April 1945, that a betatron may have been used at
Strasbourg University during the German occupation from 1940 to 1944.

S E C R E T

46. The problem of harnessing the released energy in the sense of using it as power for engines, factory machines, transportation (ground, water, air), has not been practically solved as yet. This side of uranium research is clearly a post war problem.

47. A man named ZINSSER, a Flak rocket expert, mentioned what he noticed one day: In the beginning of Oct. 1944 I flew from Ludwigslust (South of Luebeck), about 12 to 15 km from an atomic bomb test station, when I noticed a strong, bright illumination of the whole atmosphere, lasting about 2 seconds.

48. The clearly visible pressure wave escaped the approaching and following cloud formed by the explosion. This wave had a diameter of about 1 km when it became visible and the color of the cloud changed frequently. It became dotted after a short period of darkness with all sorts of light spots, which were, in contrast to normal explosions, of a pale blue color.

49. After about 10 seconds the sharp outlines of the explosion cloud disappeared, then the cloud began to take on a lighter color against the sky covered with a gray overcast. The diameter of the s still visible pressure wave was at least 9000 meters while remaining visible for at least 15 seconds.

50. Personal observations of the colors of the explosion cloud found an almost blue-violet shade. During this manifestation reddish-colored rims were to be seen, changing to a dirty-like shade in very rapid succession.

51. The combustion was lightly felt from my observation plane in the form of pulling and pushing. The appearance of atmospheric disturbance lasted about 10 seconds without noticeable climax.

52. About one hour later I started with an He 111 from the A/D at Ludwigslust and flew in an easterly direction. Shortly after the start I passed through the almost complete overcast (between 3000 and 4000 meter altitude). A cloud shaped like a mushroom with turbulent, billowing sections (at about 7000 meter altitude) stood, without any seeming connections, over the spot where the explosion took place. Strong electrical disturbances and the impossibility to continue radio communication as by lightning, turned up.

53. Because of the P-38s operating in the area Wittenberg-Merseburg I had to turn to the north but observed a better visibility at the bottom of the cloud where the explosion occured.
Note: It does not seem very clear to me why these experiments took place in such crowded areas.

FOR THE COMMANDING OFFICER:

HELENES T. FREIBERGER
HELENES T. FREIBERGER
Captain   AC

DISTRIBUTION:

30	copies	G-2, Hq, USFET, Att: Capt. E.L. Wing
10	"	U S Army Air Forces in Washington, D.O.I.
12	"	USSTAF (Main), A-2 Section
12	"	USSTAF (Rear), A-2 Section
15	"	Ninth Air Force, A-2 Section
3	"	IX T.A.C., A-2 Section
3	"	XII T.A.C., A-2 Section
3	"	XXIX T.A.C., A-2 Section
3	"	Ninth Air Defense Command, D.O.I.
3	"	Ninth Air Division, D.O.I.
1	"	3rd U S Army, G-2 Section
1	"	15th U S Army, G-2 Section
80	"	A.D.I.(K), Air Ministry
10	"	AF.IU, 2nd TAF Main
35	"	Ninth Air Force Service Command, Disarmament Division, APO 149
2	"	Ninth Air Service Command, A-2
25	"	Files & Spares.

-6-

S E C R E T

Figure 37. A US Intelligence report of 24 January 1946, describing the apparent witnessing of a nuclear test by flak expert Zinsser.

TNT, but in fact the yield was over 17 kt. This increase was attributed to several causes. There was no experience of exploding large nuclear devices, and one possibility for the increase was that because the tamper was uranium oxide, some of the U.239 formed during the explosion might have increased the Pu.239 fission process, the U.239 acting as another fissile material. The problem was that U.239 has a half-life of only 23.5 minutes, which meant that there were no results from previous experimental work which gave figures for its fission cross-section or the ease with which it would fission. Thorium has a similar nuclide formed by neutron capture, Th.233, which has a similar half-life of 22.2 minutes and which would also act as a booster to U.233 in the same fashion as U.239 acts as a booster to Pu.239. Was there any chance that Germany (or Japan) had been able to produce enough U.233 from thorium to make at least one bomb, say about 10 lb (4.5 kg), or even a similar amount of Pu.239? There is the document produced by Fritz Houtermans (Figure 1), dated 3 September 1945, only days after the end of the war, and certainly too soon for him to have obtained the information from other sources. In the document he refers to the production of U.233 from thorium, and the information contained indicates that a considerable amount of work must have been done on the subject.

This document is in complete contrast to the Farm Hall discussion between Hahn, Gerlach and Bagge on 11 August. Gerlach stated that 60 kg of ionium was produced in Belgium, and he added some mystery to the story by mentioning the SS and physicist George Stetter. Ionium, thorium isotope 230, is used for dating, like carbon 14, and its use as weapon or reactor material is about as unlikely as using C-14 – another example of the Farm Hall 'Oscar performance'. In the USA in the 1950s, work was carried out irradiating thorium Th.232 in two uranium reactors, to produce U.233. They used the 3 MW LITR (Low Intensity Test Reactor) at Oak Ridge and the 40 MW MTR (Materials Testing Reactor) at Idaho. (This work is reported by L.J. Templin, in the Selected Bibliography.)

The published results of this work show that, depending on the neutron flux in the reactor, 1 gm of U.233 was produced per kilo of Th.232 after an irradiation period of 50 days. To produce enough U.233 for a bomb, say a minimum of 5 kg (11 lb), you would need to irradiate 5,000 kg (5 tons) of thorium for this period. The production of U.233 from thorium is complicated by the high levels of gamma radiation from one of the decay products, thorium 228, which has a half-life of 1.9 years. In some of the above experiments the U.233 was allowed to cool down for 3.5 years before it was removed for analysis, to reduce the radiation problems, but obviously in the Second World War that amount of time was not available and some form of remote handling would have been required. The use of slave-labour would have changed this situation, and since the effects of the radiation would not have become apparent immediately, this would have made the working conditions appear normal in the first instance.

The problem with obtaining U.233 is that a working reactor is required in the first place, and for 5 kg, quite a large reactor. Particle accelerators such as the betatron can produce small amounts of U.233, but a reactor of several megawatts thermal power is really required. Such a reactor does not need enriched uranium, and either uranium oxide or uranium metal can be used. The Windscale reactor in the UK was 160 MW, and reactor G-3 at Marcoule in France was 150 MW, using natural uranium fuel. Plutonium Pu.239 is produced in a similar manner to U.233, except that the uranium reactor produces Pu.239 directly from the uranium, but with a much lower conversion rate.

Typically, for a 40 MW reactor to produce 5 kg (11 lb) of Pu.239 would take at least 120 days, almost two and a half times longer than the time needed to produce the same amount of U.233, and by 1944/5, for the Germans and Japanese, the time factor was critical to the outcome of the war. In both cases, the U.233 and Pu.239 are obtained from the other radioactive material by chemical processing. The author believes that, in both Germany and Japan, by the middle of 1944 the nuclear weapon options had been reduced to just two possibilities. There was the radioactive material package using one or more betatrons to produce the material. This radioactive material would be mixed with sand or similar, and packed with conventional high explosives, ideally to be detonated above ground for maximum distribution. The choice of radioactive isotopes would be important, because some have long half-lives; cobalt 60, for example, has a half-life of 5.9 years, which would effectively mean any territory sprayed with Co. 60 would be almost unusable for years. In 1944, if the British invasion ports where the D-Day armadas were assembling could have been attacked with radioactive material spread over large areas, this would have effectively cancelled the D-Day landings for months, if not permanently. From the ALSOS investigations in Brussels shortly after it was liberated in 1944, we know that the Germans had suddenly developed a keen interest in thorium. The German metal-refining company Auer had left papers behind in Brussels which showed that they had shipped all the French thorium stocks to Germany in August 1944, the actual quantity not being known. ALSOS managed to 'capture' an Auer chemist named Jansen near Brussels who had been involved in this thorium transfer to Germany, and he told ALSOS that the material was required to make an especially white toothpaste, an absurd explanation that was accepted by the ALSOS scientists.

Not only that, but Jansen had rail ticket stubs in his papers that showed he had made a trip to Hechingen, which is the nearest rail link with Haigerloch, where Heisenberg and his team were building their final reactor experiment. Once again, his explanation, of visiting his mother, was accepted by ALSOS. Thorium never appeared on the order list in the messages sent between Tokyo and Berlin, but from Figure 27 it can be seen that Japan had ample sources of monzanite in North Korea, the ore from which thorium is extracted.

Japan may or may not have had the capability to produce radioactive material, but there is mention of cyclotrons there: these are a type of particle accelerator, different from the betatron, but which will produce the same end result. Otherwise there is the nuclear cargo on U-234, which was either radioactive material to be used as such with the submersible aircraft carriers, or a highly radioactive neutron source derived from beryllium and radium. Neutron sources which use radium have a very long life, because the half-life of the radium isotope used is 1,620 years. Such a neutron source could have been used as a 'trigger' to initiate a nuclear weapon, and it may have been such a trigger that the Japanese were waiting for, as mentioned in Wilcox's book. Alternatively, U-234 was carrying detonators (fuses), and it may be that these were special detonators intended for the explosive charges on an implosion weapon, in which case they could also be described as 'triggers'.

It is possible, then, that apart from radioactive material weapons, the second nuclear devices built by Germany and Japan were atomic bombs based on U.233 derived from thorium. They used a 'tamper' on the outside of the nuclear core made from thorium and beryllium. This tamper would ensure that as large an amount of the fissile material as possible was fissioned before the tamper vaporized in the heat of the explosion. The beryllium would ensure that the smallest number of neutrons possible escaped from the core, and the thorium would provide some Th.233 to add to the yield of the explosion. At the centre of the core of fissile material, there would be a neutron source of radium, or polonium mixed with beryllium. If tritium had been produced from the lithium shipped to Japan, this, together with deuterium, would have been at the centre of the core to add fusion to the fission and provide what is described as a 'boosted fission' weapon, added to by the beryllium fusion neutrons. In this case the neutron source would have had to be moved from the centre of the weapon to just beyond the fissile core.

Figure 38 is a German atomic bomb target map of central New York showing the radii of damage from the 'ground zero' (GZ) detonation point. For all nuclear weapons there is an optimum detonation height to achieve either the optimum heat/contamination effects or blast effect. For a 20 kt bomb similar to that dropped on Hiroshima and Nagasaki, these heights correspond to 600 ft and 1,100 ft respectively. If we assume, that due to the high buildings in New York, an above ground detonation was definitely intended, then from Figure 38, the maximum destruction (heat or blast) is shown as occurring at a radius from GZ of 1.33 km or 0.83 miles. From post-war nuclear weapon tests we know that a radius of 0.83 miles from GZ for the maximum heat or blast damage corresponds to a weapon of about 20 to 30 kt explosive yield and hence this is approximately the size of the bomb featured on the target map.

This weapon could have been delivered by an aircraft or missile but once again a requirement would have been for an accurate proximity fuse. Perhaps the V1 U-boat threat against New York was not a decoy but a real project, complementing the use of V2s in U-boat towed submersible containers.

The source of Figure 38 is attributed to a report by Dr Eugene Saenger on the Long-Range Rocket and Bomber Project of August 1944. Dr Saenger was one of the early aeronautical researchers in Germany and he continued his work after the war, as a professor at Stuttgart and Director of the Institute of Jet Propulsion. As late as 1958 he was working on rocket/space projects using nuclear power for the propulsive force, as was Dr Stuhlinger in the USA. The difference was that Dr Stuhlinger's ideas were based on actual projects being considered by NASA and the US Atomic Energy Commission (AEC).

But the submarine mysteries went on beyond the end of the war, and we return to U-873, which was given the codename 'Anton-1' by the Germans. The problem was that another U-boat, U-843, had been given an almost identical codename,

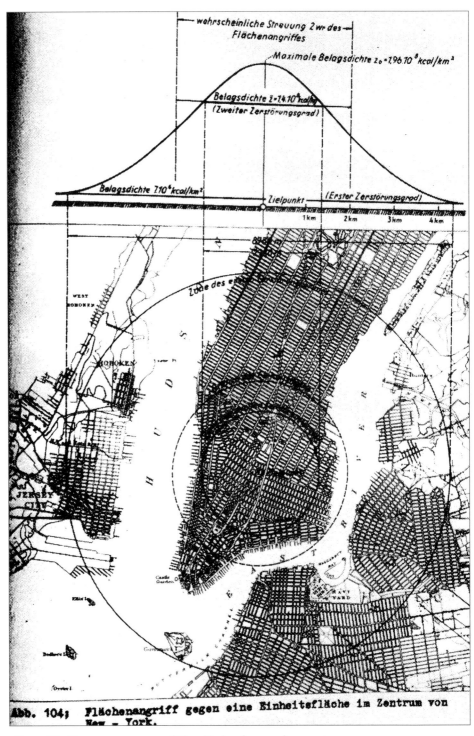

Figure 38. German target map of New York – for a nuclear weapon.

'Anton', but U-843 had been sunk on its return from Djakarta on 9 April 1945 while transferring from Kristiansand to Flensburg. The ULTRA message 1809 of 15 April 1945 was the loading list for Anton-1 (U-873), but the US codebreakers appear to have initially confused Anton (U-843) with Anton-1 (U-873) and originally identified U-843 as being the recipient of the cargo in ULTRA 1809, a mistake that was later corrected. However, in post-war Germany, there may have been some confusion about exactly which U-boat had the cargo given in the loading list of 15 April from Berlin to Tokyo, which included the very valuable beryllium. As a rule, no sunken U-boats were raised after the war if they contained dead crew members. U-843 was sunk with the loss of 44 crew, but on 22 August 1958, U-843 was located and recovered, and later broken-up at Gothenburg, Sweden. Was this unusual action taken because some one believed that the beryllium had been loaded on U-843? Certainly the USA never admitted that part of the cargo on U-873 was beryllium, and the ULTRA-decoded messages were not released for many years after 1958, so the fate of the beryllium was always a mystery, but it was certainly too valuable to leave on the sea bed. Or was U-843 carrying something from Japan that was also too valuable to leave on the sea bed?

THE PICTURE IS COMPLETE

This heading is a slight exaggeration, but even though there are still some pieces of the jigsaw missing, this does not spoil the view too much, and the picture is clear.

The missing pieces would tell us where Germany was building the reactors using the materials also being sent to Japan, and where the bombs were being designed and built, as Stadtilm was to a large extent just one of the pieces in the nuclear picture, and we know that Germany had V-weapons designed for a nuclear payload. They would also tell us what actually was going on at Skoda and the fate of General Kammler, and would explain the mystery of the flights to Japan and the Junkers truck.

We would also see exactly what type of nuclear weapon Japan had produced by the summer of 1945, and what precisely were the plans for the submersible aircraft carriers.

But for the time being, this is the end of the story. If the new 'enemy', Russia, and the Cold War dictated that many aspects of the Second World War presented to the public were far from the truth, perhaps now is the time to really put the record straight.

Karl Jaspers, philosopher and critic of the Nazi regime, lived in Germany throughout the war and never deviated from his ideas that man should have freedom of choice and action, and wrote in 1945,

'That which has happened is a warning, to forget it is guilt.'

For this reason alone, we need to know what really happened.

Glossary

Apogee	The highest point of a trajectory.
ASDIC	Acronym for Allied Submarine Detection Investigation Committee, used to describe equipment for locating underwater objects by high-speed sound waves.
Atom	The smallest particle of which all matter is composed. An atom of matter resembles a tiny solar system. The central sun of the atom is the nucleus around which electrons move, the planets of the system. The nucleus itself is composed of particles called protons and neutrons. Although the diameter of the nucleus is is only about 1/10,000 of the atom, almost all the mass of the atom is contained in the nucleus. Electrons have a negative electric charge, protons positive and neutrons no electric charge.
Atomic Number	The number of protons in an atomic nucleus. Symbol Z.
Atomic weight	The weight of an atom of an element, based relatively on the common isotope of carbon, which is 12.
Ballistic missile	Generally used to describe a missile which is guided or controlled for the first part of its trajectory but which afterwards continues along a natural uncontrolled trajectory.
Beryllium	Metallic element, symbol Be. Atomic number 4. Atomic weight 9.0122. Relative density 1.85. A very important metal in the nuclear industry. An excellent 'moderator', with a high scattering cross-section and a low neutron-absorption cross-section. When bombarded by alpha particles it becomes a neutron emitter (neutron source). When struck by a high-energy neutron it releases two neutrons of its own, and hence can be used to boost fission and fusion weapons. Extremely toxic.
Boosted fission	The process by which the explosive yield of a fission weapon is increased by the presence of tritium and deuterium in the core of the weapon, which produces fusion and very-high-energy neutrons.
Boron/boric acid	Non-metallic element, symbol B. Atomic number 5. Atomic weight 10.81. Relative density 2.34. Obtained from sodium borate and kernite. Used in flares, propellants, abrasives, alloys, and boric acid as an antiseptic. It has a very high thermal neutron-absorption cross-section, and diluted boric acid is used as a neutron 'poisoner' in PWRs.
Breeding	The process by which a nuclear reactor produces more fissile material than it consumes Plutonium Pu.239 can be bred more efficiently in a 'fast' reactor than a thermal reactor because there are more fast neutrons available for fission than slow neutrons, 2.9 against 2.15. Uranium U.233 can be bred almost equally well in either a fast or a thermal reactor because there are almost equal numbers of both types of neutrons, 2.29 and 2.40.
Centrifuge	A mechanical device for separating U.235 from U.238, consisting basically of a spinning cylinder rotating about its longitudinal axis and containing uranium hexafluoride. Centrifuges are grouped together in cascades, with several thousand in each group.
Chain reaction	A self-sustaining nuclear reaction in which the release of neutrons following fission exceeds those lost by absorption, capture and leakage, leading to the fission of an increasing number of nuclei and the further release of neutrons.
Control rods	Rods used in a nuclear reactor, usually located above the core and used to control the neutron population and hence the reactivity in the core. They are composed of material with high thermal neutron-absorbing cross-sections, such as alloys of boron, silver, cadmium, indium and hafnium.
Cross-section	The concept of the probability of a particular nuclear reaction occurring, following the collision between a neutron and nucleus. There are four types of cross-section in nuclear reactions scattering, absorption, fission and capture, where the total absorption cross-section of an element is the sum of the fission and capture cross-sections. Cross-sections are expressed in 'barns' where a barn is 10^{24} cm^2.
Critical energy	Following the absorption of a neutron by a nucleus, fission will not occur unless the new compound nucleus has enough energy to split into two fission fragments, and expel neutrons. The energy required for fission is called the 'critical energy'. The energy contained in the compound nucleus is provided by the 'binding energy' of the colliding neutron plus any energy it contained before absorption.

Decay heat	After the shut-down of a reactor, large amounts of heat continue to be produced from the kinetic energy of the fission fragments, fission neutrons, gamma radiation and the alpha and beta decay process.
Doppler effect	The returning frequency of sound or magnetic waves directed at a moving object is proportional to the speed at which the object is moving away from the transmitter. It results in an apparent change in frequency, especially of sound waves, to an observer.
Electromagnetic separation	A modification of the mass spectrometer technique for the detection, identification and measurement of isotopes, in which larger-scale equipment is used to separate U.235 from U.238.
Electron	Sub-atomic particle with a negative electric charge.
Element	A substance that cannot be split chemically into a simpler substance. The atoms of an element all have the same number of protons in their nuclei.
Enriched uranium	Natural uranium consists of two main isotopes, U.235 and U.238 in the proportions of 0.72 per cent and 99.28 per cent respectively. For some types of reactors and all nuclear weapons, the U.235 content is increased to about 3 per cent for reactors and 90 per cent for weapons.
Fertile material	Nuclides which can be converted into fissile material. The only known examples are thorium 232 and uranium 238, which can be converted into U.233 and Pu.239 respectively.
Fission	The release of large amounts of energy by the splitting-up of atomic nuclei into two lighter nuclei, called fission fragments, accompanied by the liberation of neutrons. The fission of U.235 is composed of approximately 82 per cent kinetic energy of the fission fragments and 18 per cent energy of gamma radiation, neutrons, alpha and beta particles and neutrinos.
Fissile material	Nuclides that will undergo fission with neutrons of any energy. The only known examples are U.233, U.235 and Pu.239.
Fissionable material	Nuclides that will undergo fission with neutrons of a specific energy only. Examples are Th.232 and U.238 which will undergo fission only with fast neutrons with energies above about 1 MeV.
Fizzle	An incomplete or premature nuclear explosion in which very little fissile material is fissioned.
Fusion	A nuclear reaction in which certain light atomic nuclei combine to form the nucleus of a heavier atom. Such materials are the nuclei of deuterium and tritium. The fusion process results in the release of large amounts of energy. Some fusion occurs in a fission explosion, and as fusion produces high-energy neutrons, these can be used to cause fission in U.238 and Th.232, as well as boosting the fission of U.235, U.233 and Pu.239.
Gaseous diffusion	Originally the main commercial method of separating U.235 from U.238, in which uranium hexafluoride diffuses through a porous barrier. This method is now being superseded by advances in centrifuge technology.
Gold	Metallic element. Symbol Au. Atomic number 79. Atomic weight 196.97. Relative density 19.3. Gold has three important nuclear properties: firstly, due to its density, it is an excellent attenuator (stopper) of gamma radiation; secondly it had several resonance periods when the thermal neutron-absorption rate is very high; and finally it is the most efficient absorber of alpha particles available, gold being used as the 'standard'.
Ground zero	The point on the ground immediately underneath the centre of a nuclear explosion.
Gun-type weapon	A nuclear weapon in which a conventional explosive charge is used to force a mass of fissile material along a modified gun-barrel into another mass of fissile material. This forms a supercritical mass of fissile material, producing a nuclear explosion.
Gyroscope	A mechanical device using a spinning mass (flywheel) in which the spin axis tends to remain fixed in space. The flywheel is mounted in gimbals which allow it one or two degrees of freedom.
Hafnium	Metallic element. Symbol Hf. Atomic number 72. Atomic weight 178.5. Relative density 13.31. Found in zirconium minerals. Because it has a very high thermal neutron-absorption cross-section, it can be used as an alloy for nuclear reactor control rods. Hence, when zirconium is used for reactor fuel tubes, virtually all traces of hafnium must be removed. First commercial production by J. Kroll, Luxembourg, 1941.
Heavy water	Deuterium oxide. Water composed of the hydrogen isotope deuterium, which has a mass twice that of hydrogen and oxygen, of which 'light' water is composed. Heavy water has a high thermal neutron-scattering cross-section and a low neutron-absorption cross-section, making it an excellent reactor moderator. It was originally produced by the electrolysis of water, but this has been superseded by the cheaper fractional distillation method.
HTP	High Test Peroxide. Concentrated hydrogen peroxide which when used with a suitable catalyst – calcium or potassium permanganate – produces high-energy steam. HTP systems are often used

	in rockets, particularly to drive auxiliary power units. In a very diluted form it is used as a bleaching agent for hair, peroxide blonde. HTP is very volatile and reacts violently with many substances, especially ferrous metals.
Hydrogen	Colourless, highly inflammable gas with three isotopes: protium, tritium and deuterium. Used in many chemical processes. It was originally produced by the electrolysis of water.
Hydrogen bomb	A nuclear weapon utilizing the fusion process, in which isotopes of hydrogen and lithium are fused together, producing a massive release of energy. Also referred to as a thermonuclear, or fusion, bomb.
ICBM	Inter-Continental Ballistic Missile. The term is usually applied to a missile with a range of more than 5,000 miles.
Ionization	The process by which radiation is induced into material by the passage of alpha or beta nuclear particles. Gamma rays, X-rays and neutrons produce ionization indirectly.
Implosion	The opposite of explosion. It describes how explosives are used to compress fission or fusion materials into a supercritical mass.
Inland Sea	Japan comprises four main islands, Kyushu, Honshu, Shikoku and Hokkaido. Between the largest island, Honshu, and the smallest, Shikoku, is a stretch of water called the Inland Sea. It has two outlets into the Pacific and one into the Sea of Japan.
Isotope	Atoms of an element with the same atomic number but with different numbers of neutrons in their nucleus. Isotopes can occur naturally or they can be produced as a result of nuclear reactions. All artificial isotopes are radioactive, and some elements, such as uranium, have both natural and artificial isotopes.
Kamikaze	From the Japanese meaning 'Divine Wind', and usually applied to suicide attacks from the air.
Lead	Metallic element. Symbol Pb. Atomic number 82. Atomic weight 207.2. Relative density 11.35. Has many industrial uses, and is a cheap and effective radiation shield material, especially for gamma- and X-rays.
Lithium	Chemical element in alkali metal group. Symbol Li. Atomic number 3. Atomic weight 6.941. Relative density 0.534. Lithium has many uses in industry, but when the natural isotope lithium-6 is bombarded with slow neutrons it produces helium and tritium.
Mach number	The ratio of the speed of sound of a body divided by the speed of sound in the air through which the body is moving. Mach 1 implies that the body is moving at the speed of sound. At sea level the speed of sound in air is approximately 750 mph.
Manhattan Project	Name given to American Second World War nuclear weapons programme which was under US Army control and led by Major-General Leslie Groves, of the Manhattan District Engineers.
Mass number	The total number of protons and neutrons in an atomic nucleus. Symbol A. Uranium U.235 has a mass number of 235, 92 protons and 143 neutrons.
Mean free path	The average total distance covered by a neutron before it collides with a nucleus. In most substances the distance is 1–4 inches. The mean free path defines the size of the fissile material, in that it has to be larger than the m.f.p., otherwise neutrons will run out of material before hitting a nucleus, although not all neutrons produce fission, and this has to be taken into account.
Moderator	In a nuclear reactor using uranium, the probability of the fission of U.235 by slow neutrons is much higher than for fast neutrons. Hence the neutrons are slowed down by substances with small thermal neutron-absorption and high thermal neutron-scattering cross-sections. The energy of slow neutrons depends on temperature, and so they are called thermal neutrons, and reactors utilizing fission by slow neutrons are called thermal reactors. Many modern power station reactors use ordinary 'light' water as a moderator since it absorbs more neutrons than heavy water, beryllium or graphite; therefore the fuel used has to be enriched to about 3 per cent with U.235.
Neon	Gaseous element. Symbol Ne. Atomic number 10. Atomic weight 20.183. Apart from its use in neon tubes, it has considerable use in nuclear research. It is used in spark chambers and liquid-hydrogen bubble chambers to detect the passage of nuclear particles.
Neutrino	An electrically neutral particle which has zero mass and which carries off surplus energy in the beta decay process.
Neutron	Atomic nuclei contain two particles, protons and neutrons, symbol 'n'. Neutrons have no electric charge and are slightly heavier than protons. Neutrons are stable when bound in nuclei, but free neutrons have a mean lifetime of about 15 minutes before a nuclear interaction occurs. During fission, 99.25 per cent of the neutrons, 'prompt neutrons', are liberated very quickly, and the remainder, 'delayed neutrons', are liberated in six groups over a longer period of time.

	Prompt neutrons are of high energy and velocity, and delayed neutrons of lower energies, but all neutrons eventually slow down as a result of collisions with nuclei.
Neutron energy	Neutron energies are expressed in electron volts, eV, and they can vary from almost zero to several million, MeV. Thermal, slow neutrons have energies of less than 1 eV.
Neutron absorption scattering	In neutron to nuclei collisions, there are two results, elastic scattering and inelastic scattering. In elastic scattering the result is similar to two billiard balls colliding, there is an exchange of energy and the neutron remains free. In inelastic scattering the neutron is absorbed by the nucleus: the two most important nuclear reactions resulting from this neutron absorption are radiative capture, and fission. If sufficient energy is available, the 'excited' compound nucleus formed can fission into two separate nuclei, fission fragments, and liberate neutrons. If insufficient energy is available for fission, the compound nucleus, with the 'captured' neutron, is now an isotope of the original material, with the same atomic number but with one unit higher in mass number. The capture process has some important results in that following neutron capture by U.238 and Th.232, they eventually produce Pu.239 and U.233 after four stages of beta decay. The excess energy of the compound nucleus is usually emitted as gamma radiation.
Neutron flux	This is a measure of the neutron concentration and activity at any time, and is the product of the neutron population times their velocity.
Neutron multiplication factor, 'k'	The value of 'k' for the fission reaction indicates the number of neutrons available for fission compared to those lost by capture and leakage into the surrounding structure. If 'k' is less than 1.0, the reaction is sub-critical and the fission process will die out. If 'k' is 1.0, the reaction is critical and a self-sustaining chain reaction will occur. If 'k' is greater than 1.0, the reaction is supercritical, and unless it is controlled (by control rods), the neutron population will grow without limit, possibly very quickly, a potentially dangerous situation. Once the value of 'k' is 1.0, a reactor can operate at any power level, e.g. 100 W or 1,000,000 W.
Neutron source	The action of alpha and gamma particles on some materials results in those materials emitting neutrons. Beryllium, mixed with an alpha emitter such as radium or polonium, is probably the most widely used neutron source. Some nuclides, such as californium 252, decay by spontaneous fission, and this results in them being a powerful source of neutrons. 1 g of Cf 252 produces 3,000,000,000,000 neutrons per second.
Nucleon	A photon or neutron forming part of an atomic nucleus.
Nucleus	The positively charged centre of an atom composed of protons and neutrons, and containing virtually all the mass of the atom.
Nuclide	An atomic nucleus with a specific atomic number, atomic mass number and energy state.
Oralloy	An acronym for Oak Ridge Alloy, weapons-grade uranium with at least 90 per cent U.235 and produced at the American Oak Ridge nuclear plant.
Particle accelerators	A nuclear reaction is produced when two nuclei contact each other. These are usually positively charged, in which case they tend to repel each other. To overcome this repelling force the colliding particle is given a very high velocity in order to bring it into contact with the nucleus repelling it, hence the need for particle accelerators. There are several types of particle accelerator intended to produce the disintegration of nuclei by bombardment with particles: Van de Graaff generator for protons, deuterons and helium nuclei; cyclotron for protons; betatron for electrons; linear accelerators for electrons and protons. High-energy versions of these accelerators have been produced in which synchrotron is added to the title.
Photon	A basic particle having no mass or electric charge but having angular and linear momentum or energy. Commonly used to describe the energy in gamma radiation.
Pit	Term used in the USA to describe the inner assembly of a nuclear weapon. Usually comprising the fissile core, air gap, and tamper, plus neutron source.
Polonium	Metallic element. Symbol Po. Atomic number 84. Atomic weight 210. Relative density 9.32. Polonium is a highly radioactive alpha emitter, the most useful isotope being Po.210, with a half-life of 138.4 days. Used with beryllium as a neutron source. Po is produced as a by-product of radium disintegration (decay) or by bombarding bismuth or lead with neutrons.
Plutonium	A range of artificial isotopes which are only produced in quantity in a nuclear reactor. The most important plutonium isotope is Pu.239, which fissions by neutrons of all energies and has a half-life of 24,400 years. All plutonium isotopes are radioactive.
Proton	Particle of atomic nucleus with a positive electric charge.

Radioactivity	The spontaneous emission of radiation from atomic nuclei. Radiation is of four types: alpha, highly positively charged heavy particle with little penetration power, stopped by a sheet of paper, but producing ionization in material it travels through, produced during the fission and decay processes; beta, high-speed electrons produced during the decay process with slightly more penetration than alpha particles and producing little ionization; gamma rays, produced during the fission and decay processes, and extremely penetrating so that steel, concrete or lead shields are required, the thickness depending on the gamma ray energy and the degree of protection; X-rays, similar to gamma rays but with less power and produced outside the fission process. Neutron radiation is mainly produced during the fission process, and it is very penetrating and capable of ionizing material it passes through. Neutron sources also produce neutron radiation.
Radioactive decay	Some naturally occurring isotopes, especially with high atomic numbers, are unstable and undergo radioactive disintegration (decay) at various rates. In addition, many artificial isotopes are produced in reactors, or in particle accelerators or by neutron capture. The decay process continues until a stable configuration of neutrons to protons is reached, about 1:1. During the decay process, gamma and beta radiation is emitted, and in some cases alpha rays. The term 'half-life' is used to describe the time in which the radioactivity of a source has decayed to half its original amount.
Radioactive series	There are three naturally occurring radioactive series and one artificial. The natural series are uranium, thorium and actinium, and the artificial one is neptunium. The uranium series begins with U.238 and by alpha and beta decay ends with lead 206. The thorium series starts with Th.232 and ends with lead 208. The actinium series begins with U.235 and ends with lead 207. Neptunium begins with Pu.241 and ends with bismuth 209.
Radium	Radioactive chemical element. Symbol Ra. Atomic number 88. Relative density 5. Main source is pitchblende, and uses were originally medical for its gamma radiation, in luminous paint and for its alpha radiation with beryllium as a neutron source.
Reactor	Equipment which utilizes the fission chain-reaction process to produce heat and power. It usually comprises a core of uranium oxide, uranium metal or uranium enriched with about 3 per cent U.235 as the fuel. The fuel is surrounded by a moderator and reflector, which are sometimes the same material. Either above or below the core are control rods, and surrounding the core is the coolant for removing heat, the entire assembly being enclosed within vessels of steel and concrete. The coolant is used to produce steam, which then passes to a turbine-generator to produce electricity.
Reactor period	If all neutrons released during fission were 'prompt', the increase in neutron population following an increase in reactivity due, say, to control rod removal, would be very rapid, making the reactor impossible to control. In such circumstances the 'reactor period' would be less than 1.0 sec. Because of 'delayed neutrons', the reactor period can be arranged to be around 100 seconds, allowing time for the control rods to adjust the activity in the core. If the increase in activity is greater than the delayed neutron fraction, then the neutron population will increase by prompt neutrons alone and the reactor will be classed as 'prompt critical'.
Reflector	Containment surrounding the reactor or weapon core to prevent the escape of neutrons into the surrounding material. Reflector materials have a low neutron-absorption cross-section and a high neutron-scattering cross-section. Materials used are light and heavy water, graphite, and the most efficient – beryllium.
Relative density	The density of a substance relative to the density of a standard substance, usually taken to be water at 4°C.
Resonance absorption and Doppler effect	Many elements have a period of resonance absorption in which the absorption rate of neutrons increases rapidly at certain neutron energies and temperature increases. This increase in neutron absorption is due to the resonance peaks broadening because of the Doppler effect. Hence, any increase in core temperature, and consequently fuel temperature, reduces the neutron population, removing activity from the core and acting as a first-stage safety measure.
Re-entry Vehicle, RV	The main part of a ballistic missile to re-enter the atmosphere, usually containing the warhead and associated guidance equipment. Other variations are: MRV: Multiple RV, a missile which separates into several warheads, usually intended for the same target; MIRV: Multiple Independently Targetable RV, a missile in which each warhead can be guided independently or to different targets; MARV: Manoeuvring RV, a missile in which each warhead can change its trajectory after re-entry, in order to confuse the enemy defence system.

Scabbing	When a missile hits a target such as a concrete bunker, the stresses generated can result in a large portion of material being ejected from the back face of the target, even though penetration has not occurred.
Silo	A circular emplacement with lid, usually made from reinforced concrete sunk into the ground and designed to accommodate one ICBM vertically.
Snorkel (Ger. *Schnorchel*)	Used initially by German U-boats, this Dutch invention allowed the diesels to be run while the boat was partially submerged. It consisted of a tube with a non-return valve at the head, the tube being extensible above the surface of the sea. The snorkel allowed batteries to be recharged and provided air for the crew.
Spalling	When a missile hits a target, spalling occurs when material is ejected from the target's surface without penetration necessarily occurring.
Spontaneous fission	Some artificially produced nuclides, especially those with even atomic and mass numbers, can fission without contact with additional neutrons, resulting in the release of further neutrons. The most powerful example with a practical half-life is californium 252.
Tamper	A dense metal casing surrounding the fuel in a fissile weapon, which delays the release of the explosive energy until it reaches its design value. The tamper may also serve as a reflector, and in a boosted fission or fusion weapon, as an additional source of fissile material. Materials used are beryllium, uranium, thorium and gold.
Thallium	Metallic element. Symbol Tl. Atomic number 81. Atomic weight 204.4. Relative density 11.85. A highly toxic metal, originally used as a rodent poison. Its only commercial use is in infra-red lenses, photoelectric cells and radiation detectors. It is used in the scintillation counter, the most accurate method of detecting alpha, beta and gamma radiation. Crystals doped with thallium produce visible blue light when exposed to radiation, generating a measurable voltage.
Thorium	Metallic element. Symbol Th. Atomic number 90. Atomic weight 232.04. Relative density 11.66. Thorium has thirteen radioactive isotopes of which only one, Th.232, occurs naturally. Obtained from monzanite ore, Th.232 is fissionable but only with fast, high-energy neutrons, above 1 MeV. The fissile U.233 is produced following neutron capture by Th.232 and four stages of beta decay.
Test vehicles	Used to describe any rocket or missile launched to obtain data or to confirm design information, as opposed to those used operationally.
Tritium	A radioactive isotope of hydrogen. Atomic weight 3. Half-life 12.5 years. Can be produced in reactors or by bombardment of lithium-6 by a powerful neutron source.
Tube Alloy	The original Manhattan Project code name for uranium metal, often abbreviated to TA, and used to indicate any work associated with nuclear weapons.
Uranium	Metallic element. Symbol U. Atomic number 92. Atomic weight 238.03. Relative density 18.95. Obtained from pitchblende, carnotite and monzanite ores. Natural uranium contains three isotopes, U.234 (0.005 per cent), U.235 (0.72 per cent) and U.238 (99.28 per cent). U.235 is fissionable by neutrons of all energies (slow or fast), whereas U.238 will fission only by high-energy (fast) neutrons, above about 1 MeV. However, U.238 is responsible for Pu.239 production via neutron capture and beta decay, during the fission process. There are at least fourteen known isotopes of uranium.
Urchin	American name given to neutron sources made from beryllium and polonium, and used as triggers to initiate fission weapons.
Yield	The explosive power of a nuclear weapon. Usually expressed in kilotons, kt, implying that the weapon is equivalent to 'x' thousand tons of high explosive.
Zirconium	Metallic element. Symbol Zr. Atomic number 40. Atomic weight 91.22. Relative density 6.5. Zirconium was first commercially produced in 1941 by J. Kroll, Luxembourg, and is obtained mainly from zircon. Zirconium is an important metal in the nuclear industry due to its resistance to corrosion and high-temperature strength, and most importantly it has a very low thermal neutron-absorption cross-section. Used particularly for the tubes holding the fuel in Pressurized and Boiling Water Reactors (PWRs and BWRs). It is usually alloyed with small amounts of tin, iron, chrome and nickel. Zirconium hydride, zirconium heated in hydrogen gas, has both the small neutron capture cross-section of zirconium and the high scattering cross-section of hydrogen. Zirconium hydride moderator mixed with uranium fuel ensures that the moderator temperature follows that of the fuel with little delay. In its nuclear use, virtually all traces of the neutron absorber hafnium must be removed.

Appendices

APPENDIX 1

US Report on the Interrogation of U-234 crew, dated 27 June 1945, including technical details of U-234, preparations for the voyage to Japan and a list of officers.

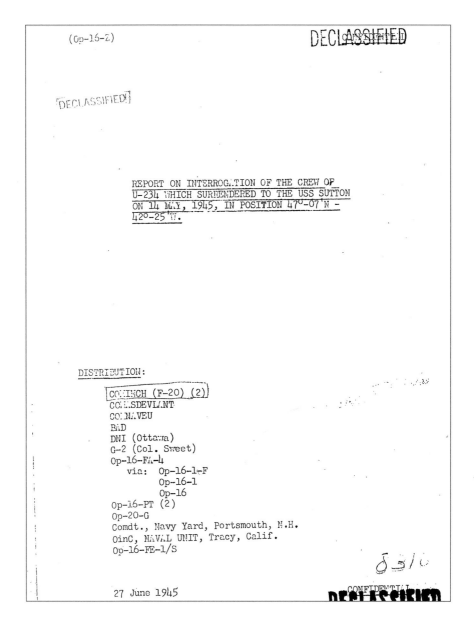

(Op-16-Z)

DECLASSIFIED

DECLASSIFIED

REPORT ON INTERROGATION OF THE CREW OF
U-234 WHICH SURRENDERED TO THE USS SUTTON
ON 14 MAY, 1945, IN POSITION 47°-07'N -
42°-25'W.

DISTRIBUTION:

COMINCH (F-20) (2)
COMSDEVLANT
COMNAVEU
BAD
DNI (Ottawa)
G-2 (Col. Sweet)
Op-16-FA-4
    via: Op-16-1-F
          Op-16-1
          Op-16
Op-16-PT (2)
Op-20-G
Comdt., Navy Yard, Portsmouth, N.H.
OinC, NAVAL UNIT, Tracy, Calif.
Op-16-FE-1/S

27 June 1945

CONFIDENTIAL
DECLASSIFIED

(Op-16-Z)

REPORT ON INTERROGATION OF THE CREW OF
U-234 WHICH SURRENDERED TO THE USS SUTTON
ON 14 MAY, 1945, IN POSITION 47°-07'N –
42°-25'W.

D E T A I L S

Number: U-234.

Type: IX-B.

Tonnage: 1650 Tons (actual tonnage with cargo aboard was
                            stated to be between 2100 and 2200 Tons).

Yard Number: G 664.

Building Yard: Germania Werft, Kiel.

Keel Laid: September 1942. (In May, 1943, U-234 was hit by
                     an aerial bomb while on the building ways. A
                     forward section of about 9 meters in length
                     was severely damaged and had to be completely
                     replaced.)

Launched: 23 December, 1943.

Commissioned: 3 March, 1944.

Commanding Officer: Klt. Johann Heinrich FEHLER, (P/W).

Armament: 2 Torpedo tubes aft.
                     2 Double-mount 20-mm guns on Platform I.
                     1 Double-mount 37-mm gun on Platform II.
                     (1 10.5-cm gun was removed from the forward
                     deck after the U.A.K. trials.)

Torpedoes: 7 Torpedoes carried, consisting of 2 T-1 (FAT)
                     3 T-3 A (FAT), 2 T-5s.
                     Torpedoes were stowed as follows:
                     2 in the tubes
                     3 under the floor plates
                     2 on the floor plates.

Torpedo Pistols: 3 Pi-1
                     4 Pi-2
                     3 Pi 4C.

Scuttling Charges: 12 1/2 Kilogram scuttling charges carried in
                     ammunition locker.

Mine Shafts: 6 3-mine shafts forward amidships.
                     12 2-mine shafts located port and starboard.

(Op-16-Z)   DECLASSIFIED CONFIDENTIAL

S.B.T: Fitted.

Diesels: 2 G.W. Diesels of 2100 HP each without super-
                      charger.

Supercharger: Kapsel type with Vulkan clutch for Schnorcheling.

Schnorchel: Fitted, Deschimag Type 2.

Cut-away Deck: Not fitted.

Electric Motors: A.E.G. of 560 HP each.

Switchboard: A.E.G.

Batteries: 33 MAL.

Pressure Hull: 22 mm thick amidships, tapering to 18 mm forward
                      and aft.

R.D.B: Carried.

G.S.R: 1 "Hela" type for Runddipol antenna.
                      1 "Naxos" type for Tunis antenna.
                      1 "Borkum" for Runddipol antenna.
                      1 "Hela" carried in reserve.
                      2 Tunis type antenna.
                      1 Southern Cross type antenna carried in reserve.
                      1 Runddipol mounted on the bridge and one atop
                        the Schnorchel mast.
                      2 Runddipole carried in reserve.

Radar: Hohentwiel type. 2 Sets carried in reserve.

D/F Gear: Fitted; type designation T-3PL LA 38, from 15-33
                      kilocycles and from 70 - 12,000 kilocycles, by
                      Telefunken.

Transmitters: 1 "Rhein" type designated as T-200 FKW 39. Wave
                      lengths from 3,000 kilocycles to 24,000 kilo-
                      cycles, by Telefunken.
                      1 40-Watt reserve transmitter, 20 - 80 meters, by
                      Lorenz.
                      1 150-Watt transmitter, 600 - 800 meters, by
                      Telefunken.
                      1 Emergency transmitter for rubber life rafts,
                      600 meters with automatic S.O.S.

"Kurier" Transmitter: Fitted and 1 carried in reserve.

(Op-16-Z)   DECLASSIFIED

Receivers: 1 "Grosschiff" type 18 - 100 meters, by Telefunken.
                             1 "Köln" type short-wave receiver from 1.5 to 25
                             megacycles, (GAF Model).
                             1 All-wave receiver, 20 - 20,000 kilocycles,
                             by Telefunken.

Echo Sounding Gear: 1 Echolot type Flachlot, 80 kilocycles, by Elac.
                             1 60-kilocycle Flachlot by Elac.

Hydrophones: G.H.G. fitted (Balkongeraet).

Underwater Sound: Elac U.T. fitted, 84.5 - 87 cycles.

Ultra Short-wave: Fitted, Type Fu.G. 17, 6 - 7 meters, by Lorenz.

Rubber Boats: 5 6-man rubber boats.
                             72 1-man rubber boats.

Diving Time: Best diving time 37 seconds to 20 meters.
                             Average diving time to 20 meters 40 - 45 seconds.

Flotilla: Belonged to the 4th U-boat Flotilla at Stettin
                             until June, 1944, and from then on assigned to
                             the 5th Flotilla in Kiel.

E A R L Y   H I S T O R Y

U.A.K. trials took place in Kiel and lasted about 14 days.
U-234 then went back to Germania Werft to rebuild the pressure oil
system which required about 35 days. From this point on, her trials
were frequently delayed because of mining operations throughout the
Baltic area. From Kiel she went to Warnemünde for three days and
then proceeded to Rönne for underwater sound testing which lasted
7 days. Flak trials followed in Swinemünde. She then proceeded to
Danzig, arriving there on 7 May, 1944, for additional U.A.K. trials
and repairs to the electric air compressor and bilge pumps. She
then proceeded to Hela and carried out surface mine laying trials. Sixty-
six mines were laid and while these mines were being recovered, she
did part of her Agru-Front trials. This was followed by underwater
mine laying trials and upon the completion of these trials, she
finished her Agru-Front training period. She then proceeded to
Danzig and entered the Holm Werft to have additional repairs made,
particularly to the electric propulsion equipment and to the main
transmitter. After a short run to Hela, she again was forced to
return to Danzig for additional repairs to her radio equipment.

From Danzig, she went to Pillau for tactical exercises which
lasted about eight days and then proceeded to Libau for the
commanding officer's torpedo trials. This was followed by another
period in dock, this time in Königsberg, necessitated again because
of difficulty with her radio equipment.

(Op-16-Z)   DECLASSIFIED

On 5 September, 1944, U-234 returned to Germania Werft for the usual overhaul and redesigning of the vessel as a transport, rather than a mine laying craft. During this time, the following changes and repairs were made:

(1) Schnorchel was built in.

(2) Pressure oil system was again changed and a temperature regulating device built in.

(3) G.H.G. was changed to Balkon type.

(4) The starboard propeller was replaced. (The original one had proven noisy at 100 rpm).

(5) Mine shafts $\frac{31}{33}\ \frac{35}{37}\ \frac{39}{41}\ \frac{43}{45}\ \frac{47}{49}\ \frac{51}{53}$ on the starboard side were removed and cargo stowage compartments made. The aft compartment was fuel oil flooded and the forward compartment was water flooded. On the port side corresponding mine shafts were removed. The outer keel plates were removed and the keel duct loaded with cargo, said to consist mainly of mercury and optical glass.

The final overhaul, loading and conversion of U-234 as a transport vessel, lasted until 25 March, 1945.

The actual loading of U-234 and the type of cargo she was to carry was determined by a special commission formed in December, 1944. At this time, it was made known to the officers of U-234 that they were to go to Japan. The special commission known as the "Marine Sonder Dienst Auslands", headed by K. K. Becker, was in charge of all details and determined what cargo was to be carried. Klt. Longbein from this commission was the actual loading officer. Loading containers were designed of the same diameter as the vertical mine shafts and were loaded in the shafts and held in place by the original mine releasing mechanism. The four compartments, two on either side, were loaded with horizontal tubes, (these tubes were originally above deck torpedo containers and were merely shortened somewhat and used as cargo containers). U-234 then carried six cargo containers in the mine shafts forward and amidships; six vertical containers in the mine shafts on either side, and in each of the four cargo spaces were eight horizontally placed cargo tubes. Four cargo containers, two on either side, were carried topside. The ship's officers estimated that 240 tons of cargo were aboard in addition to fuel and provisions for a six to nine months' trip.

After the loading was completed, some additional trials were carried out in the vicinity of Kiel. One was a silent run test near Apenrade at which time grounding rings were fitted to the propeller shafts. She returned to Kiel at which time most of her passengers came aboard. These were primarily technicians and GAF officers, in addition to Lt. Cdr. Hideo Tomonaga and Lt. Cdr. Genzo Shoji from the Japanese Navy.

(Op-16-Z)   DECLASSIFIED

        During the late evening hours of 25 March, 1945, U-234
left Kiel with U-516 and a VII-C boat. They arrived in Horten two
days later and during the following eight days, carried out
Schnorchel trials. During the trials and while proceeding at
Schnorchel depth, U-234 rammed a VII-C boat also carrying out
Schnorchel trials. Neither boat was badly damaged, diving tank
No. 1 and fuel oil tank No. 1 of U-234 were holed but she was
able to continue her trials. The other boat suffered very minor
damages. U-234 arrived in Kristiansand on about 5 April where
repairs were made and she topped up with provisions and oil.

FIRST AND LAST PATROL

        U-234 left Kristiansand on 15 April, 1945, with a conviction
among all hands that Japan would never be reached. In fact, the
commanding officer was stated to have told his crew that although
they were officially destined for Japan, he was firmly convinced in
his own mind that their destination would never be reached. U-234
proceeded submerged and at Schnorchel depth for the first 16 days
and surfaced for the first time shortly before the Rosengarten, because
of a severe storm. From then on she usually ran two hours on the
surface at night and spent the balance of the time submerged to depths
between 40 - 100 meters. She had orders not to make any attacks, so
about the only incident before news of Germany's surrender came was
when she almost rammed a large steamer, but U-234 herself was not
observed. The first ominous sign was when the Goliath station fell
out and shortly after passing the Rosengarten no further signals were
received from Nauen. From then on, all signals received were short
wave. They had no radio contact for several days after the last
message was received from Nauen. The U-boat series had been changed
over to "Distel" series of which U-234 was ignorant. Then on the
4th of May, she got a fragmentary repeat from English and American
stations about Donitz's elevation to supreme command in Germany. She
was finally forced to surface in order to receive complete signals.

        On 10 May, U-234 picked up the order for all U-boats to
surrender and to proceed to an Allied port depending upon their position
at that time. Upon receipt of this message, considerable discussion
arose among the officers and passengers as to what course they should
follow. Eire was first mentioned and this proposal was enthusiastically
received by the two Japanese officers aboard. The discussion was
particularly heated because at the time the surrender signal was
received, U-234 was exactly on the dividing line which determined
whether she should proceed to England or to an American port. During
the following two or three days after the surrender order was
received, she proceeded southerly, surfacing at night and sub-
merging during the daytime. Messages from other U-boats obeying the
surrender order were picked up by U-234 and led her to report her
position. She first tried the international short wave band but
her signals apparently were not received so she switched to the 600
meter wave band and it was several hours before an answer was received

CONFIDENTIAL

to this signal. U-234's first direct orders were from England on short wave, received on the 12th of May at about 0800. Then late that evening, she received orders from Halifax to report her position and speed hourly.

When it became apparent to the Japanese officers that FEHLER intended to obey surrender orders, they informed the commanding officer of their resolve to commit suicide. FEHLER made some attempt to dissuade them from this, particularly by citing the surrender of Gen. Oshima and his staff as an example. But the pair requested that they be allowed to remain undisturbed in their cabin, which was granted. Previously, numerous gifts had been distributed among the officers and passengers. FEHLER received a Samurai sword, which he later threw overboard, and a sizeable sum in Swiss francs. A guard was placed outside their compartment, and the two took an overdose of Luminol. They were still alive some 36 hours later, much to the disgust of the crew, and efforts on the part of the ship's doctor to revive them failed. They were buried at sea on 11 May. Letters of thanks and appreciation addressed to FEHLER were found afterwards, also a request that an enclosed signal be sent to Japan. FEHLER did not comply with this request.

The first report made by U-234 as to her position and speed was accurately given but from then on she gave her speed as eight miles when she actually was doing between 12 and 15 and she was proceeding more westerly than indicated. Observation of her position by an airplane apparently resulted in the order from Halifax that she was to report hourly. The commanding officer of U-234 assumed that none of his hourly reports reached Halifax. At 2300Z on 14 May, U-234 was contacted by the USS SUTTON and a prize crew was placed aboard her. She arrived in Portsmouth on 17 May.

O F F I C E R S   O F   U - 2 3 4

At the time of commissioning, officers of the U-234 were:

    C.O. - Klt. Johann Heinrich FEHLER, (Class of 1935).
1 W.O. - Olt. d. R. Alfred KLINGENBERG.
2 W.O. - Lt. Karl Ernst PFAFF, (not in G.N.L.).
    L.I. - Klt. (Ing) Horst ERNST, (Class of October 1937).
    W.I. - Olt. (Ing) Günter PAGENSTECHER, (Class of December 1939).
Medical Officer: Stabsarzt Günther BESUCH.

In January, 1945, KLINGENBERG was replaced by Klt. Richard BULLA, (Class of 1935). Klt. BULLA had originally known the commanding officer of U-234 when they both served aboard the Raider "ATLANTIS" and when it became necessary to replace KLINGENBERG, FEHLER selected BULLA from the passenger list primarily in order to have one less person aboard.

In October, 1944, BESUCH was replaced by Stabsarzt Dr. Walter FRANZ.

APPENDIX 2

Cargo unloading list for U-234 at Portsmouth, New Hampshire, on and from 23 May 1945.

    Source: US National Archives, Box RG-38, Box 13. Document OP-20-3-G1-A, Dated 23 May 1945.

Injection pumps.
Documents.
Atabrin – 465 kg.
Aircraft warning device.
Direction finding (DF) set.
All-wave receiver.
Searchlight drawings.
Planospheric lenses.
Uranium oxide (10 cases, 56 kg, marked for Japanese Army).
Coils (presumably electrical coils).
Benzyl cellulose.
Silk ribbons.
Recoilless anti-tank munition plus igniter.
Junkers drawings (many).
Vacuum tubes.
Computer parts for fire-control computer.
Drawings for Me-323.
Thallium metal (106 kg).
23 cases of various munitions.
Steel (6,110 kg).
Fuses (for munitions).
Lead (11,151 kg).
Zinc.
Mercury (1,926 kg).
etc., etc.

In the Keel
Belts for machine guns (38 kg).

1,474 bars of lead (55,758 kg).
564 bottles of mercury (22,186 kg).

Grand Total 162,352.9 kg

APPENDIX 3

US Interrogation Report of General Kessler, dated 31 May 1945, after the surrender of U-234.

REPRODUCED AT THE NATIONAL ARCHIVES

SECRET

\# 5255

Report on Interrogation of: 1 June 1945.
P/W: KESSLER, Ulrich   Capt. Halle
Rank: General der Flieger (Major General)
Unit: Kampfgeschwader 1 (Hindenburg)
Captd: 15 May 1945; surrendered to the Americans at sea.

Veracity: Believed reliable.

REPORT: Memorandum for Capt. Harvey dated 31 May 1945. Subject: Interro-
        gation of Genlt. Kessler, submitted by H. Priestley, Wing Commander,
        RAF.

Questions 1 and 2: What is known of air transport flights between German
occupied Europe and the Far East? How many such flights were carried out and
when were they made? What cargoes were carried on such transport flights,
both personnel and materiel? Information about cargoes is required for
flights in both directions.

Answer: There have never been any flights between German occupied Europe
and the Far East, as far as German planes and German pilots are concerned.
There was only one flight made by Italian officers which started west of
Stalingrad in 1942. P/W does not know whether they flew directly to
Tokyo or landed in Manchukuo, but P/W does know for certain that the
Japanese Government objected strongly to this flight, even to such a degree that they treated the pilots very discourteously. The Japanese also
started one flight via India but it is unknown what became of the plane and
its crew as they never arrived at their destination. The intention of
making flights existed from the beginning of the war and was intensified
after the German-Russo war. The General staff of the Luftwaffe even contemplated establishing regular air traffic between Japan and Germany, with
the idea of sending to Japan information, designs, and even models, if
possible of new technical developments in return for scarce materials such
as antimony, tungsten, etc. This idea had materialized to such an extent
that three Ju 290's were modified to cover the long distance and were expected to carry two tons of material on the return trip. Even the pilots
who belonged to P/W's command and had been with the Lufthansa in peace
time were ordered to prepare to perform this flight. P/W, too, with a
considerable number of experts was supposed to make the initial flight and
to remain in Tokyo as Chief of Luftwaffe Liaison Staff. It is astonishing
but typical for Luftwaffe Staff procedure that all preparations were made
without advance consultation with the Japanese who strongly vetoed any
idea of an airline between Germany and Japan which might touch Russian
territory. It is typical of the Luftwaffe, too, that the plan was dropped
and the planes disposed of without ascertaining whether the objection was
to regular air traffic only (as it was) or also to single or occasional
flights to which they would have protested officially to save face but which
they secretly would have both condoned and desired. P/W found out that
they expected the Germans to make the flight up until as late as the fall
of 1944 but as a result of a speech made by Mr. Stalin against the aggressor
nations, they objected to any flight at all that might touch Russian territory after that date.

SECRET

1.

P/W KESSLER (Cont'd)   1 JUNE 1945.

Questions 3 and 4: (3) What types of aircraft were either contemplated
for use in or actually used in transport flights to the Far East? It the
aircraft was a specially modified type of aircraft, what modifications
were carried out? (4) What routes were contemplated or actually used for
such flights? Did they avoid Soviet Territory or was no particular consideration given to such a question?

Answer: The types of aircraft contemplated for this flight were Ju 290
(cf above), BV 2 2 2 (a flying boat) which might have covered the distance
from Rhodes to India and the Me 264, the plane constructed for the
Japanese Olympic Games in 1940, designed to cover 10,000 km and was capable of making the flight to Japan via India. The possibilities of a
flight via India were studied over and over again as the Japanese kept urg-
ing that we should establish air communication but avoid Russian Territory.
Owing to the experiences of Freiherr von Gablentz in peace time and owing
to the scientific research done by our meteorologists, this route was always rejected as meteorological and geographic conditions were described
as being too difficult, whereas meteorological conditions were excellent
in both Summer and Winter, especially on the West-East Trip, and geographic conditions were favorable too as there are no high mountains. It so
happens that the BV 222 and BV 398 (a plane that was 95% completed and designed to cover more than 10,000 km) and the Me 264 were never modified
for this flight.

Question 5: What bases were used as termini for transport flights (a)
in Europe, and (b) in the Far East?

Answer: For the northern route, Petsamo and Bardufoss were contemplated
as bases, whereas Tokyo was the eastern terminus with possible emergency
landings at Harbin or Hakodate. When Petsamo was occupied by the Russians and fuel supply had become difficult for the Norwegian Region,
Gotenhafen, near Danzig and even Rechlin, were considered as starting
points. If the India route had not been rejected, Simferopol in the Crimea
was to have been the starting point.

Question 6: What was the attitude of the Japanese in Europe towards such
flights? What indications did they give of the attitude of Japanese in
the empire proper toward such flights?

Answer: The attitude of the Japanese has already been touched upon. It
is the impression of the P/W and even his conviction, that the Japanese
ambassador OSHIMA and his aides in Berlin, Admiral Abe, Admiral Koshima,
and General Komatsu, were sincere in their desire that a flight even via
Russia should take place. Admiral Koshima told F/W that he could not understand the way the Imperial Japanese Government in Tokyo thought. He
emphasized that out flying or not flying via Russia would never affect the
Russian attitude of never allowing the United States to use Soviet air
fields for attacking Japan. He maintained that the discrepancies between Russia and Japan were negligible in comparison with those existing

2.

P/W KESSLER (Cont'd)   1 June 1945.

between Russia and the U.S. To substantiate this statement, he pointed
out that Russian and Japanese Intelligence in Turkey exchanged information
concerning the United States.

Question 7: A former G.A.F. pilot now in Allied hands claims to have made
two return flights between Poland and Manchukuo in early 1944 and that two
other pilots from his unit each made one similar flight. Did such flights
actually take place, and if so, what is known about (a) cargoes carried,
(b) routes followed, and (c) actual dates of flights?

Answer: After making every allowance for the possibility that one section
of the German Luftwaffe may not be acquainted with all the activities of
another, it is quite impossible that such a flight took place as P/W con-
ferred with all sections which had anything to do with such flights. Of
course, the Japanese, too, would have known something about such flights
and there would have been no need to approach them on this matter if there
had been any precedent. The only unit which performed flights far to the
East but not to the Far East, was K.G. 200 which had been given the three
Ju 290's. At that time, these Ju 290's were capable of covering only
7,000 km. This squadron was assigned the special task of dropping agents
and made flights even as far east as the Urals. Observations made during
these flights concerning magnetic declinations, weather conditions, etc.
were given to P/W in a condensed form by the scientists who helped P/W
prepare the intended flight.

APPENDIX 4

Letter from Robert Oppenheimer to Enrico Fermi on the subject of using radioactive material as a nuclear weapon, dated 25 May 1943.

CANCELLED

LOS ALAMOS

SANTA FE, NEW MEXICO

P. O. BOX 1663

May 25, 1943

Dr. Enrico Fermi
Metallurgical Laboratory
University of Chicago
Chicago, Illinois

Dear Fermi:

 I wanted to report to you on the question of the radio-actively poisoned foods, both because there are some steps that I have taken, and because Edward Teller has told me of the difficulties into which you have run.

 When I was in Washington I learned that the Chief of Staff had requested from Conant a summary report on the military uses of radioactive materials and that Conant was in the process of collecting the material for that report. I therefore, with Groves' knowledge and approval, discussed with him the applica-tion which seemed to us so promising, gave him a few points of detail and some orders of magnitude. I raised the question of what steps, offensive and defensive, should be taken in this connection. It is my opinion, and it was also Conant's, that the defensive measures would probably preclude our carrying out the method ourselves effectively, and therefore I asked that in his report the question of policy be raised as to which of these lines we should primarily follow. This report, and you will undoubtedly have heard of it in other connections, is to go directly to General Marshall so that it will have authoritative if not expert consideration. I hope to discuss the question further when Conant visits here in ten days.

 I also plan to go into the matter a little more deeply with Hamilton, although of course only on the physiological side. As you know, he has already made studies of the strontium which appears to offer the highest promise, and he expressed his willingness to look into these questions more fully. I think that I can do this without in any way indicating the nature of our interest, but it will be some time, perhaps three weeks, before I get to see him.

 I understand the difficulties that you have had in getting this subject developed without telling anyone about it,

Dr. E. Fermi
Page 2
May 25, 1943

and it is hard for me to give very sound advice on what to do.
I think that there is at least one quite well defined radio-
chemical problem, which is the separation of the beta-strontium
from other activities. It is my impression after talking it over
with Teller, that this is not a very major problem except in so
far as provision would have to be made for carrying it out by
remote control at the actual site of operations. I do not see
how this can be done without letting a number of people into
the secret of why we want the strontium. I should therefore
like to ask you what you think the latest safe date is for the
solution of this and other problems. It seems to me that we
have a much better chance of keeping your plan quiet if we do
not start work on it until it is essential to do so. If, in
your opinion, the time for such work is now, I believe that you
should discuss it with Allison and Franck and on their advice,
if absolutely necessary, with Compton, and that perhaps this
group of people will be enough to get the work done without
more wide-spread discussion. In a general way I think we have
better facilities here for keeping things of that kind within
a well definied group, namely, the scientific personnel of the
laboratory. On the other hand,
I do not think that we are equipped to tackle the problem
with anything like the expedition that you can in Chicago.

To summarize then, I should recommend delay if that
is possible. (In this connection I think that we should not
attempt a plan unless we can poison food sufficient to kill
a half a million men, since there is no doubt that the actual
number affected will, because of non-uniform distribution, be
much smaller than this.) If you believe that such delay will
be serious, I should recommend discussion with a few well-
chosen people. Finally, I should postpone this action until
I have had an opportunity to reopen the question with Conant
and if possible to obtain information on the decision of the
General Staff.

Things here are going quite well and we are still
remembering with pleasure and profit your fine visit. I hope
that you can come again late in June, and that we shall have
at that time some less programatic problems to discuss with
you.

With all warm greetings,

Robert Oppenheimer

RO:pg

Selected Bibliography

Agoston, T. *Blunder, How the U.S. Gave Away Nazi Supersecrets to Russia*, William Kimber, London, 1986.
——. *Teufel oder Technokrat? Hitler's graue Eminence*, Mittler, Berlin, 1993.
Allen, L. *Japan, The Years of Triumph*, American Heritage Press, New York, 1971.
Bernstein, J. *Hitler's Uranium Club*, American Institute of Physics, New York, 1996.
Blackett, P.M.S. *Military and Political Consequences of Atomic Energy*, Turnstile Press, London, 1948.
Bormann, M. *Bormann–Vemerke, Hitler's Secret Conversations, 1941–1944*, Signet Books, New York, 1961.
Bower, T. *The Paperclip Conspiracy*, Michael Joseph, London, 1987.
Boyd, C. & Yoshida, A. *The Japanese Submarine Force and World War II*, Airlife, London, 1995.
Brooks, G. *Hirschfeld, The Story of a U-Boat NCO 1940–1946*, Leo Cooper, London, 1996.
Butow, R.J.C. *Tojo and the Coming of War*, Princetown University Press, 1961.
Collier, B. *The Defence of the United Kingdom*, HMSO, London, 1957.
Dornberger, W. *V2*, The Scientific Book Club, London, 1952.
Ermenc, J.J. *Atom Bomb Scientists, Memoirs 1939–1945*, Greenwood Publishing Group, Westport, 1989.
Glasstone, S. & Sesonske, A. *Nuclear Reactor Engineering*, Volumes 1 and 2, Chapman and Hall, London, 1994.
Green, W. *War Planes of the Second World War*, Volume 10, Macdonald, London, 1968.
Groves, L. *Now It Can Be Told*, Harper and Row, New York, 1961.
Guillaume, A. *The German Russian War, 1941–1945*, War Office, London, 1956.
Gwaltney, R.C. *Missile Generation and Protection in Light Water Cooled Reactor Power Plants*, US Atomic Energy Commission, 1968.
Hansen, C. *U.S. Nuclear Weapons*, Aerofax, Arlington, Texas, 1988.
Hashimoto, M. *Sunk. The Story of the Japanese Submarine Fleet, 1942–1945*, Cassel, London, 1954.
Holsken, D. *V-Missiles of the Third Reich. The V1 and V2*, Monogram Aviation Publications, Sturbridge, Mass., 1994.
Irving, D. *The Mare's Nest*, William Kimber, London, 1964.
Jones, R.V. *Most Secret War*, Hamish Hamilton, London, 1978.
Kramish, A. *The Griffin*, Macmillan, London, 1987.
Manchester, W. *The Arms of Krupp, 1587–1986*, Michael Joseph, London, 1964.
Michel, J. *DORA. A Survivor's Story of the Third Reich's Hell-Hole Death Camp*, Weidenfeld and Nicolson, London, 1979.
Powers, T. *Heisenberg's War. The Secret History of the German Bomb*, Cape, London, 1993.
Rose, P.L. *Heisenberg and the Nazi Atomic Bomb Project*, University of California Press, California, 1998.
Rusbridge, J. & Nave, E. *Betrayal at Pearl Harbor*, Simon and Schuster, New York, 1991.
Sharpe, P.R. *U-Boat Fact File 1939–1945*, Midland Publishing, UK, 1998.
Shirer, W.L. *The Rise and Fall of the Third Reich*, Secker and Warburg, London, 1961.
Templin, L.J. *Reactor Physics Constants*, Argonne National Laboratory, University of Chicago, US Atomic Energy Commission, 1963.

Walker, M. *German National Socialism and the Quest for Nuclear Power*, Cambridge University Press, New York, 1989.

——. 'Heisenberg, Goudsmit and the German Atomic Bomb', *Physics Today*, American Institute for Physics, January 1990.

——. 'National Socialism and German Physics', *Journal of Contemporty History* 24, SAGE 1989.

Wilcox, R.K. *Japan's Secret War*, Marlowe, New York, 1995.

Williams, P. & Wallace, D. *UNIT 731. The Japanese Army's Secret of Secrets*, Hodder and Stoughton, London, 1989.

Index